MARJORIE BLAMEY'S
FLOWERS OF THE COUNTRYSIDE

MARJORIE BLAMEY'S
FLOWERS OF THE COUNTRYSIDE

Written by Philip and Marjorie Blamey
Illustrated by Marjorie Blamey

Collins
London and Glasgow

We would like to record our thanks to Rennie Bere who kindly read the manuscript and gave freely of his advice in the preparation of this book. We are most grateful to Diana Dent and Mavis Davey who accepted the task of typing the manuscript, to our daughter-in-law Paula for helping us with the initial draft and to our daughter Anne who read the proofs and compiled the index. We thank them all and the rest of our family who uncomplainingly accepted hurried visits, lack of baby-sitting duties and fewer parties whilst we went into hibernation in order to produce this book. Above all, we thank each other for the enjoyable months we spent working together – which is the way we like it.

© Philip and Marjorie Blamey 1980
First published 1980 by William Collins Sons and Company Limited

ISBN 0 00 411663 1

Colour and black and white reproduction by Adroit Photo-Litho,
Birmingham
Filmset by Typesetting Services Ltd,
Glasgow
Printed in Great Britain by William Collins Sons and Company Limited

CONTENTS

THE WOVEN PATTERN · 7
EARLY DAYS · 11
THE FLORAL PATH · 18
BEGINNER'S BOTANY · 21
WAYSIDE WEEDS · 38
TRAPPERS, PARASITES AND POISONERS · 48
FIELD FARE · 53
PERFUMES AND PLEASANTRIES · 67
WILD FLOWER GARDENING · 72
PLAYTHINGS AND PASTIMES · 88
PAINTING FLOWERS · 98
RECORDING AND PHOTOGRAPHING FLOWERS · 107
A PLACE FOR FLOWERS · 113
THE PROTECTED FLOWERS · 118
HABITATS FOR FLOWERS · 125
PORTRAITS OF WILD FLOWERS · 141
GLOSSARY · 214
BIBLIOGRAPHY · 216
INDEX · 217
FULL CIRCLE · 224

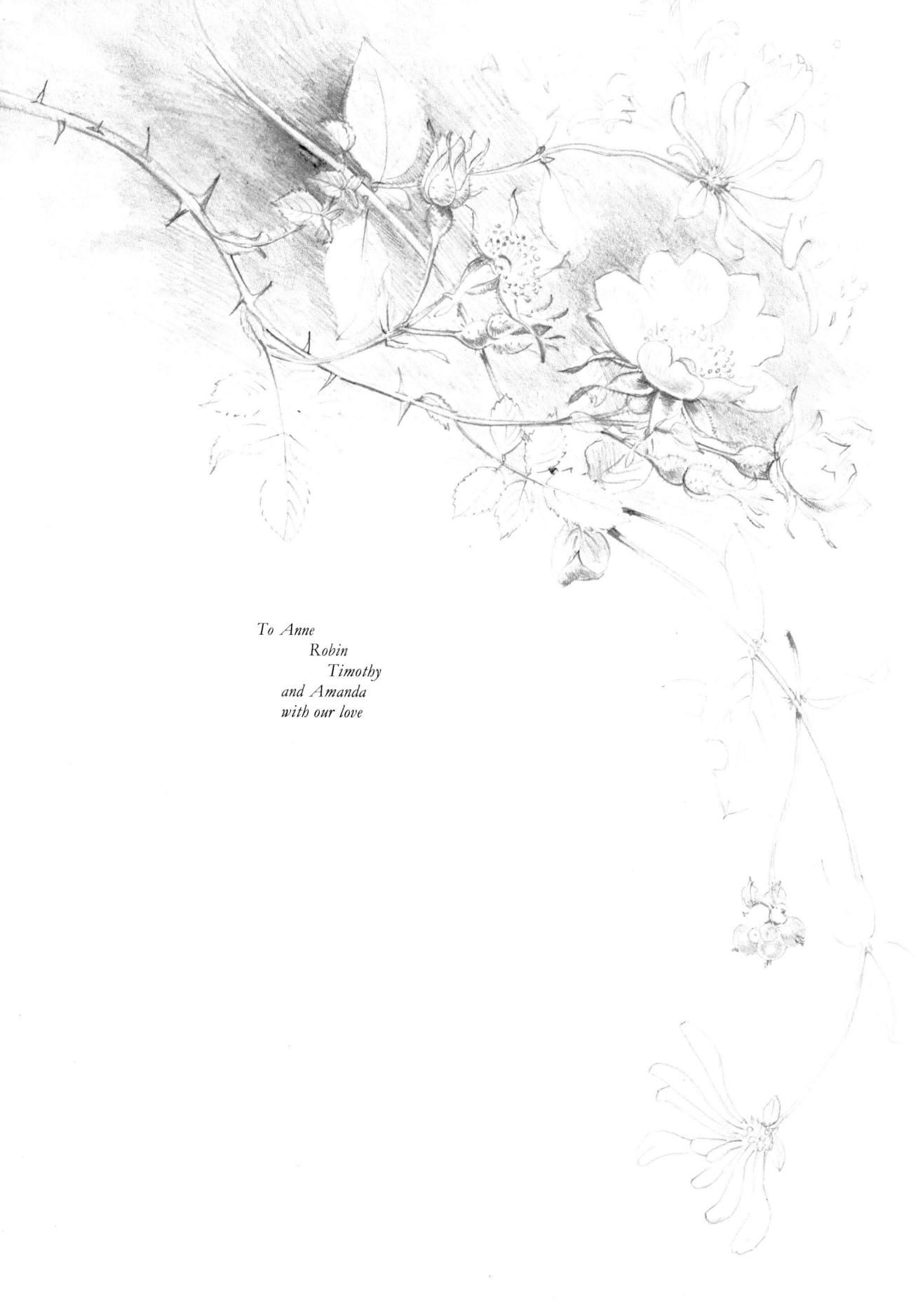

*To Anne
   Robin
      Timothy
 and Amanda
 with our love*

THE WOVEN PATTERN

This is a book about wild flowers. Into it I have woven a mixture of ideas and thoughts, facts and figures, my likes and dislikes. The choice of flowers is a purely personal one. I have included all those I love to paint, from the large scarlet poppy to the smallest pansy. Some flowers are included because they are strange and sinister, others because they are insignificant and easily overlooked yet deserve a second glance. I have painted many of our rare and vanishing species because I may never again have the opportunity of doing so.

In my enthusiasm for wild flowers I strayed into so many subjects connected with them that I found I had enough work for two people. At this point my husband Philip joined me in the project and wrote on conservation, about which he knows far more than I do through his work on the Council of the Cornwall Naturalists' Trust. He became as enthusiastically involved in the book as I was and explored further into the history and uses of plants while I wrote on other subjects and steadily painted my way through one chapter after another. But although we divided the work, the book is our joint effort. We are of one mind and generally think alike where wild flowers are concerned, particularly when their wellbeing and continued existence are endangered.

Because we believe that all the threads of life on earth are interwoven, we have tried to include many of the resulting patterns in the book. Although our original idea was to write only about wild plants—from the pleasure they have given us by their very existence to the problems and dangers we, the human race, have put in the way of their continued survival —we very quickly discovered that we could not separate them completely from the

caterpillars which were feeding upon their leaves, nor could we concentrate on the flower itself and ignore the butterfly which was supping nectar from it or the bee acting as the pollen carrier.

We have tried to show how we feel about the role of man, his dominion over the creatures of this earth and the importance of positive conservation as opposed to negative preservation. We hope that we have also conveyed some of the joy we experienced while looking for the flowers about which we have written and which I have painted with such pleasure.

Introduction to Flowers
If anyone had predicted, on that particularly wet July day in 1966, that flowers would soon change the course of my life, I might have gloomily rejoined that they had already done so. It would not have been the flowers of the field about which I was then thinking but the beasts which trampled upon them as they passed me on their leisurely way to the meadow. I, in my mud-splashed jeans, had no kindly thoughts at that moment for any of our wild-flower-named cows who always seemed to take so much longer to walk from the milking shed to the field on a wet day than on a fine one. They filed slowly past me, looking as though their own butter would not melt in their mouths, led as usual by Bluebell followed by three of her daughters—Hyacinth, Holly, and Mistletoe—then Buttercup, Daisy, Thistledown, Marigold and the rest of the herd.

At last I was free to return home through the fields, and by the door I picked the last flower from a clematis. I gently shook the rain from its bedraggled face, little knowing that I was waving not a flower but a magic wand. I suddenly decided that I would like to paint it. From that moment on the spell was cast. I borrowed my daughter's paintbox and a brush that could have passed as a doll's dish mop, and I failed so totally and dismally to produce anything approaching a good painting that it left me feeling annoyed and frustrated.

I had not touched any paints—apart from gallons of whitewash for the cowshed walls—for over thirty years, but I knew I could have painted that flower far better at the age of eight than I did that evening at the age of forty-eight. I had imagined that painting was something one never forgot—like swimming or riding a bicycle—but apparently not. I was determined, however, to continue, and I chose flowers as my subjects only because it was easier to pick a fresh one each evening after the farm work was finished than to find time during the day to paint birds or anything else which then interested me more. As a child I had drawn with great accuracy from the time I was old enough to hold a pencil and had made small detailed sketches of all the objects I so passionately loved to collect, from seashells and empty snail-shells to caterpillars and moths. My sketching came to an abrupt end at the age of sixteen when a new art teacher told me that there was no point in wasting my time drawing a perfect replica of a prickly conker, and that there was no future for me in the world of art. He said I was merely a human camera, recording in an hour of concentrated work what a mechanical instrument would click in a hundredth of a second. If he expected me to be disappointed by his remarks he could not have been more wrong. I was suddenly and totally overwhelmed with desire to become a photographer; the idea was as bright and sudden as a flashlight exploding before my eyes. Like Mr Toad of Toad Hall, a new hobby to me at that time was a joy for ever. A year later I won my first major prize with a close-up photograph of a prickly conker!

I had never had any wish to take up art as a career in the first place; my eyes were firmly fixed upon the stage and, after training, I acted in plays in London in the evenings and concentrated on my camera work during the day. My paints were put away and forgotten. After my marriage in the early years of the Second World War and the start of our farming life in Cornwall in 1948, my camera too was inclined to be left on the shelf. I always promised myself that one day I would return to it. I never had any desire to return to painting, and I hardly remembered the hours I had 'wasted' on my sketches until I held that clematis in my hand.

After three months, my second-childhood attempts at painting had slowly and painfully progressed from the appalling to the mediocre, with perhaps a slight glimmer of life here and there. I had acquired some artist's watercolours, a few good brushes and better quality paper which accepted the paint without wilting under the first impact of a drop of water. I therefore no longer had any excuse to blame my tools. I worked for a few hours each week and began to make a collection of paintings of flowers from our garden. When winter came, I sketched the dying leaves and bare branches until the supply of interesting material diminished and with it my enthusiasm for my new hobby. I might, I thought, start again in the spring if the farm allowed me any time off. A small but intensive dairy farm, with deep-litter poultry, calf-rearing, pigs, ducks, geese and pounds of Cornish cream to be made, left little time to spare for hobbies. We employed no one, and our working days numbered seven in each week throughout the year. The delightful ties of four small children had been loosened; our elder daughter Anne was married with a daughter of her own, but we still enjoyed the company of three near-adults under our roof. Neither of our sons wanted to farm and we did not encourage them because, by 1966, small farms were rapidly becoming less attractive propositions than they had been.

With much regret and even more apprehension, we decided to sell the farm after one more year and to build a house nearby, find new work, fresh hobbies, even take up photography again. But as soon as the spring flowers began to bloom I felt the urge to paint them. In April of that year I was asked if I would exhibit my paintings at the County Flower Show in Truro. With no frames or mounts, we fastened them to the wall with sticky tape in a most unprofessional way. The magic wand, still waving, produced an author who asked me to illustrate a book. I could not have been more astounded.

As planned, we sold our farm and built our house by the stream, but everything else that happened that year and ever since has been totally unexpected, exciting and almost unbelievable to us both. That book was to be the first of many. Because I no longer had an entire lifetime ahead of me in which to paint at leisure, I attacked my new-found career with red-hot enthusiasm. One book overlapped the next; I worked fourteen hours a day, every day, and enjoyed every minute of it, but there was always more work than I could manage. After a year, Philip took over the business side, arranging exhibitions, designing our new systems of recording, pressing, filing and photographing all the flowers I painted, and he mastered the craft of framing my pictures. Before long he decided that my work was far more interesting and satisfying to him than the political world in which he was involved, and he joined me full time so that I was freed from all the paperwork and could concentrate on painting. We enjoy working together again as we have throughout our married life.

One of the first things I was told when I nervously agreed to do the illustrations for my first book, was that my paintings must be better than anything a camera could produce, with every detail sharp and clear. If I could always achieve that my future as an illustrator would be assured. I vividly remembered the remarks of my art teacher and felt that my life had turned full circle. I was getting back into the art scene for the very reason I had been rejected all those years ago.

Since then we have discovered many things. We have found that there is no substitute for hard work and that a thoroughly professional attitude towards it is essential at all times; that we can work at high pressure for weeks and months on end without a day off because we enjoy it to the full. Even though I never stop sketching while I am away, we now have the opportunity of visiting many beautiful places in this country and abroad merely to look at flowers. What better could one find to look at? We are fully aware that we live in the best of both worlds, for we work in our own home and in our own time. After our down-to-earth farm life this is indeed a flower-strewn path we tread, and we still find it difficult to realize that we not only have the time but also a valid reason, in fact a positive duty, to look at flowers for the rest of our lives.

EARLY DAYS

It was the medicinal power of wild plants which first prompted their study. To the people of those days disease was the outward sign of evil spirits within the body, which had to be expelled before a cure could be effected, and it was believed that certain plants endowed with particular powers could do this. Other plants were credited with the power to prevent evil spirits entering the body, the house, the byre or the beasts belonging to the household. Such passionately held beliefs of hundreds of years ago are at the root of many present-day superstitions and fancies. Equally, we owe to many of these beliefs a great debt of gratitude because all through botanical history—closely tied to the work of apothecaries, herbalists and physicians—they encouraged research which often resulted in the production of invaluable drugs and cures.

About fifty years after the birth of Christ, two men were working independently on the study of flowers in the Mediterranean area. One was a Greek physician called Pedanius Dioscorides Anazarbeus, the other a Roman named Gaius Plinius Secundus, or Pliny the Elder, hereinafter, as the lawyers say, referred to as Dioscorides and Pliny. *De Materia Medica,* written in AD60 by the Greek, mentions 600 plants; *Historia Naturalis,* written by Pliny at about the same time, is a work of over thirty books, fifteen of them devoted to botanical subjects. More than any others, these two works form the base upon which the study of plants has been built.

Name This Flower
Throughout the early days of botany—and let us take that as starting with Dioscorides and Pliny—the naming of flowers was a science based only on the uses or virtues ascribed to each plant. Here we find the first appearance of legend and magic. The powers of fairies, devils and hobgoblins were manifest in wild flowers, and religions too gathered their symbols. In the Greek and Roman religions flowers were linked by their names with individual gods and had their place within the mythologies, and as Christianity developed, so were flowers dedicated to the Holy Family, and many nowadays have names which reflect this dedication, such as Lady's

Slipper and Lady's Tresses, 'Our Lady's' having become in time 'Lady's'. It seems that many 'evil' flowers were given holy connotations to counteract their wickedness.

With the advance of the Roman Empire came the flowers of the Mediterranean and their Latin names which were either accepted as they were, translated or adapted to the local languages. Roman soldiers wore garlands around their heads, which were called *coronas*. The flowers from which these particular garlands were made were known thereafter as coronations, later shortened to carnation. In some parts of Britain the flower is still called coronation.

As people travelled about Europe they found that folklore, legend and myth, and even medical practice, were much the same from country to country. Direct translation therefore gave the international names in different languages. The Dandelion is an interesting example. The Romans called it *dens leonis* after an old physician's name for the plant. This came about because the shape of the lobes of the leaf are similar to a lion's tooth. The French translated it to *dent de lion,* and the English anglicized this to dandelion. This is not the end of the story. It was found that the plant had strong diuretic qualities and so it was also named in many languages for this property. The English called it Pittle-bed or Piss-a-bed, the French *Piss-en-lit* and the Dutch *Pisse-bed*. No eminent botanist here, and no words spared, in the days when flowers were being named.

After the time of Dioscorides and Pliny, little comes to us of any value in the study of flowers until the 15th century. Then the Elizabethan period produced a considerable number of works on the subject, mainly medical books, their interest in flowers based on the theory of signatures.

Alongside the mythology and folklore of flowers grew the idea that their power could be identified by their appearance, touch or smell, an idea based on the belief that when God created man He also created disease. Having endowed man with intelligence, He created the cure in flowers and gave each a 'signature' as a clue to its potential value. Over the years interpretation of these signatures often became more and more bizarre, but at the same time it is extraordinary how many seem to have been effective. Henbane, for example, is an extremely dangerous plant containing that virulent poison hyoscine. The seed capsule was seen to resemble a jaw so the signature ascribed to the plant was the cure for toothache. Probably a drastic cure but effective nonetheless for quite a different reason—hyoscine as a drug is a very powerful sedative. Toadflax, that lovely hedgerow flower, is another which has a signature but here it is the colour. Because it is such a bright yellow colour, it was decided that it had diuretic qualities and would cure all malfunctions of the kidney and bladder (at one time it was even called Urinalis).

The Herbalists
With the upsurge of interest in botany came several works of great significance. Travel was becoming less hazardous and specimens of flowers from other parts of the world were being brought back for study and identification. The main emphasis, however, was still on the use to which wild plants could be put, and few books were devoted to flowers for their own sake. A Flemish botanist born in 1517 by the name of Rembert Dodoens and known as Dodonaeus, wrote his great book, the *Cruydeboek,* in 1554 from which came many English plant names. In 1583 Dodonaeus produced his *Stirpium Historiae Pemptades Sex,* known as *Pemptades,* which became the source of numerous subsequent works. There was no copyright law in those days and plagiarism, or literary piracy, was rife. Next came Clusius, as he is known. Born Charles de L'Ecluse in 1526 he became France's leading botanist of his day. Among his publications was the translation of *Pemptades* into French.

Henry Lyte, born in 1529 to a very old Somerset family, met and worked with Clusius and translated his version of *Pemptades*. Lyte called his translation *A herball or Historie of Plantes* and it was published in 1578. He also anglicized many Dutch and German plant names and coined new ones himself. A few years later came the biggest piece of literary piracy yet. John Gerard, who lived from 1545 to 1607, a Cheshire-born surgeon-barber, moved to London and wrote his world famous *The Herball or Generall Historie of Plants* in 1597. It was another translation of Dodonaeus' *Pemptades* but with no acknowledgement whatsoever. It was published as Gerard's own work and contains many changes to the original which are far from accurate. However, in spite of this, Gerard's *Herball* is still frequently referred to.

Born in 1567, John Parkinson grew up in London and became an apothecary and botanist. He had a passion for wild flowers and in time transferred that passion to gardening. He wrote a famous book *Paradisi in Sole Paradisus Terrestris* (dedicated to Charles I's queen, Henrietta Maria), whose title, when translated, shows his punning sense of humour. *Paradisi in Sole* literally means 'park in sun' and *Paradisus Terrestris,* 'paradise on earth'. He was a brilliant botanist, devising many names for new plants introduced from across the Atlantic. He gave up his apothecary's work in order to write his book, became a full-time botanist and was appointed King's Botanist, a post he held for some years. He died an old man (for those days) of eighty-three.

Whilst John Parkinson was concentrating his work on flowers, vegetables, orchards and the herb garden, William Turner, born in 1510, was busy studying and writing about those plants which were 'in their proper place'. Turner is still cited for his work in naming and recording wild flowers. He started by studying 'simples'—bunches of flowers and herbs, hung indoors for various culinary and medicinal purposes. He recorded 300 different British species and named many of them. He died in 1568. As a naturalist of great standing, Turner was followed by John Ray who lived from 1627 to 1705. He did a tremendous amount of work for botanic nomenclature and classification, achieving international fame, and completed several local floras, that of Cambridgeshire being one of his major works.

In Britain, botany then went out of fashion, becoming a subject of interest only to a few professional academics until the advent of William Curtis in the second half of the 18th century. Born in 1746, at an early age he was virtually in charge of the Chelsea Physic Garden. After completing publication of his *Flora Londinensis* in 1787 he started *Curtis's Botanical Magazine,* describing and illustrating cultivated plants and using the best artists of the day. Believed to be the longest running magazine in existence, it is still published as the *Botanical Magazine* by the Royal Horticultural Society.

Meanwhile, in Sweden, Carl von Linné had revolutionized the study of plants. Born in 1707 and better known as Linnaeus, he was appointed Professor of Botany at Uppsala University at the age of thirty-four—his first claim to fame. His second was his method of naming and classifying plants.

Up to the time of Linnaeus and the acceptance of his binomial system, the naming of plants had been haphazard. For professional use the names were in Latin, the international academic language, and gave a full description of the plant, which could vary from botanist to botanist. Vernacular names were just as confusing—some plants had as many as a hundred names, from different parts of the country. To take just one example, John Parkinson called the common Cowslip, which has over forty vernacular names, *Paralysis vulgaris pratenis flore flavo simplici odorato*. *Paralysis* was originally *herba paralysis* due to its reputed efficacy as a remedy for the palsy, aches and pains; *vulgaris pratensis* because it was common in fields; and *flore flavo simplici odorato* says that the flower is 'yellow, single and scented'. But thanks to Linnaeus, plants now have Latin, or scientific, names basically made up of two words—in this case *Primula veris,* 'spring-flowering primula'—and botanists around the world know exactly what the others are talking about.

The Linnaean System

The system developed by Linnaeus and improved since his time classified plants into four main divisions, only one of which—the spermatophytes, or seed plants—concerns us here. The seed plants are divided into two classes—dicotyledons, those with two seed leaves, and monocotyledons, with only one seed leaf. The classes are divided into orders consisting of closely related families, which in turn are made up of related genera (the plural of genus) comprising similar species. Under the binomial, or two-name, system each plant is given what may be likened to a first name and a surname, back to front. The generic name, or 'surname', which always starts with a capital letter, comes from how the plant is classified and is placed first, followed by the specific name of the individual species, which does not have a capital and which indicates what makes this particular plant different from others in its genus. It can indicate habitat, as in *aquaticus* meaning 'of water' or *arvensis,* 'of fields'; habit, as in *repens,* 'creeping'; geography, as in *pyrenaicum,* 'from the Pyrenees' or *scotica,* 'from Scotland'; or colour, as in *lutea,* meaning 'yellow'; or it may commemorate forever the botanist who first recorded that particular flower. The botanist Leonhard Fuchs found and first recorded the Common Spotted Orchid which was named *Dactylorhiza fuchsii*. What better way is there to be remembered?

The binomial system becomes even more complicated when wild and garden hybrids come into the picture, and in fact Linnaeus himself would have nothing to do with hybrids. There is a group of eminent botanists who form the International Nomenclature Committee which constantly studies and revises names as modern technology exposes errors in previously established relationships.

The Illustrators
Paleolithic man appears to have concentrated all his artistic abilities on drawing the wild animals around him but rarely, if ever, did he depict the plant life. The ancient Egyptians, too, paid little attention to plants, preferring to draw figures, and merely added a few stylized flowers here and there to fill up the spaces. Other highly developed races ignored plants or painted them inaccurately only as decorations on pottery and friezes, and it was not until the arrival of the herbals of two thousand years ago that flowers were illustrated in a more natural manner. The very early herbals, dating as far back as 300BC, were probably illustrated, but none of these has survived. The first illustrated book of great importance, dating from *c*512, was the *Codex Vindobonensis,* an illustrated copy of Dioscorides' *De Materia Medica,* now in the State Library in Vienna. It contains nearly 400 detailed, lifelike and accurate botanical illustrations. Such splendid works were few and far between and there was to be a lapse of over a thousand years before such a high standard was seen again.

Towards the end of the 14th century an occasional painting would depict a border of recognizable flowers; the white lily was the main one to be shown in a natural manner and the only one to appear with any regularity in an indentifiable shape. Very few plant illustrations appear to have been drawn from living specimens, and many were copies—often repeated from book to book—of earlier illustrations, with all their imperfections and mistakes.

Gradually, the Florentine painters added flowers to their landscapes, but no studies of individual plants seem to have survived from this period. Altarpieces in France, Holland and Germany featured certain flowers, other flowers appeared in borders of manuscripts, and a few were beginning to be treated with a little more design. The *Book of Hours* painted by Jean Bourdichon at the very start of the 16th century for Anne of Brittany contains 340 flowers, all recognizable and accurately named in French and Latin. About the same time, the German artist Albrecht Dürer was painting flowers in a delightful and delicate manner. His famous watercolour of a small piece of meadowland, in close up, showing every blade of grass and every weed in magnificent detail, is a joy to behold and has a timeless quality about it.

Many of the early printed herbals were illustrated with woodcuts and it was difficult in those days to produce delicate work by such means. Inevitably, the lines were coarse and the treatment stilted and heavy, and it was not until the 16th century that botanical illustration reached a high standard of beauty with finer lines and more detail.

By the late 16th century the great gardens were beginning to provide the setting for flowers which were merely beautiful as opposed to useful, their size and colours changing under the skilled hands of the expert plantsmen. Flowers from the four corners of the world were planted in profusion, and the botanical painters of the day were at last supplied with as much work as they could possibly wish for. Woodcuts were superseded by metal engravings—often coloured by hand—and far greater detail and finer lines became possible.

Thus began the heyday of flowers and gardens, books and paintings. Yet many of the great works of art produced at that time, which often took a lifetime to do, now lie hidden in museums and private collections. The original paintings of many of the botanical artists of the 17th century have not survived at all for us to see; only inferior engravings remain, but we can imagine how exquisite the original works must have been because some paintings which have survived—for example, those of the French artist Daniel Rabel—are greatly superior to the engravings taken from them.

The first woman to emerge as a serious botanical and entomological artist was the German-born Maria Merian who, in 1678, published the first of three books on European insects, delicately painted amongst their appropriate food plants or the flowers with which they are associated. At the age of fifty-one, Maria, with the help of one of her daughters, made the hazardous journey to South America to study, collect and paint the insects and flowers of the area.

One of the most famous botanical artists was Georg Ehret (1708–1770), a genius among flower painters, with a strength of style that brought feeling into the art. Much of his exquisite work lies unseen in museums. Pierre-Joseph Redouté, a Belgian, born in 1759, was another famous artist of the 18th century but his work can readily be seen as prints and on table mats. His roses, although beautifully painted, are in my opinion, not of quite such a high standard as the work of Georg Ehret, the Bauer brothers, or Pierre Jean Turpin (1775–1840), one of the greatest painters.

The Bauer brothers, Francis and Ferdinand, of German nationality, made England their home during the 18th century. Both were brilliant painters, very similar in style. Francis became the permanent artist at the Royal Botanic Gardens at Kew and worked there for fifty years; by contrast, Ferdinand was more of a wanderer and roamed the world painting flowers until he eventually returned to Germany. It is, however, Francis Bauer whose work is considered by many to be the greatest ever produced by one person.

Botany became such a popular pastime of the 19th century that every young lady began to paint her little flower pictures, illustrate verses and poems with garlands of over-pretty posies and to colour-in line drawings of flowers in books specifically designed for the purpose. A great many not very gifted amateurs painted a vast amount of over-fanciful and inaccurate flower pictures. There were, however, a few notable artists who rose above the ranks of the amateurs, particularly Walter Fitch (1817–1892) whose published paintings totalled almost 10,000 and who worked at Kew as sole illustrator for the *Botanical Magazine* for over forty years, continuing a tradition which included James Sowerby and Sydenham Edwards.

The silly sentimental age, the fun years of flowers, eventually gave way to the no-nonsense, serious and well-informed books on plants around the world. The invention of lithographic printing began a revolution which has culminated in colour reproductions of a very high standard. And with the high technical standards have come the artists. The 20th century has brought women to the fore, and several have worked at Kew for the *Botanical Magazine* as well as acting as freelance artists and illustrators of books. Notable among them are Lilian Snelling, Stella Ross-Craig, Margaret Stones and Mary Grierson whose paintings I greatly admire.

By the middle of this century the age of the field guide had arrived: small, plastic-covered, pocket-sized books designed to contain as many colour illustrations as possible to aid beginners and botanists alike in their pursuit of flowers. Perhaps not as exquisite as some beautiful books of earlier ages, they are nevertheless taken on walks, on holiday, find their way into schools and libraries and bring flowers into the homes of everyone who welcomes them.

THE FLORAL PATH

The path between the flowers is not an easy one to follow. On one side are the wild ones, the few indigenous plants mixed with the casual aliens and the escaped and introduced species. On the other side of the path are the flowers strictly for the garden, and I cannot allow many of these to stray across and into this particular book. Those that I do accept consist of a few of my favourite alpines and some common wild flowers of Europe which grow fairly contentedly in the wilder parts of the garden and which have not been changed in shape or colour by the hybridizers.

Throughout the ages, wild flowers played a far more important role in the life of the community than they do now. They provided food and, unknowingly, vitamins and minerals; they were the source of warpaint for primitive man, provided the colours for his art and crafts. They were invested with the power to ward off evil spirits, they poisoned man's enemies, cured his ills and played an essential part in the endless fertility rites. They carried warnings of untimely death and destruction according to how they were arranged, and to this day some flowers, such as Hawthorn blossom and Snowdrops, are considered omens of bad luck if brought into the house. Sweet-smelling herbs and rushes were gathered daily to strew over floors—Cleopatra was said to have rose-petal carpets eighteen inches deep. Some herbs were collected to stuff into small pillows to induce peaceful sleep, others were used to flavour food and mask the rancid taste of meat. Nosegays of flowers were carried by the fastidious, into whose fragrant faces they could bury their own in the hope of overcoming the unpleasant odours of the unwashed population and the open sewers in the street and of escaping infection. Some plants provided the ingredients for primitive insecticides to combat bed-bugs and body-lice, others the medicines which were supposed to cure all ills. But rarely were they loved for their beauty alone. Before the 16th century any flower, however beautiful, which did not provide some useful service was virtually ignored.

In the Beginning
The great ice ages which engulfed Britain left the land devoid of much of its vegetation. A few plants still survived in southern England and in Wales, which were less affected by the ice, and some alpine plants managed to cling to rocks and to life on the Burren in Ireland and Ben Lawers in Scotland where their descendants survive to this day.

It must have looked a bleak and barren land, as if the devastation had spread into eternity, but gradually over the centuries plants began again to carpet the ground. Seeds from more southerly lands were carried by the wind or on the feet or in the crops of migrating birds; others were brought by man, accidentally carried in the clothing of the earliest Paleolithic hunters or, later, deliberately introduced. Thousands of such introduced species did not flourish for long; but many did survive to escape into the wild, as did the medicinal herbs so carefully cultivated by the monks of early Christian times. And so our flora grew and multiplied as violet and Feverfew, Rosebay and chickweed, buttercup, oxalis and Ox-eye and many other early introductions crossed the path to become the flowering delight of the rich or the free food of the poor or the weedy pest of the farmer.

It was during the reign of Elizabeth I that our flora became much enriched as quantities of new and exotic plants, flower seeds, herbs and vegetables were brought back from expeditions to the far corners of the world in the Queen's fleet of ships. At long last flowers were enjoyed for their beauty as well as for their other virtues and were planted in ever-growing numbers to enhance the great gardens of the gentry.

A new breed of man began to emerge, one which was aware of the need to separate the sciences of medicine and botany. The new botanists began to create order out of the prevailing chaos, and gradually the power of superstition diminished as knowledge advanced.

In the 17th century the first professional plant hunters, men like John Tradescant and his son, searched the world for new species. The magnificent gardens blossomed anew with strange and beautiful blooms from the New World, from China and from any country whose flora was more exotic than our own.

The Floral Famine
Plants are often very accommodating and many settle happily in conditions very different to those in which they normally grow; even so, the wastage in transplanting them must have been enormous. Some flower hunters in the past obsessively gathered all the plants of a rare species that they could carry, destroying what was left lest someone else should find them and grow rich or famous from the same discovery. Although, as a result, our gardens became places of

great beauty, it also led to the death of floral rarities. To this day, the practice goes on in large or small measure, whether it is a plane-load of exotic plants dug up from one of the fast-diminishing rain forests to decorate a London club, or a few humble alpine plants smuggled home in the bottom of a sponge bag.

Over the years wild flowers have been destroyed in vast quantities, exterminated by the acre as roads and cities become concrete gravestones above them. When people ceased to need the common plants for food or medicine, they picked the beautiful ones in large numbers to sell for coppers in markets or by the roadside, thus helping to make flowers like Lady's Slipper Orchid the great rarities they are today. As agriculture and its technology spread, more fields of flowers were ploughed in or sprayed out, to the verge of extinction and beyond. Many species once common in this land have now been reduced by one means or another to a mere handful of plants, their exact locations a closely guarded secret.

Since the beginning of life on earth, species of both flora and fauna have been evolving; new ones appear and many disappear and this will always be so. To cope with changes in climate and other conditions, natural selection and survival of the fittest have always been the way of the world, but over the last century many species have disappeared which need not, and should not, have done so, for their destruction has been entirely man-made. Plants once used by man as food or as medicine, and now regarded as a pest, are not for us to destroy out of hand—or out of ignorance. Nearly every one is the food plant of some animal, bird or insect, yet we think we have the right not only to control such plants—which is often a necessary measure—but to exterminate them as well.

I hold no brief for the oversentimental who want nothing controlled, for good husbandry and sound land-management have conserved nature and not destroyed it, but I cannot forgive the mass removal of wild plants, be they trees of the rain forest or a few cornflowers in the wheat. In this country we take our flowers too much for granted—they are always there, until we suddenly realize that they are not.

Flowers still play an important part in our lives even if we swear we don't know a dandelion from a buttercup. They arrive at our cotside to welcome us into the world; they are held under our noses as soon as we can understand the word 'smell'; daisies are made into chains for small necks; posies are picked by small hands for Mother's Day; bouquets are traditionally carried by brides and are presented to mark all anniversaries, to cheer invalids and to acknowledge acts well and truly performed. Whatever we do, flowers are thrust upon us in some form or other—even plastic ones. Eventually we leave this world, as we entered it, surrounded by flowers.

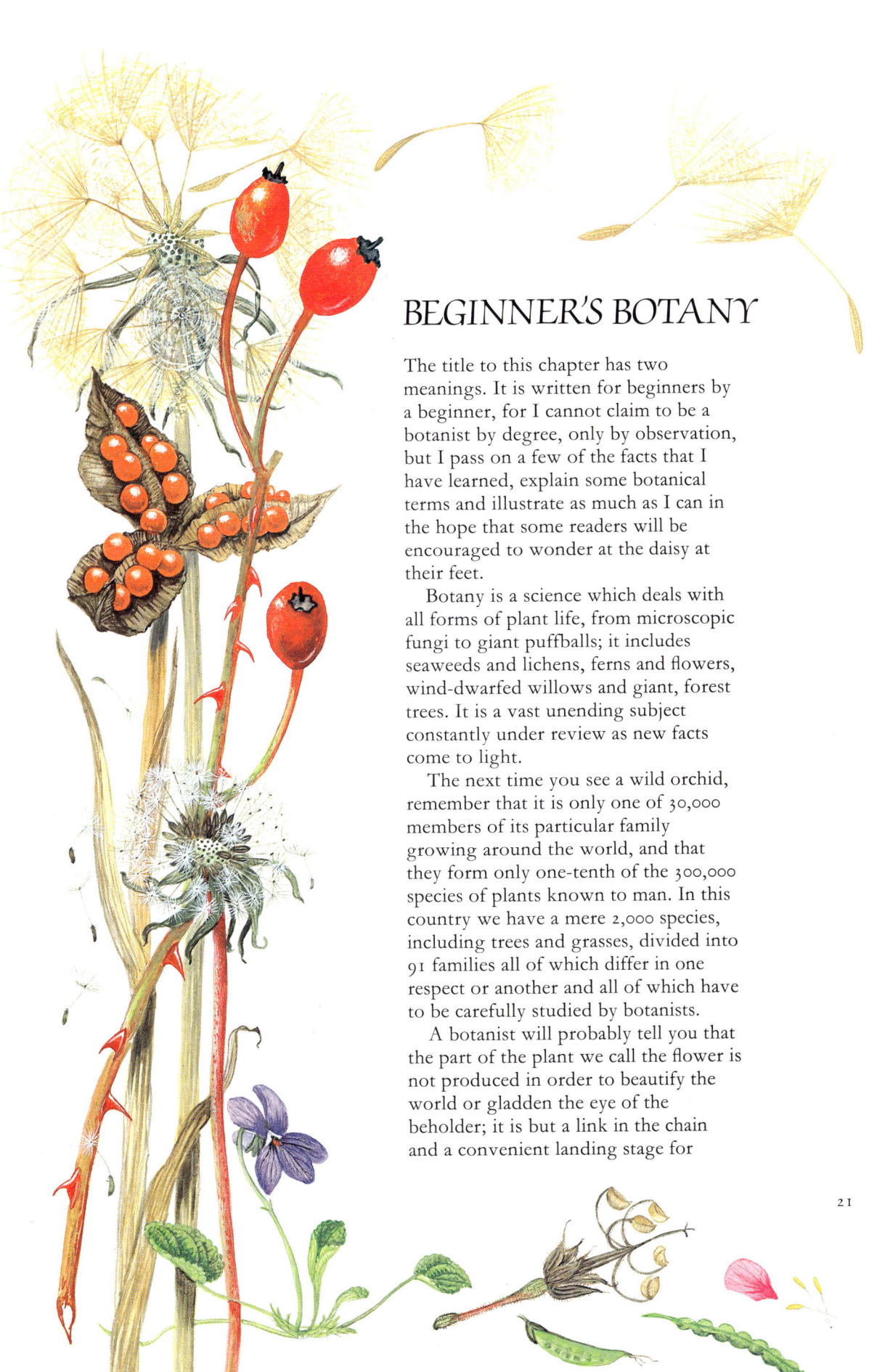

BEGINNER'S BOTANY

The title to this chapter has two meanings. It is written for beginners by a beginner, for I cannot claim to be a botanist by degree, only by observation, but I pass on a few of the facts that I have learned, explain some botanical terms and illustrate as much as I can in the hope that some readers will be encouraged to wonder at the daisy at their feet.

Botany is a science which deals with all forms of plant life, from microscopic fungi to giant puffballs; it includes seaweeds and lichens, ferns and flowers, wind-dwarfed willows and giant, forest trees. It is a vast unending subject constantly under review as new facts come to light.

The next time you see a wild orchid, remember that it is only one of 30,000 members of its particular family growing around the world, and that they form only one-tenth of the 300,000 species of plants known to man. In this country we have a mere 2,000 species, including trees and grasses, divided into 91 families all of which differ in one respect or another and all of which have to be carefully studied by botanists.

A botanist will probably tell you that the part of the plant we call the flower is not produced in order to beautify the world or gladden the eye of the beholder; it is but a link in the chain and a convenient landing stage for insects which squeeze between the tight lips of toadflaxes or disappear up the long throats of foxgloves in their quest for pollen-food or nectar, and at the same time carry out—unknowingly—the cross-pollination of the plant which is essential for the survival of the species. The only reason for the flower's existence is to produce the seed which will ensure for the future at least one more generation.

The seed is the last link in the botanical chain. But this is a rather cold matter of fact, and I still prefer to believe that the seed is the beginning of life and not the end product, that it is the flower which finishes the whole cycle with its burst of beauty. I remain unashamedly convinced that it blooms to give us pleasure. A landing stage is not enough.

To understand a few basic facts and botanical terms may not make one appreciate a flower any more than before, but a little learning, in this case, is not a dangerous thing. Beneath the cold facts one can appreciate the amazing and stubborn persistence of such a delicate object which has battled successfully through the ages to keep its hold upon this earth despite flood and drought, ice ages and storms and all that man can do to destroy it with his poison sprays, flame guns and bulldozers. Even after man has devastated an area by overgrazing or war and left it barren, flower seeds which have lain dormant for perhaps a century may suddenly germinate and cover the scars left by our ignorance or stupidity.

Plants have been fighting for survival for considerably longer than man, and while many have perished over the ages, unable to continue to adapt to changing conditions, others have spread and multiplied. With modern techniques it is now possible to ascertain from the fossil remains of plants that some have remained virtually unchanged over millions of years. Some organisms capable of photosynthesis have been found in layers of rock more than three billion years old. Remains of later stems, leaves and seeds have been found and identified, with members of the Buttercup and Water-lily families among the earliest; and seeds from late Bronze Age settlements include those of poppies, nettles, sandworts and Pennycress.

The study of botany goes back a long way, yet most of the mysteries which have been solved, and the subsequent advances made in knowledge, have been done so comparatively recently. The idea of male and female flowers was vaguely thought about during the time of the Greeks and Romans, and it is astonishing to realize that no one appears to have pursued this theory further until some seventeen hundred years had elapsed, when the reason why insects visited flowers was studied. Even then, no one arrived at the correct solution for not only did they continue to believe that no sexual organs were present in flowers, they also did not realize that cross-pollination was taking place, or that the fusion of the male and female parts of the flower was necessary for the production of seed. They merely came to the conclusion that the insects were collecting food for themselves and their hungry broods.

Then, in 1672, Nehemiah Grew, an English botanist, read a paper to the Royal Society on the anatomy of flowers, in which he referred to the stamens as the male part of the bloom. John Ray, the great naturalist, waited until 1686 before cautiously voicing his opinion that there might be some truth in the statement but that he would require more proof before he could be certain.

The existence of the male and female organs, their function and the use of pollen were eventually accepted by some eminent botanists around the world but rejected by others. As late as the beginning of the 18th century a famous French botanist still believed the extraordinary idea that pollen was the excess sap from the plant oozing out of the stamens, and it was not until the middle of the century that Grew's hypothesis was finally accepted as the truth. What nature had decided millions of years ago was essential for the survival of the plant species, man only discovered a mere two hundred and fifty years ago.

By the middle of the 18th century, Linnaeus was systematically classifying and naming wild flowers; other botanists were also advancing knowledge, and many of them contributed valuable information. By means of careful work many important facts were added between the time of Linnaeus and the early years of the 19th century which saw the emergence of great men such as Charles Darwin and later Fritz Muller who studied in detail the pollination of plants by insects. By the beginning of the 20th century, laboratory techniques and new scientific methods of studying plants had taken over from the enthusiastic amateur.

Photosynthesis
One of the most important chemicals discovered to be present in green plants is chlorophyll, a pigment manufactured in the leaves, which is responsible for the colour of the plants and which is capable of absorbing the red, orange and blue bands of the spectrum. In a process called photosynthesis, the chlorophyll uses this solar energy to combine carbon dioxide and water to produce food in the form of sugar while the plant gives off oxygen. The amount of sunlight that is available governs the amount of food which can be produced. The production ceases during the hours of darkness when the process is reversed; carbon dioxide is given off and oxygen is 'burned' up. The energy created during the day is used to increase the growth of the plant by producing more leaves and extra roots. If, after that, there is still a surplus of the energy, it goes into the making of more of the nectar which attracts pollinating insects.

Roots

The root systems of plants vary greatly in size and shape. Some are woody, others fleshy; they may have long, thin taproots or a network of hairlike roots. Some plants produce new tubers, bulbs or corms annually, and in these the food is stored for the following year.

The main tasks of the roots are to provide sufficient water for the production of sugar and to keep the plant firmly in the soil. Anyone who has tried to pull out a large dock or even a small dandelion will know just how efficiently even a tapering root system can anchor the plant.

Surplus water is given off by the plant in a process known as *transpiration* and it is estimated that 99 per cent of the liquid taken up by the root is returned to the atmosphere in this way.

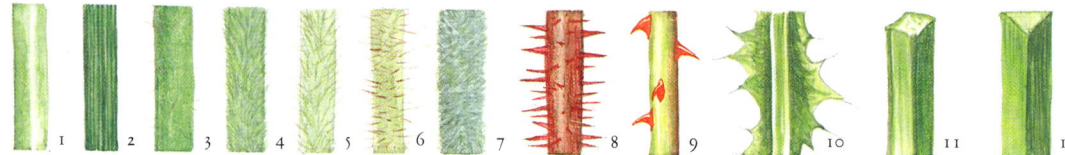

1 *Smooth and glabrous*
2 *Striate or furrowed*
3 *Pilose*
4 *Pubescent*
5 *Hirsute*
6 *Hispid*
7 *Tomentose*
8 *Spines*
9 *Thorns*
10 *Winged*
11 *Square*
12 *Triangular*

Stems

The stem is not only a structure which has to bear the weight of a plant, it also has to convey the sap to all parts of the system. Stems may be hollow or solid, stiffly erect or soft and prostrate, branched or unbranched, and, in cross-section, round, triangular or square. The surface, known as the *epidermis*, may be smooth, hairless, rough, sticky or thickly covered with hairs, bristles or thorns. The botanical names to describe these sometimes form part of the plant's name as well. If a plant has *hirsuta* as its specific name, for example, then you know that either the leaves or stems are covered with short stiff hairs.

Plants have evolved a number of devices on their skins to protect themselves, thorns being particularly effective against browsing animals; they also prevent small creatures, such as snails, from crawling up the stems but they do not deter mice—I have watched them climb extremely thorny rose stems to bite off the hips. In some cases, leaves have also developed protective spines, and these continue down the stems, like the familiar sharp 'wings' on thistles. Some of these thorny weapons are straight, others hooked, and in some parts of the world they have developed into savage and wickedly dangerous pieces of armoury, capable of withstanding the onslaught of large animals. People have taken advantage of such thorns by making stock-proof fences from their branches. In Britain, our thorns are mild by comparison and merely leave a few scratches on the arms of blackberry or rose-hip pickers.

The stalk that joins a solitary flower to the stem is a *peduncle,* which is also the term used for the main stalk leading up to a bunched head of flowers. The small stalks within that bunch are *pedicles*.

Leaves

The leaf's basic shape is usually flat and very thin, so designed that it can receive the maximum amount of sunlight over the largest area. Each and every leaf is a small, efficient chemical factory, working at all times with its fellow leaves for the good of the plant. Leaves are arranged around the plant to the best advantage, some in the form of rosettes with the lowest ones always on the longest stems, others spiralling up the stem, but each one spreading out to the light in order to assist photosynthesis and the production of chlorophyll.

Leaves have a waterproof skin which may be thin and transparent, thick and waxy or covered in protective hairs which help to insulate it, keeping it cool and thus preventing too much loss of water. Succulent plants, such as sedums, actually store water in their leaves.

Young leaves in spring can look as though they are made of semi-transparent silk because the sunlight can penetrate right through the very thin cells, but as the summer progresses the cell walls thicken, causing the leaves to lose that wonderful spring-green colour.

As with the stems, there are many standard terms in use to describe not only the shape of the leaf but also its edge, surface, habit of growth and its position on the stalk. The main part of the leaf is the *blade* or *lamina*. If there is a stalk, this is the *petiole*; small leaflike growths at the base, not always present, are the *stipules*.

1 Hottentot Fig
2 Round-leaved Common Sundew
3 Oblong-leaved Sundew
4 English Stonecrop
5 Stinging Nettle
6 Violets
7 Alpine Lady's Mantle
8 Clovers
9 Spear Thistle
10 Marsh Pennywort
11 Lungwort
12 Cyclamen
13 Stitchworts
14 Lady's Mantle

25

There are also names to describe the surface of the leaf; a *scabrous* leaf is covered with rough hard bristles, a *rugose* one is wrinkled because of the close network of veins leading from the midrib, and so on.

There are even more names to describe the actual shape of the leaf and its margin. One with a clean-cut, straight edge is simply termed *entire* and when it is also wavy-edged it is *undulate*. But when it looks as though pinking shears have been used along the margins, the names become complicated and numerous. There are names to describe the smallest variation, from regular straight teeth to double-teeth, uneven and rounded or sharp backward-facing ones.

The margins of leaves
1 Entire: smooth edge
2 Undulate: wavy
3 Crenulate: small round teeth; Crenate: larger round teeth
4 Serrate: sawtoothed; Serrulate: small sawtoothed
5 Dentate: toothed and at an angle
6 Sinuate: round, broad and irregular teeth
7 Ciliate: hair-fringed
8 Lobed: wide-toothed

Leaves are frequently too irregular in outline even to be called *toothed*, and a further list of descriptive names has to be applied to explain the general shape, but not the edge, of the leaf. Thus an undivided leaf is known as *simple* and this may have an *entire* edge or one of the many *toothed* variations. If the leaf is divided into several fingers, like Green Hellebore, it becomes *compound*, and it may have an *entire*, *toothed* or *crenate* edge or any permutation that nature dictates. A common shape for a leaf, and a much used word to describe it, is *lobed*; lobes are too large to be called teeth—an oak leaf is a typical example. After this, the list of leaf shapes becomes long and complicated at first glance, but most terms are self-explanatory, such as oblong, ovate, rhomboidal and so on. A selected few are illustrated here. There are also special terms to describe the shape of the tips and bases of leaves and these too are shown.

Some leaves have virtually changed their shapes over the years and now resemble thorns. Gorse and Butcher's Broom are typical, while Holly and

The shapes of leaves
1 Sagitate: arrowhead-shaped
2 Lanceolate: narrow and tapering at each end
3 Orbicular: circular
4 Ovate: egg-shaped
5 Cordate: heart-shaped
6 Reniform: kidney-shaped
7 Peltate: stalk attached to the underside centre
8 Trifoliate: divided in three
9 Palmate: shaped like a hand

Tops and bases of leaves

26

thistles still keep their leaves but surround the edges with fierce *spines* pointing in all directions; yet other leaves cover their whole surface with spines—for example, cacti—and several have a second line of defence, as many an innocent-looking hairy leaf can cause skin irritation and rashes as well as stings. A good example is the Stinging Nettle which is the worst offender in this country but mild compared with many tropical plants.

The scientific names of many plants tell immediately what shape the leaf is or what its surface is like. If, for instance, you find a leaf shaped like an

Spiny leaves

Butcher's Broom

Holly

Thistle

arrow, i.e. *sagittate,* a quick glance down the index will give you *Sagittaria sagittifolia,* 'the Arrowhead', and the illustration will confirm your identification.

The featherlike *pinnate* leaves may have more divisions to each leaflet and so become *bi-pinnate, tri-pinnate,* and so on, until they become such a confused mass of divided leaflets that the term *deeply divided* is frequently used to cover a multitude of complications.

Stipules are very easily overlooked but if present they are valuable aids to identification. The majority are small, simple leaflike structures found growing where the true leaf joins the stem; other stipules sheath the stem, and some join together to form a tube around it. *Bracts* are also small leaflike forms, usually simple in outline, which appear at the base of a flower. Sometimes several such bracts form a circle around the base of the umbel. The *calyx* is a leafy case tightly enclosing the bud, which, when the flower begins to open, either falls off or stays open behind the flower, acting in a supporting role. The number of separate *sepals*, or leaves, of the calyx varies, and in many cases you will find the same numbers as there are flower petals.

Sepals are usually green, the shape varying from the simple concave ones that enclose a buttercup to the long, unevenly shaped leaflike sepals of the rose. Some flowers lack petals altogether, their place being taken by brightly coloured sepals which look remarkably like petals. A very good example is the Marsh Marigold whose brilliant yellow sepals are the same shape as the petals of its relatives, the buttercups.

Flowers

It is nearly always the flower which attracts our attention and admiration, and it is at this small part that we first look if we wish to identify a plant. The many different shapes, colours and patterns of flowers can help to sort them into their correct families, but sometimes these vary greatly even within a family, which for the beginner can make identification a little difficult. The purple Pasque Flower, for example, is not in the least like a wild clematis, and neither looks very like a buttercup, yet all are members of one family, the Ranunculaceae. It is less difficult to see a similarity in growth and flower shape between the Wild Carrot, the Hogweed and Wild Parsnip, even if the colour is different; these are all Umbelliferae, members of the Carrot family.

Among the flowers illustrated here are three from the Caryophyllaceae family, or pinks as they are commonly called. The Maiden Pink and the Small-flowered Catchfly have a certain family likeness, but the third member, Ragged Robin, has petals of a very different shape. The various violets and pansies resemble each other closely, but at first glance one might also include the Common Butterwort as well, although this belongs to quite a different group.

This great variety of colours and shapes of flowers—with all their

1 Field Bindweed
2 Perforate St John's Wort
3 Large-flowered Butterwort
4 Marsh Violet
5 Wild Pansy
6 Foxglove
7 Germander Speedwell
8 Ivy-leaved Toadflax
9 Birdseye Primrose
10 Cowslip
11 Maiden Pink
12 Small-flowered Catchfly
13 Cyclamen
14 Ragged Robin
15 Marsh Gentian
16 Large-flowered Hemp-nettle
17 Red Hemp-nettle
18 Bastard Balm
19 Meadow Clary
20 Lady Orchid
21 Burnt Orchid
22 Common Spotted Orchid
23 Military Orchid
24 Grass of Parnassus
25 Greater Meadow-rue

spots, stripes and shadings, their perfumes or unpleasant smells—is not produced by any haphazard game of chance, it is the result of gradual natural selection; each and every feature, down to the smallest spot, is there for a purpose. To us, it may seem to be 'just a pretty face'. To the plant, it is the lure, the bait, the insect's larder, the seedmachine and the promise of the survival of the species.

A complex and highly technical piece of natural engineering, each flower is designed specifically to fulfil its function. In some cases it is custom-built to fit only one particular insect and should the insect fail to arrive at the right place at the right time then the future of that species may be endangered. No other insect is built in the correct shape to reach the nectar or transmit pollen from the stamen to the stigma of that particular plant.

A flower may be either *dioecious*, having all male flowers on one plant and all female on another; *monoecious*, having separate male and female flowers but both growing on the same plant; or *hermaphrodite*, with both male and female organs in the same flower.

The most obvious parts of a flower are the *petals* which collectively form the *corolla*. In the centre there is a varying number of *stamens* (the male organs of the flower), each of which is made up of a *stalk* or *filament*, topped by the pollen-bearing *anther*. Also in the centre is the *ovary* which contains the undeveloped seeds and from which rises the *stigma*. These together are known as the *pistil* (the female organs of the flower) whose primary function is to receive the pollen.

The colour of the petals of a flower is due to pigments. The yellow shades come from living bodies inside the cells, which are called *plastids*; the red, blue and purple tones come from pigments which are dissolved in the sap of the cells. Some colours are more attractive to insects than others, and many markings, such as a ring of a different colour around the 'eye' of a flower, act as a homing device to guide the insect straight to the pollen-bearing stamens. Stripes, spots, circles, ridges and other marks, even hairs and grooves, which we may not see well, are familiar and easily recognized signposts to a bee, as clear as a brilliantly lit flarepath is to a pilot.

Flowers which are pollinated by a hovering fly or moth need no landing stage, and the shape is therefore not important so long as the tubelike entrance to the pollen or nectar is clearly defined. Beetles often select flat, open flowers, and many may be seen feasting on the white, lace-covered

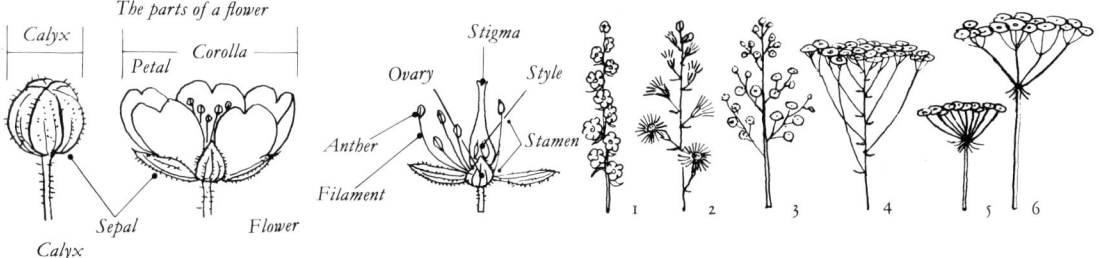

Positions of flowers on a stem
1 *Spike*
2 *Raceme*
3 *Panicle*
4 *Corymb*
5 *Umbel*
6 *Compound umbel*

tables of the Carrot family. The outer row of large, sterile florets of Cow Parsley and the long rays of Ox-eye Daisies act as homing devices for insects which might not otherwise notice the tiny, fertile flowers in the centre. Flies seem to love rather unpleasant-smelling plants, those with the odour of bad meat or fish being particularly appealing, which is perhaps only natural. Bees are among the most prolific collectors of pollen and visit many flowers in rapid succession for they have but a short time in which to feed a large family of larvae, and pollen is a highly nutritious and protein-rich food. They and other insects can see colours more brilliantly than man is able to and can also detect ultraviolet light, which makes the guidelines clearly visible to them but not to us. Even stamens, it has been proved, stand out like well-lit beacons within the corolla.

Other small parts of a flower may have considerably more influence on insects than we realize; hairs, grooves and spots all play a part in directing the visitor along the right path, and may be likened to roads and signposts or to a map, well designed to point in the direction of the honey pot.

A few plants give off a powerful scent, mainly at night, to attract a passing moth, and many of these flowers are white which helps the insect to home in on them quickly. Butterfly Orchids rely on their vanilla scent and white flowers to attract their moth pollinators after dark. The Bee Orchid is said to smell like a female bee, and the lip is very like the brown furry body of that insect.

Pollination is merely the transference of pollen by insects or windpower from one plant to another, or, in the case of self-pollination, within the plant. Once the pollen has adhered to the sticky receptive stigma, fertilization, which is quite a separate process, can, or should, follow. As a general rule, nature dislikes self-pollination, but many flowers do have a last-minute fail-safe device which ensures that its own pollen is shed on to the stigma should a suitable insect fail to arrive.

In spite of all the elaborate precautions taken by many flowers to avoid self-pollination, others continue to do just that year after year and remain remarkably healthy. These, however, may well be doomed to eventual extinction for they breed such pure lines in small localized communities that almost new species have evolved which cannot adapt to changing conditions because, without variation in the seedlings, natural selection and the survival of the fittest cannot take place.

Some flowers, such as violas, Wood-sorrel and Common Chickweed, are cross-pollinated but produce very little seed because they often grow in deep woodland or under taller plants and need this alternative means because they are difficult for insects to find. Later in the season the plants produce a number of non-opening flowers with very small petals, called *cleistogamic* flowers, which are entirely self-pollinating and produce a great deal of seed.

The way flowers prevent self-pollination varies: some do not produce both ripe pollen and receptive stigma at the same stage of the flower's development; others have different heights and arrangements of these parts. The Primrose is an excellent example. In some flowers the stigma is uppermost and can clearly be seen at the mouth of the corolla with the stamens hidden below in the tube. In other flowers the arrangement is reversed and the stamens are easily visible at the top. These are called *pin-eyed* and *thrum-eyed* flowers respectively. An insect pushing its tongue down the tube of the corolla will collect pollen from one stamen at

Arrangements to avoid self-pollination

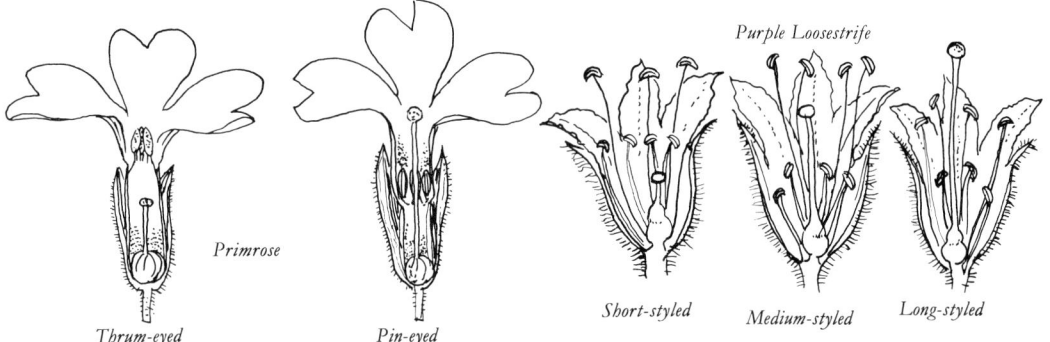

a certain level to ensure that it is deposited on the stigma of another flower of the opposite position. Purple Loosestrife arranges its stamens in three ways, at the top in some flowers, halfway down or at the bottom in others, thus really hedging its bets.

It has been said that through inbreeding self-pollination could well be the cause of self-destruction at some time in the future. Another possible cause is extreme specialization and over-adaption of the pollinating mechanism to one specific insect. If that insect is not in the right place at the right time and no other insect can take its place, then that plant could face extinction.

Consider Monkshood, a wild flower which man has also taken into his garden. It is completely dependent upon bumblebees for they are the only insects which can reach the nectar and collect pollen on their furry bodies, so the plant is limited in its range to that of the bees. 'Where the bee sucks there grow I' is the byword of the Monkshood—there and no further.

Nectar is the sugary secretion which is an important food for insects. Various parts of the plant are capable of producing nectar—in the flower, at the base of leaves, and so on. The amount of nectar varies from plant to plant; in some it is absent, others have very little, and a few actually drip with sweetness. In orchids, nectar is stored in their long spurs and specialist feeders are required to reach the supply. The most famous is the Madagascan Orchid (*Angraecum sesquipedale*), with a fourteen-inch-

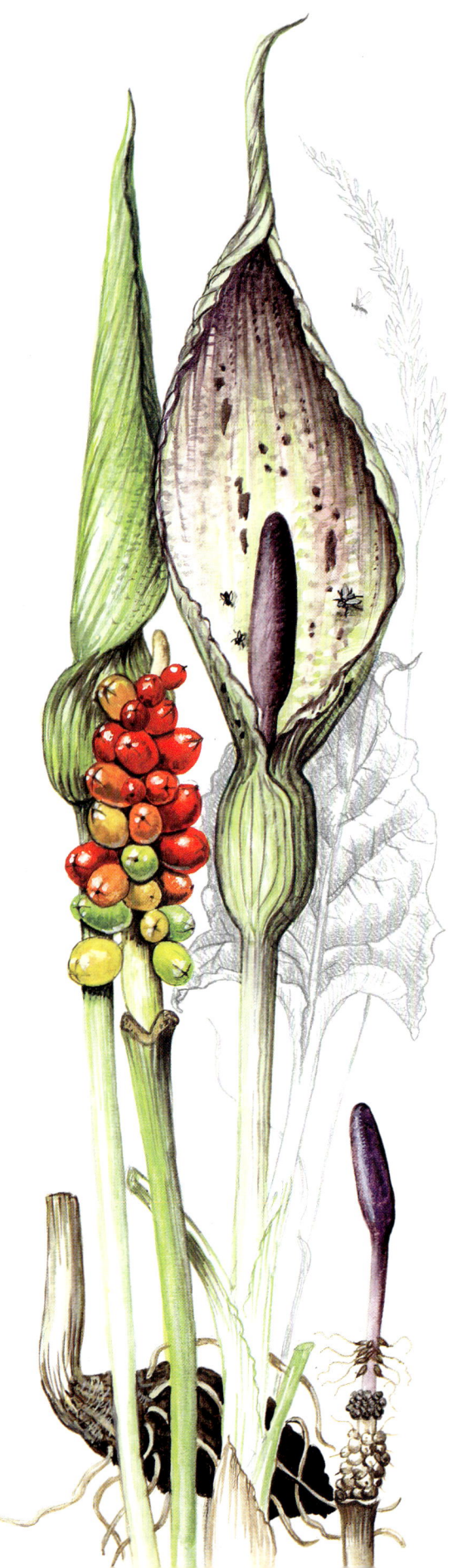

Lords and Ladies

long spur, of which Charles Darwin predicted that one day a moth would be found with a proboscis long enough to sup the nectar at the foot. True enough, in 1934, a large hawkmoth with a tongue almost fourteen inches long, was discovered drinking and pollinating the white orchid.

There are thieves in all walks of life, and even insects have discovered that they can outwit the complicated procedure laid down by some flowers and rob them of their nectar by biting through the back of the flower. These 'bite-and-run' vandals, such as bees, not only rob their victims but, what is worse, they bypass the stamens and leave the flower unpollinated. Some flowers have anti-thief devices in the form of guard-hairs to stop insects which are not the true pollinators from obtaining the nectar; other flowers have false nectaries in various positions, enabling all-comers to partake of the feast while the true pollinator can reach the central larder with less competition.

Yet another form of attractant is heat. Lords and Ladies is one such plant which produces this heat, for inside its *spathe* (the leaf-like part enclosing the flower cluster) the temperature is higher than the air outside. Add to this a very strong smell of rotting meat, and small flies are irresistibly lured into its cosy, warm interior. Once they have descended into the lower dungeon where the smell is even more delectable, they are unable to get out for the prison walls are clothed in downward-pointing hairs and are also very slippery. Any pollen which the flies may have brought in with them is transferred to the sticky stigma as they move around, and when this has been achieved the 'walls' dry up. In payment for their service, the flower gives the donors a small drop of nectar each, to keep them going for the next day or so until the pollen is ripe. Then the flower showers this over the prisoners, after which they are allowed to make their getaway. In all probability they will immediately fly to the next flower in good condition—emitting yet more mouthwatering smells—and so face yet another prison sentence.

Many more examples of strange and highly individual behaviour exist in the plant world. I particularly love the small, orange-yellow Bog Asphodel, found in many marshes and peat bogs in Britain, of which Anthony Huxley writes in his book *Plant and Planet,* that it relies on rain water, which settles on the hairs of the filament, to form a bridge over which the pollen can flow from the anthers to the stigma— too delightful a happening to miss.

I have written about self- and cross-pollination, but there is a third method which is common and successful; this is wind pollination. Flowers which lack a *perianth* (the floral envelope made up of the calyx or the corolla or both), or have very insignificant petals, and those which lack scent and nectar and therefore have little or nothing to attract insects, often produce an abundance of pollen. Many of these flowers hang downwards, such as Hazel catkins; you have only to shake the loosely jointed column of flowers to see clouds of ripe, golden pollen dust borne away in the air. There are more than five million grains of pollen in every single catkin, and as there is probably a group of two or three catkins growing together, and these groups are only a little apart all over the branches, the amount of pollen produced by each bush is astronomical and seems to be a

January

February

Hazel

October

33

great waste of energy. It also seems like gross overproduction when but a few grains are sufficient to pollinate the small scarlet-tasselled females which grow here and there along the branches, looking totally inadequate when you consider the size of the autumn nuts into which they will grow. But wind pollination is a chancy business, a real touch-and-blow affair, so that five million grains have to be sacrificed for every one that finds its target.

The female flowers are generally completely overlooked because they are overshadowed by the more showy male. Many catkin-minded people, like myself, become suddenly spring-fevered early in February and suffer from the compulsion to pick 'lambs' tails' which daily seem to lengthen and promise that spring is here, even though the snow is on their branches. Next time you dust away yet another cloud of pollen below the vase, look for the tiny female flower and use a magnifying glass to see her scarlet tassels properly.

The catkin-like flowers of Dog's Mercury are nothing to look at compared with Hazel, but nevertheless this low-growing plant can produce well over one thousand million grains of pollen during its short life. Add to this the forest of grasses and it all becomes a hay-fever sufferer's nightmare, as I well know. It has been proved that pollen can travel up to three thousand miles and the lighter-than-dust pollen grains of the wild orchids in this country can reach the upper atmosphere before floating down to earth again.

Only one more marvel of nature needs be told, a statement which is based on fact but which must remain a delightful piece of fiction. It was perhaps first related in dry statistical terms but I think not; I believe that Charles Darwin allowed himself to be transported for a moment into flights of fancy when he wrote that an acre of land would hold 174,240 plants of Heath Spotted Orchid, each having a six-inch square of ground to itself. Making allowance for 400 infertile seeds per capsule, the progeny of one single plant could achieve this in one year's distribution of its seed. At the same rate of production, the great-grandchildren of that single plant would clothe nearly the entire landmass of the world with a uniform green carpet, to say nothing of a sea of pink flowers—what a delightful prospect! It just proves how hazardous are the existence and future prospects of one single flower—the million-to-one-against chance of survival—when changing conditions, weather and people are all against you.

Insect-pollinated flowers produce far less pollen than wind-borne ones, but the ovaries often contain more ovules, so, after successful pollination by one method or another, *fertilization* can take place. This is a process involving the fusion of a male nucleus from the pollen grain with the female nucleus in each *ovule*. These ovules (and there may be many thousands inside even a tiny ovary) are the structures which, after fertilization, develop into viable seeds.

Fruits

The fruit of flowers is a general term used by the botanist to denote the seeds and their covering, whether soft, juicy and edible—like a cherry—or dry and spiny, or any other type of container which holds the ripening seed after fertilization has taken place.

Some flowers produce and distribute their seeds with little effort and do not make much show of it, merely quietly dropping their seeds around them, while others go in for more spectacular wind-assisted methods—we can see their ripe seeds wafting in clouds of silky parachutes across thistle- and dandelion-infested fields.

The succulent-looking fruits of summer and autumn, which give country lanes so much extra colour, are often edible but some are merely unpalatable while others are exceedingly poisonous. These are listed on page 52; it is wise to study and learn which to avoid.

Fleshy types of fruits are divided into three main groups: *berries* with several seeds, or pips, within a soft fleshy cushion which is itself in a firm outer skin, for example, the Gooseberry; *drupes* which usually have only one seed covered in a hard shell surrounded by a soft fleshy substance, the whole within a firm skin, such as the Cherry (Raspberries and Blackberries, which produce several small drupes in one cluster, also come under this heading); and *pomes* whose fleshy parts surround one or more seeds, each encased in a hard cover, the whole of which is composed of the swollen calyx tube, as in the Crab Apple. Roses also have a swollen calyx tube, but they are a special case as their seeds are loose inside the calyx and not covered with a hard casing. Strawberries are different again, as the fleshy part forms the centre, and the small seeds, which are really achenes, are embedded in the outer surface.

Dry fruits in containers which split open spontaneously on one or more sides to release their seeds are called *dehiscent*. Seed heads, such as those of the poppy, St John's Wort and the crucifers, all come under the heading of *capsule* and open in various ways. The poppy, for instance, develops a row of holes around the top of the capsule which turns it into an efficient dispenser, rather like a pepper pot; as the wind moves it, the seeds are scattered around.

A seed tightly enclosed within a woody exterior needs little explanation, as everyone recognizes a *nut*, and a single seed loosely enclosed in a dry covering is an *achene*. These may be joined together in a group, as in the buttercup.

The names which describe the shapes of seeds are similar to those for leaves and are mainly self-explanatory, that is oval, cylindrical, and so on. The covering of the seed has also been given an extensive list of names and again these are easy to understand; such names as ridged, reticulated, pitted, and so on.

The manner in which seeds reach their resting places varies from plant to plant. Some forcibly eject them, the balsams and various crucifers in particular. Geraniums use the slingshot method to throw a single seed from each of their five pockets. Their near relations, the erodiums, when their seeds are freed from the central column, actually corkscrew into the ground from where their barbs prevent their being easily pulled out again. Remove a seed from a ripe capsule and watch it twist and turn in circles within a few seconds.

Seeds of the Daisy family parachute to earth; Sycamores and maples 'helicopter' their way down while other plants rely on their hooked seeds catching on the fur of animals or the clothing of man, to be distributed far afield in this manner. These 'hitchhikers' include the well-known burrs and cleavers which are so difficult to remove from one's clothing. Forgetmenots have hooks on their calyx, Wood Anemones have hooked styles and Enchanter's Nightshade has hooks on the sides of the seed casing.

Rivers and the sea can carry seeds from one shore to another where they will still be able to germinate if they land on suitable soil. Birds and animals also play their part in the distribution of nuts, particularly acorns, which they bury and then forget.

And so, in one way or another, millions of seeds are scattered far and wide every year so that a few thousand will germinate and grow to maturity—weather, grazing animals and man permitting.

1 Crab Apple (pome)
2 Wild Cherry (drupe)
3 Rose Hips
4 Wild Strawberry
5 Gooseberry (berry)
6 Hazel (nuts)
7 Blackberry (drupe)
Dry dehiscent fruits:
8 Poppy (capsule)
9 Hairy Bittercress
10 Buttercup (group of achenes)
11 Thistle
12 Field Pennycress
13 Cleavers
14 Shepherd's Purse

Coltsfoot and daisies

WAYSIDE WEEDS

How can one best define, and indeed defend, a weed? It has been described as a plant which flourishes where you do not want it to grow, and to the average person it is a wild flower when it blooms in the countryside and a weed when it appears in the garden. It always seems to produce a vast amount of seed at a precocious age and to distribute them just before you get around to pulling it up, and every one of them appears to germinate and thrive where well-brought-up garden flowers refuse!

Many weeds are condemned as uneconomic occupants of valuable farming land. Their root systems impoverish the soil around them, and so their control and early removal is advisable. But control sometimes means extermination for in Britain every acre must be set aside for food production, roads or housing estates, and there is little room to spare for wild weeds—or so it is said.

Some weeds act as hosts for the diseases of cultivated farm crops. Fat Hen can become infected with a virus which it passes on to Sugar Beet. Shepherd's Purse, Groundsel and Pennycress can also infect crops with virus diseases. These and many other plants are therefore dangerous on arable land.

Tall flowers growing on road verges restrict the visibility of the motorists and are a hazard, so they must be cut down, or worse, sprayed out of existence. When the rank weeds die, so too do the Cowslips which we have seen along some road verges in Gloucestershire, twisting grotesquely after their dose of herbicide. These are flowers we cannot spare.

The Lost Flowers of the Cornfields

When the poppies were banished, the Corn Cockles and Cornflowers went also, but there were valid reasons for their removal, for the Corn Cockle had become one of the most noxious weeds of farmlands as early as the 16th century. Its seeds contain a poison which, when mixed with wheat, taints the resulting flour. It was common in cornfields until the early years of the 19th century but since then has become very rare.

Cornflowers, too, were numerous. In the 19th century John Clare wrote of them that they were 'troubling the cornfields with their destroying beauty'. It is sad that two such beautiful flowers had to be destroyed and that they were so loathed as weeds though still so much loved as garden plants.

So pestilent a weed was the brilliant yellow Corn Marigold to farmers that King Henry II decreed it should be destroyed whenever it appeared, probably the first flower to receive the royal death warrant. It can still be found on disturbed ground.

The small Summer Pheasant's-eye used to be abundant on arable land. It probably did little harm and its cherry-red, black-patched flowers were gathered and sold in Covent Garden. Now it is seldom seen, the victim of careful seed-screening.

The tall wild Larkspur must have looked particularly beautiful when it turned meadows to a blue haze of flowers. Over the last 150 years this flower too has decreased, and the same fate has befallen many other cornfield weeds, including Field Cow-wheat, Blue Woodruff, Thorow-wax and Small-flowered Catchfly.

1 *Corn Cockle*
2 *Cornflower*
3 *Corn Marigold*
4 *Summer Pheasant's-eye*
5 *Larkspur*
6 *Field Cow-wheat*
7 *Blue Woodruff*
8 *Thorow-wax*
9 *Small-flowered Catchfly*

'The Persistent Hordes'
If the 'destroying beauties' of the last few centuries have been exterminated, other, less attractive ones remain. These include docks and thistles, Charlock, Wild Radish, Black Mustard, chickweed and Shepherd's Purse, Ivy-leaved Speedwell, Knotgrass, Persicaria, the vegetables of bygone days—Fat Hen and Good King Henry—and the familiar mayweeds and sow-thistles. The less plaguesome weeds are probably as common as ever: Groundsel and Silverweed, Field Forgetmenot, Creeping Cinquefoil, various buttercups, deep-rooting Field Bindweed and the prostrate pimpernel which is usually scarlet but may also be found in shades from white through palest pink and lilac to purple and occasionally even a true, clear blue. Hairy Tare, once the scourge of cornfields, destroyed crops by smothering less vigorous plants so earning its old name of Strangler Vetch. Over the last hundred years, its hold has been broken and its numbers greatly reduced.

1 *Black Mustard*
2 *Wild Radish*
3 *Charlock*
4 *Field Forgetmenot*
5 *Creeping Cinquefoil*
6 *Stinking Mayweed*
7 *Scentless Mayweed*
8 *Shepherd's Purse*
9 *Silverweed*
10 *Ivy-leaved Speedwell*
11 *Hairy Tare*
12 *Scarlet Pimpernel and colour variations*

The Wild Weeds of Europe

In parts of Europe where the land is broad and the population sparse, wayside and farm weeds do not have to fight for survival. Cornflower still flourishes as a dash of brilliant, cold sapphire blue among the cool green leaves of young wheat, and poppies compete freely with the corn for a place in the sun.

Meadows are full of flowers and if the farmers have to cut two fields to obtain the same amount of hay as one would provide in this country, it does not seem to matter, for there the sun is shining and life is more leisurely. The milk yield is not quite as important, and the cows seem to like their diet of dried meadow flowers.

In one small valley of the Dordogne we found twenty-five species of wild orchids, all but one of which could be found in Britain if you were prepared to travel the length of the country and knew where to find them. Here they can be seen in less than an hour's stroll, growing abundantly among the meadow flowers. Many are cut in their prime for hay, and I have picked up bunches of Bees and Butterflies, Pyramids and Spiders but there are always many left uncut along the roadside to disperse seed far and wide. Each year they are as plentiful as ever.

There is little traffic on the smaller roads of France, so the verges remain uncut and for hundreds of kilometres there is a changing ribbon of colour. Viper's Bugloss and royal-blue Clary, Red Helleborines among tall spikes of Lizard Orchids and armies of Military Orchids, all growing in such profusion one almost, but never quite, takes them for granted. The wild 'weeds' of France are the rarities of Britain.

1 Meadow Clary
2 Cornflower
3 Creeping Bellflower
4 Common Poppy

The Old Contemptibles

For centuries, weeds in general and thistles, docks and nettles in particular have plagued gardeners and farmers alike and have been much discussed. Geoffrey Chaucer complained of nettles in 1380, Thomas Tusser in 1557 wrote much about weeds in his book *Five Hundred Pointes of Husbandry*. William Shakespeare in *Richard II* wrote, 'I will go root away the noisome weeds that without profit suck the soil's fertility from wholesome flowers'. In 1731, Jethro Tull in his book *The Horse Hoeing Husbandry* said, 'It is needless to go about to compute the value of the damage weeds do, since all the experienced husbandmen know it to be very great and would unanimously agree to extirpate their whole race as entirely as in England they have done the wolves, though much more innocent and less rapacious than weeds'. He also described the offspring of weeds as 'savage, wicked broods'. Finally, in 1812 James Grahame cautioned all farmers, '... yet let them not be spared, still as they rise unconquered let the hoe or ploughshare crush them. In your field permit no wild flower to expand its teeming bloom'. After such furious calls to arms it is a wonder we have any weeds left, and I can only admire their powers of survival.

The most common species of dock, *Rumex crispus*—Curled Dock—is not only still with us but it is a widespread and pernicious weed around the world, as much of a pest in New Zealand as it is here. Its roots can descend some six feet into the ground and if you break off the top it will happily grow again from the stump. Each plant can produce about 25,000 wind-pollinated seeds which can remain dormant for fifty years if necessary. The

1 Curled Dock and Small Copper butterfly
2 Spear Thistle
3 Ragwort and Cinnabar caterpillar
4 Creeping Thistle
5 Nettle and Tortoiseshell caterpillar

flower—if you can call this green and shapeless thing a flower—is not attractive and I dislike its leaves and habit of growth. Dock is an ugly name for a rather ugly and persistent weed which produces tons of useless green stuff annually. However, if I complain of the way others destroy all weeds which do not appear to benefit us, then I must find something to justify its existence or I will find that I, too, am dismissing it out of hand merely because it is not pretty and because its use, if any, is not apparent at the moment.

I decided to enlist the help of friends and experts like Richard Mabey and Michael Chinery to tell me the good qualities of Curled Dock. I also checked through old herbals for its healing properties, but few were listed, and many ignored the plant altogether. According to Nicholas Culpeper, it was used 'to cleanse the blood and strengthen the liver', and the boiled roots help the 'itches, scabs and breaking out of the skin', but a hundred other plants were listed in those days as suitable cures for such common ailments. He also described it as a 'wholesome pot herb', but I can think of many others I would prefer to eat; I find it exceedingly bitter, though Richard says the very young shoots are quite pleasant if cooked as a green vegetable.

The plants do contain massive amounts of vitamin A, far more than the carrot, but I know which of the two I like better. In North America the seeds are eaten by free-food enthusiasts, and they can also be ground into a flour not unlike buckwheat. Richard also reminded me that dock leaves were used to wrap up butter and keep it cool, but so were those of Butterbur and other large leaves, and Michael Chinery confirmed that Goldfinches and Siskins are partial to the seeds; House Sparrows will also eat them, and they are one of the main foods of the Bullfinch, though gardeners surveying their stripped fruit buds may well disbelieve this.

Our own cows would not touch them; no one can be certain whether or not rabbits eat them. Insects, however, do find them palatable, but in no case are they the sole food of any caterpillar. The Small Copper is probably the most devoted consumer of dock leaves though they also eat Sorrel, another common weed. Ermines and Tigermoths may be found on docks, and according to Michael, 'many members of the Noctuid family, Yellow Underwing, Angleshades, Old Lady and many rustics' may be discovered champing their way through docks, but they also eat any other low-growing herbage around. Many plant bugs are found on docks but are not in any way confined to them. Despite these uses, I confess that I still do not like the dock as a plant. If Mother Nature had given us daffodils in place of docks, I would not have had to work so hard to justify their existence, their beauty alone would have sufficed. As to the dock's powers of healing the stings of nettles, I am doubtful if it deserves this claim to fame. Perhaps, years ago, someone like myself also tried to justify its existence and invested in it the properties of healing stings for want of something better.

Rumex acetosa is quite another matter. A member of the Dock family, it is true, but its common name, Sorrel, is as pleasant as its flowers can be if looked at when the sun is low—all fire and orange and green, delicate as the Curled Dock is coarse. The tan-brown seed heads are worth gathering for winter decoration.

Thistles and nettles I also view quite differently to docks. The Spear Thistle is at least statuesque, with its colourful flowers, even if its arsenal of spears is unpleasant to handle in a bale of hay. Its seeds provide even more of a banquet for the goldfinches than docks do. It is a controllable, annual farmland weed if cut before it seeds, but its relative, the perennial Creeping Thistle, is difficult to eradicate if it invades fields and gardens, for its roots go down deep and branch sideways as well, to produce more plants in a very wide circle around their parent.

I am enthusiastically in favour of nettles, not in flower beds or vegetable plots but in odd corners where they won't be too much of a nuisance. They are weeds which have followed man around for centuries and grow wherever he disturbs the soil. They thrive in various parts of our garden and in patches around the compost heaps where each year we watch swarms of caterpillars consuming them, and every summer we reap the benefit of their presence through a harvest of butterflies which bedeck buddleias, Michaelmas Daisies and other flowers we plant for their enjoyment. Five of the most beautiful butterflies in Britain depend upon these dull-green stinging weeds for their very existence. They are the only food plant of the Small Tortoiseshell and the Red Admiral and one of the main foods of the Peacock, Comma and Painted Lady. For their sakes alone, we leave nettles in the garden, for we no longer use them for their medicinal properties as we would have done a few hundred years ago. In those days we would have boiled the leaves or roots to cure our aches and pains. We would have drunk the liquor in which they were boiled if we were poisoned by Hemlock or Deadly Nightshade; they would have cured the effects of bites from mad dogs and cleansed all wounds and skin ailments, and most probably we would have died in spite of them. If we had lived in Roman times we might have beaten ourselves with stalks of Stinging Nettles to cure rheumatism and spun the fibres to make fine bed sheets. Throughout the ages we would certainly have gathered the young shoots to cook as a vegetable or to make into soup.

It is a very different story to that of the docks. Because we, the human race, have decided that a particular species is of no more use to us, we think we have the right to eliminate it, regardless—or perhaps in ignorance—of the fact that it is the food plant of other occupants of this earth.

Some of the more attractive and least injurious weeds we have removed all too efficiently in the past. The poison-spraying 1960s reaped a heavy toll of wild flowers but the main, injurious plants listed in the 1959 Weeds Act do not seem to be in any more danger of disappearing now than they were a few hundred years ago. The five weeds listed are Spear and Creeping Thistles, Curled and Broad-leaved Dock and Ragwort.

Ragwort manages to keep going and periodically has a season of enthusiastic flowering—1978 was such a year. Many of the plants were covered with the wasp-striped Cinnabar caterpillars which can strip the plants quite bare—but what is one hundred caterpillars' meat is one cow's poison. These plants are best removed from fields where cattle graze and, more particularly, from meadows to be cut for hay. Although cows do not readily eat them when they are growing, they will do so if they are made into hay, and they have a dangerous cumulative effect. Ragwort can reproduce its kind several times in one year and as each plant can produce up to 50,000 seeds we are not likely to see the end of these cheerful golden flowers in our lifetime.

Crop spraying and the efficient screening of farm seed has removed many more wild flowers which really would not have harmed the land or the economy, but if one has to go, all of them go. Those that have managed to survive belong to quick-growing and abundant seed-producing plants or to species which can spread rapidly by means of underground stolons or surface runners. The former group includes many crucifers and composites, such as Wild Radish and Charlock, mustard and daisies which thrive on arable land, and the familiar Groundsel, Common Chickweed, Dandelion and smaller crucifers such as Shepherd's Purse. Some of the underground travellers are unwelcome, to say the least, when they invade the garden. Ground Elder and Field Bindweed are extremely difficult to remove from beds and borders because their roots are deep and care not if they are broken.

Some weed seeds begin to germinate before they even leave the parent plant. Rosebay Willowherb may be found thus, still in its capsule. Yet other seeds on the same plant are still viable if collected and sown six months later. Dandelions will germinate in a few days or in a couple of years, and Kidney Vetch seeds are said to be able to grow ninety years after they have been produced. Poppies are able to reappear after many years of absence, for their seeds lie dormant for as long as a hundred years and wait for ground disturbance to start them into production again. The laying of pipes through previously untouched fields has been followed by a red bandage of poppies across the landscape to cover the scars.

The Garden Visitors

The weeds of the garden we divide into three groups: some we plant in suitable places; others we tolerate, and the remainder we really will not allow to invade us. The ones we tolerate appear by accident, coming and going at will. Various small willowherbs appear along the stream and are consumed by Elephant Hawkmoth caterpillars. Violets owned the damp, shady parts of this valley long before we did. The term 'weed' applied to them might be surprising, but you have only to see how rapidly and successfully they have spread to realize the name is justified. Celandines just 'arrived' when we cleared a woodland path and stayed, but are far too beautiful to be considered a nuisance. Foxgloves are great colonizers and have set up a commune in our wild garden too. They are far more numerous than docks in the garden but again their beauty saves them from being called weeds. Not so, however, the equally beautiful Rosebay Willowherb. Burn down an area of woodland and this 'Fireweed' moves in, and gardeners should not allow it, Coltsfoot nor the scented Winter Heliotrope into a small garden or they will take over the whole area. Leave them to colonize waste ground together with hawkweeds, umbellifers and teasels, Feverfew and the everspreading Barren Strawberry, and allow only the less rampant members of the plant world into your garden.

1 *Thistle down*
2 *Field Bindweed*
3 *Broad-leaved Willowherb*
4 *Groundsel*
5 *Red Campion*
6 *Dandelion*
7 *Stinging Nettle*
8 *Common Field Speedwell*
9 *Ox-eye Daisy*
10 *Common Dog Violet*
11 *Field Buttercup*
12 *Herb Robert*
13 *Bittersweet*
—and an Elephant Hawkmoth larva

The Invaders

The decline or extermination of so many of our weeds was, in some cases, necessary, in others unnecessary and regretted. It is therefore pleasant to know that others have greatly increased, though none is so beautiful as the Cornflower, Corn Cockle or Wild Larkspur.

The plants which have spread so rapidly are mostly introduced species; they include Oxford Ragwort and Gallant Soldier, both escapees from botanical gardens. Gallant Soldier—its Latin name is *Galinsoga*—has spread far and wide. It is less hairy than its relative *G. ciliata*, the Shaggy Soldier, which is also becoming a common weed.

Canadian Fleabane, its first seeds here reputed to have 'escaped' from the torn packing used by a taxidermist to stuff a dead bird, quickly became common over southern England and Wales, much the same area now covered by Beaked Hawksbeard which was introduced in 1713 and began its rapid spread during the past century.

The tall spectacular Himalayan Balsam was brought here as a garden plant 150 years ago. It quickly escaped and took over large tracts of riverbank and wet meadows. Another riverbank and damp-wood colonizer is Pink Purslane. Although small and delicate looking, it has proved to be a rapid spreader along with the Monkey Flower from North America, which made its escape from gardens over a hundred years ago and can now be found in many areas.

Common Field Speedwell and that roadside traveller Pineapple Mayweed have both made astonishing advances across the country, the former covering Britain in the hundred years since its introduction, the latter in even less time, its advance speeded up by the way its seeds adhere to shoes and tyres.

1 *Canadian Fleabane*
2 *Pineapple Mayweed*
3 *Monkey Flower*
4 *Common Field Speedwell*
5 *Beaked Hawksbeard*
6 *Himalayan Balsam*
7 *Oxford Ragwort*
8 *Gallant Soldier*
9 *Pink Purslane*

TRAPPERS, PARASITES AND POISONERS

Trappers

Animals and man have always been hunters after meat. Animals hunt to survive, modern man has turned hunting into a sport and a method of controlling 'vermin'. He has used many perfectly legal and humane weapons but also some wholly unpleasant ones including poisoned baits and traps. It comes as something of a suprise, however, to discover that certain innocent-looking flowers can also behave in a thoroughly nasty fashion. There are over five hundred meat-eating plants in the world, some large enough to catch and digest a rat in their slippery sided urns. Others are shaped like miniature gin traps or act as sticky flypapers.

In Britain we have only three families of insect-eating plants, all small and less voracious than many of their foreign counterparts but deadly all the same. Two of them rely on their very sticky leaves to catch their prey. The first of these is the Butterwort family. Pale Butterwort is small with delicate pink flowers; the Common and Large-flowered species have strikingly beautiful purple flowers with long spurs, which at first sight resemble violets. All of them have rosettes of pale butter-green leaves which seem to sparkle with minute crystals if you look carefully at them. In the 15th and 16th centuries they were used as a milk-curdling agent, hence an alternative name of Thickening Grass, or as an ointment for curing soreness or chaps on milking cows' udders, and so called Butterwort.

A fly or midge landing on the leaf immediately becomes firmly stuck on to its flypaper-type surface; as it struggles, the edges of the leaf start to roll up and inwards, forcing the prey towards the middle where the maximum amounts of glue and digesting acids are secreted by the glands. Once the prey has been 'sucked' dry, the leaf uncurls and the cycle begins over again.

Trappers
1 *Common Butterwort*
2 *Bladderwort*
3 *Sundew*
4 *Pale Butterwort*

The second family of meat-eaters is the Sundews which also attract small flies. Their method of trapping is much the same, but the equipment is quite different. The leaves have stout red hairs which cover the upper surface, each one topped with a glistening sticky bead which immediately secures any fly that dares to alight upon it. These small tentacles—for that is what these hairs actually are—begin slowly to bend over and embrace their prey in a kiss of death which lasts for several days, the plant being in no hurry and its victim unable to escape. Eventually, the now dry-tipped hairs straighten up and allow the empty corpse to roll off the leaf. Once again the tips become sticky, and the trap is baited and ready. They wait, like minature diamond-bright lollipops on red sticks, for their next victim. Should two flies land on one leaf, the hairs can even divide into two camps and turn their attention to whichever fly is nearer to them.

The third family is the Bladderworts—Greater Bladderwort and its similar relatives, Intermediate and Lesser Bladderworts. These are the fishermen of the plant world, floating about on lakes and ponds unhampered by any roots, their delicate yellow flowers rising above the water, looking charming and innocent. Attached to the base of the stem are many thin green trailers; and on these, like the hooks of a fishing line, are fixed the tiny bladders. These are delicate hair-fringed traps which open as soon as some pond creature, such as a water flea, touches the hairspring catch. Water and creature are immediately swept into the empty bladder which closes up after them so that there is no escape. The plant waits until the creature has died from its unnatural causes before consuming its now decomposing and therefore more easily digestible body.

Parasites
1 Thyme Broomrape
2 Clove-scented Broomrape
3 Yellow Rattle
4 Cow-wheat
5 Eyebright
6 Dodder climbing up Heather

Mistletoe

Parasites

Parasitic plants are those which do not catch their own prey but which prey upon other members of the plant world, relying upon their chosen host to supply some, if not all, of their food requirements.

The partial parasites, which manufacture some chlorophyll but not sufficient for their needs, include Cow-wheat, Eyebright and Yellow Rattle. All have green leaves and, to the uninitiated, look like normally growing plants, but in fact they rely upon the roots of grasses for much of their food. Mistletoe is another partial parasite and is more easily recognizable as such as it hangs from branches of apple and poplar trees, sometimes in great bunches. Birds often help to spread mistletoe by rubbing their beaks on branches to remove the very sticky seeds that cling to them. Little do they know that this berry, which they enjoy eating, is the bringer of death to any bird that lands on the sticky birdlime-painted branches of trees in many European countries. Mistletoe-seed glue is still used for this fiendish 'sport' by some bird trappers.

Completely parasitic plants manufacture no chlorophyll at all and therefore no green leaves or food for themselves. They include the pale creamy-pink Toothwort and Dodder. The latter starts life with a small root of its own and then sends up an aerial stem which waves around until it finds its host, which is usually Heather or Gorse. As soon as its 'sucker-foothold' is gained, the Dodder abandons its own root and is away on its travels, extensively covering bushes with its sinister, red, thread-like knitting which is intersected by more suckerholds. It spoils the hot-coconut scent of Gorse with its own foetid smell, produced to attract small pollinating flies.

There are several members of the Broomrape family in Europe, each choosing different host plants and attaching themselves to the roots, actually penetrating these in order to obtain their food. Most are fawn or brown in colour, but some are diffused with purple and reddish tones. Their seeds have to come into actual contact with the roots of the host before they can germinate, for they need to send down a sucker, which is their very lifeline, in order to obtain immediate supplies of essential food and water.

Poisoners

Many plants in Britain and around the world contain poisons in one form or another, which harm both man and beast, producing symptoms of lethargy and sickness, and even causing death. Some berries can be eaten by birds, and, because they pass so quickly through the system, have no ill effect. Yew berries, for example, can be eaten by thrushes and will not harm them, whereas humans and cattle are seriously poisoned. Rabbits can eat Deadly Nightshade plants without any trouble, which seems surprising for its leaves, stems and shining black berries are all highly poisonous to man. On the other hand, young Bracken fronds can harm cattle with their cumulative effect, but not humans—not that we can envisage man eating such a plant.

Other plants which are poisonous in all their parts include Monkshood, Hemlock, Fool's Parsley—so named because it can be mistaken for the

Poisoners
1 *Monkshood*
2 *Henbane*
3 *Hemlock*
4 *Fool's Parsley*
5 *Thorn-apple*

garden plant—Henbane and Thorn-apple. Monkshood is a wild plant found in Britain and Europe, which is also much cultivated in gardens, yet even its roots are extremely poisonous and gardeners should be careful when handling it. The last two are aliens which have found their way over from America and appear from time to time.

Now that it is not essential to scour the countryside for our daily ration of vegetables, there is very little danger of being poisoned by such plants as Fool's Parsley. The harmless ones that are still regularly eaten, such as nettles, Dandelion, sorrel and chickweed, are easily recognizable. The danger is confined to the bright and attractive fruits of the hedgerow. The poisonous red berries of Lords and Ladies and Mezereon—now much cultivated in gardens—look as appetising as harmless rosehips and many such dangerous fruits are within reach of small children. Laburnum is grown in gardens and sometimes also appears in hedgerows, but wherever it may be found, beware that children do not eat the seeds for they are lethal.

Not all of the following plants are deadly poisonous, but it is advisable not to consume any part of them, particularly the berries or seeds:

Alder Buckthorn · *Frangula alnus*
Baneberry · *Actaea spicata*
Bittersweet · *Solanum dulcamara (6)*
Black Bryony · *Tamus communis (7)*
Black Nightshade · *Solanum nigrum*
Buckthorn · *Rhamnus catharticus*
Buttercups · *Ranunculus* spp.
Columbine · *Aquilegia vulgaris*
Cowbane · *Cicuta virosa*
Darnel Rye-grass · *Lolium temulentum*
Deadly Nightshade · *Atropa bella-donna (5)*
Dog's Mercury · *Mercurialis perennis*
Fine-leaved Water Dropwort · *Oenanthe aquatica*
Fool's Parsley · *Aethusa cynapium*
Foxglove · *Digitalis purpurea*
Fritillary · *Fritillaria meleagris*
Green Hellebore · *Helleborus viridis*
Hemlock · *Conium maculatum*
Hemlock Water Dropwort · *Oenanthe crocata*
Henbane · *Hyoscyamus niger*
Ivy · *Hedera helix*
Lily of the Valley · *Convallaria majalis*
Lords and Ladies · *Arum maculatum (8)*
Meadow Saffron · *Colchicum autumnale*
Monkshood · *Aconitum napellus*
Mezereon · *Daphne mezereum (2)*
Spindle-tree · *Euonymus europaeus (4)*
Spurge Laurel · *Daphne laureola (1)*
Spurges · *Euphorbia* spp.
Stinking Hellebore · *Helleborus foetidus*
Thorn-apple · *Datura stramonium*
White Bryony · *Bryonia cretica (9)*
Wild Privet · *Ligustrum vulgare (3)*
Yew · *Taxus baccata*

FIELD FARE

Food Plants for Man

Flowers, leaves, stems and roots have always been eaten by man, and by taking the naturally growing species and sowing seeds from selected plants over a period of time, we have arrived at the modern vegetable. Wild Cabbage, found now only in southern areas of Britain and a few coastal areas in northern France and described as a hairless perennial with a thick woody stem, is the plant that through the centuries has been the subject of selective breeding and concentration upon certain attributes. In this way, our garden cabbage, cauliflower, Brussels sprouts and their varieties have evolved. All our vegetables, whether they be root, stem or leaf, come from wild beginnings.

Gathering wild vegetables is not a job to be undertaken lightly, however, nor on the spur of the moment. It is time-consuming. For the vast majority of people it probably means a certain amount of travel to the country and almost always quite a bit of backaching harvesting. The gathering should be part of a country walk with the family. Recognition of the plant is the first vital hurdle to clear, and we make the plea that you use your field guide, take it to the plant and never pick unnecessarily. If you are taking leaves, remember that it is through these that the plant breathes, so remove only a few from each one; if the fruit is the source of food you seek, then remember that the plant relies on this part to reproduce, so leave enough to ensure its future generations.

Roots

Gathering wild roots entails digging up the whole plant and is therefore not one we encourage, although some will stand this treatment as

1 Rowan
2 Glasswort
3 Good King Henry
4 Sea-beet
5 Wild Plum
6 Crab Apple
7 Bullace
8 Comfrey
9 Hazelnut
10 Sea Kale
11 Fat Hen
12 Sweet Violet

they can easily be replaced. One is Horseradish, a dock-like plant whose root will regrow from any little piece left in the ground, as we know so well from experience when we tried to rid our garden of it many years ago. In Germany in the Middle Ages, it was used to make a sauce to accompany fish dishes and later became popular in Britain as a sauce for beef. It grows in waste places from where it can be dug with little trouble—providing any permission needed is first obtained. Wild Parsnip is an umbellifer that grows in grassy places. It was brought into cultivation about the time of the Middle Ages and it needs a frost to sweeten its usually rather strong flavour.

Salads and Vegetables
Plants whose leaves are good to eat raw or in salads are many. Probably the best known is Watercress, but it has a great disadvantage: unless it is picked from an extremely carefully controlled location there is a grave risk to health. In its slow-flowing water habitat also lives an unpleasant little parasite, the liver fluke, a dangerous pest to sheep and man, which lays its eggs in the hollow stems of plants.

Garlic Mustard, or Jack-by-the-hedge to give it one of its well-known other names, when finely chopped in salads gives a slight flavour of garlic to the dish. It grows in hedges and open woods throughout Europe and is sometimes to be seen as early as February. Take just one or two leaves and add to mint sauce to give that 'something extra'.

The Dandelion is so well known that it needs no description. It is widely used as a salad leaf in France where in some areas it is cultivated and reaches a great size. In Britain we do everything we can to rid our gardens of it, so one way is to eat it more. Chop the leaves roughly and add a dressing of olive oil, lemon juice and a trace of garlic to make a really refreshing salad. The flowers make an excellent wine, and the roots make a substitute for coffee—containing no caffeine but with a diuretic side-effect to consider.

More widespread than the salad plants generally, are those we use as cooked green vegetables. Wild Spinach *(Beta vulgaris)* is the original and thicker-leaved plant of the cultivated spinach and is the one from which all our domestic beets have evolved. It is stronger than the garden variety, and occasionally shows beetroot-coloured veins, proving the ancestry of the common beetroot. It pays to strip the leaves from the central rib when picking, as this will save time later.

Fat Hen, that troublesome weed of the cultivated field or disturbed ground, has been used as a green vegetable since Neolithic times, which has been proved by the discovery of remains in graves dating from those far-off days. The leaves are of no great size, making it a rather tedious task to gather sufficient to make a meal. As a vegetable of emergency it is excellent, containing as it does more vitamin B and calcium than raw domestic cabbage. A similar green vegetable is Good King Henry, a close relative of Fat Hen, which may be used in the same way.

Common Chickweed is another plant which is good to eat as greens but is the bane of the gardener. It should be a bonus because, following a day's weeding, it can be eaten rather than burned or thrown on the compost heap. Strip bunches of leaves from the main stem, wash well and simmer for ten minutes in its own liquid with a knob of butter, seasoning and a chopped onion.

Sorrel is a very good vegetable; it grows throughout Britain and Europe and is one of the first to appear in the spring. In France the species *Rumex scutatus* is used but does not grow outside that country. Sorrel is made into sauce for fish or veal, and it may be used to make soup; it is also good cooked as a green vegetable.

It is said that many dishes may be made with Stinging Nettles—the sting is immediately neutralized by cooking—and we have tried nettle soup, but frankly it was not to our liking. Perhaps we malign it. Common Comfrey is quite different. Dipped in batter and fried, the leaves are delicious.

Stems and Flowers
Stems of plants contribute to our wild vegetable larder. The young white stalks of Sea Kale have been eaten for centuries in coastal areas throughout Europe. Shingle or sand would be piled around the young shoots as they appeared in spring to blanch them, thus reducing the bitterness of the taste. If one is growing Sea Kale in the garden, this is exactly what one should still do. The stems are boiled in salted water until they are tender and they are served and eaten with melted butter, in the same way as asparagus. Sea Kale is not now common in the wild so great restraint should be exercised and only very little taken. Marsh Samphire is a vegetable to gather if you do not mind a bit of mudlarking since it is to be found between tides in estuaries around all the European coasts. The young shoots are certainly tedious to collect but they do make a pleasant crispy salad ingredient and, if simmered in a little water until tender and served with a knob of butter, they go well with poultry or lamb— remembering that with the polluted state of our seas and estuaries it is essential that your harvest is thoroughly washed before cooking.

Alexanders grows wild on the west coast of France, and there are naturalized habitats in Britain. The best parts of this umbellifer are from the naturally blanched base of the stems, which are boiled for up to ten minutes and eaten with butter. In the old days, Alexanders was eaten raw like the celery that finally replaced it. The seeds may be put into soup, as was done by monks in the Middle Ages.

This seems the right place to mention Sweet Cicely which is an umbellifer growing mainly in northern Britain and Denmark and which has been introduced into Holland and Belgium. The sweet characteristic of the plant has been remarked upon for a very long time. One of the best ways to use it is to cook it with sharp fruits like rhubarb. Place leaves of Sweet Cicely in the bottom of the pot in which you are going to cook your fruit and use half the amount of sugar you would normally. Remove the sprigs before serving and your dish will be sweet with a delicious piquancy of anise as an underflavour. Various other umbelliferous seeds also have this slight aniseed flavour.

The flowers of plants are best used for flavourings and for adding exotic perfumes to dishes and drinks. They have been used thus for many centuries; the Greeks perfumed their wine with rose water and the Clove Scented Pink which they found in Spain. By crystallizing them with sugar, violets have been eaten as sweetmeats for a very long time.

Herbs and Spices

Many plants used purely for flavouring and classified as herbs are plentiful. Meadowsweet, which fills the fields with a creamy froth and its heady scent, is so called because it was used to give an aromatic bouquet to port, claret and mead. It has an alternative name of Meadwort. Cow Parsley added in small quantities to winter soups or casseroles gives them a clean spicy flavour—exact identification here is essential because of its slight resemblance to Fool's Parsley and Hemlock, both of which are poisonous. Fennel flavouring for fish dishes makes this a plant worth searching for so that a few pieces of stalk can be taken for drying. The flavour also goes well with fruit, as does that of another umbellifer, wild Angelica.

Various mints grow in different habitats and have a wide variety of undertones to their overall flavour. Mint is too well known for much to be said, apart from suggesting that its use should not be confined to new potatoes, peas, and lamb. Try it with egg dishes, and flavour cordials with it as well. Mints hybridize easily with each other, making identification difficult, so it is a matter of trial and error. Marjoram is found in chalky and limestone areas and is another delightful herb to use with meat. Finally, Wild Thyme is well known and grows abundantly on sandy heaths and chalky grassland. It is a fiddly job to find and pick it, but the result when fresh Thyme is added to meat, vegetables or in stuffing for a chicken makes it all worthwhile, and you need only a very little. Plants of Wild Thyme can easily be purchased and this is probably the best way to ensure a good supply.

Fruit
Fruit is the part of the plant most generally associated with eating wild fare, and rightly so, but it is often forgotten that the seeds are also fruits. They are equally delicious and valuable and come to us in many different forms, including those in hard shells—the nuts.

Among the soft fruits we immediately think of the Raspberry, Strawberry and Blackberry. Wild Raspberry is widespread in Britain and Europe—but not along the west coast of France. It grows in hedgerows and on heaths and provides a good source of well-flavoured but often small fruit. The farther north you go, the better the Raspberries become. It is one of the first fruits to ripen and may be gathered from midsummer onwards. It is a close relative of the Blackberry, both being members of the Rose family. The Blackberry is ripe in September and is probably the reason for more expeditions to the countryside by town-dwellers than any other. If you want to taste Strawberry as no garden variety of monster size has ever tasted, then try the wild ones which grow in fields and hedges everywhere. Staying with the Rose family, we cannot move on without reference to the wild rose itself. The hips of the Field Rose, Dog Rose,

1 *Blackberry*
2 *Strawberry*
3 *Raspberry*
4 *Cloudberry*
5 *Sloe*
6 *Rosehip*
7 *Black Currant*
8 *Gooseberry*
9 *Red Currant*
10 *Elderberry*
11 *Cranberry*
12 *Bilberry*
13 *Cowberry*

Downy Rose and Sweet Briar, the most widespread of the European wild roses, are the major source of rosehip syrup which is still commercially made.

Growing near the ground as shrubs up to about eighteen inches tall is the little black, acid-tasting Bilberry. Picking Bilberries is a job requiring patience and a strong back but it is made worthwhile by the flavour of a fruit tart to which they have been added. An alternative is the small Cloudberry, of the Rose family, which grows in the far north, but rarely elsewhere, and is also used in pies. Once common in Britain, another low-growing shrub producing acid berries, the Cranberry, is a victim of the wholesale drainage of wetlands, which has made it very scarce in most of its old areas. The berries are red and make a delicious sauce. Its relative, the Cowberry, grows to about twelve inches and, like the Cranberry, is almost inedible when raw but makes a good sharp jelly.

If we turn our attention to taller bushes, the first we find, growing by streams and on river banks, is Red Currant. It is widespread and is worth searching out for its great value as a preserve to be eaten with meat. It has a number of pips so jelly is the best way of using the fruit. There is doubt sometimes about the identification of Red Currant. It always has the remains of the calyx attached at the opposite side to the stalk, and its fruits are in drooping, stalked spikes. A plant with which it has been confused on occasions is the Wayfaring Tree which also has red berries and which grows by streams, but its berry is clean at the end with no calyx, and they grow in more or less flat-topped umbels, drooping because of the weight of their fruits. Your good field guide makes the difference quite clear, but if you are in any doubt, don't pick! Black Currant is a relative of the Red but is somewhat scarcer; it is worth hunting for, however, as is the Gooseberry, another of the Currant family, which grows in woodland and is often overlooked. The Gooseberry was not brought into cultivation until much later than many other fruits because the wild variety is so palatable.

Moving up again, to trees, we find Elder with its froth of off-white flowers used for white wine and its fruit for red wine; it is widespread throughout Europe. The fruit can be included in pickle with advantage, and an excellent sauce can be made based on the berries, vinegar and spices. Elder will colonize bare ground very quickly and is often considered a serious weed. In no way is the next tree considered a weed. Crab Apple is generally familiar, and in spring, when in flower and the bees are feeding, it presents a picture foretelling the delights to come. The fruit is acid, and by selective breeding over many generations the domestic apple has been produced. Often trees thought to be Crab Apples turn out to be domestic varieties growing from bird-sown pips or from a core thrown down by a walker or from a car. Over the years these trees revert to Crab types. Crab Apple jelly is one of the best ways in which to use the fruit because it contains a great quantity of pectin. The addition of a few berries from a Rowan tree gives the jelly a little sharpness and a slightly different flavour; this is well worth doing but please don't take too many. Rowan and Hawthorn—whose berries also add to the pleasantness of Crab Apple—are much better left to their natural consumers, the Thrush family.

Blackthorn produces dark-blue berries, or sloes, bloomed with a paler blue, which are used primarily for flavouring that delectable liqueur, sloe gin. It is a fiddly job handling the small berries, but they make a good jelly although a considerable number of sloes are needed. Hybridization of the Bullace with the Cherry Plum produced the garden plum. Neither tree is common in Europe, unlike the Wild Cherry whose fruit, however, is of little significance to humans.

Nuts

We have seen that fruits are either soft, like the Blackberry, firm, like an Apple, or small and hard like a seed of Alexanders. Other hard fruits—the nuts—grow in our hedgerows and on the large trees in our woodlands. The nuts of three trees common in Britain and Europe—Hazel, Sweet Chestnut and Walnut—are valuable as food for man. Others which can also be eaten are far more important to the birds and animals around us.

The Hazel grows abundantly throughout Europe. In winter the catkins begin to lengthen as telltales that spring is on the way. The tiny flower on top of the stem catches the windborne pollen—provided the wind does not blow too hard—and begins to form for next autumn the nuts that are so relished by the dormouse, the squirrel and by man. It is a race each year between man and the squirrel as to who will take them when they are just right. If there is no sight of activity by the squirrel, the nuts are unripe. As soon as activity is noticed, then is the right time to gather in the Hazel harvest. Collect the nuts in bags and store them in their shells in a good dry airy place. In this way, the likelihood of them drying out will be minimized. Use them chopped or grated in salads, or eat them raw with breakfast cereal and make full use of their bounty. They contain 50 per cent more protein, seven times more fat and five times more carbohydrate than hens' eggs on a weight for weight basis. Then there is the Sweet Chestnut, and few of us have not had the pleasure of eating roasted chestnuts at some time or other. Gather them in October for eating later in the winter, but do not try to store them for more than two months as they do not keep well. Eat them raw as well, making sure that the inner skin is removed first since it is rather bitter. When roasting, cut a slit in the skin of all but one in the batch. They will be ready when the uncut one explodes. The Walnut was introduced by the Romans and is not very widespread in its range but is a worthy nut all the same. It is ripe when it begins to fall in October and should be collected then, scrubbed perfectly clean of all traces of husk and stored until Christmas when, with the roasted chestnuts, you can eat them and enjoy the fruits of nature together with a glass of sloe gin.

The gathering of wild plants in these days of convenience foods is certainly a hard way of getting a meal, and, whilst not wishing to diminish the delights and value of our field fare, it is necessary to keep it well in perspective. Consider it as a bonus and be thankful it is there. Gather your wild food, remembering that others depend on it more than we do, and enjoy the time spent in the country. Respect those who live there and obey the Country Code. Our wild foods are valuable and should be appreciated and not wasted. There are many mouths to feed.

Food Plants for Insects
The Caterpillar Crèche

To deal with the plant foods of all species of insects would fill a book on its own, and most insects can survive without our help. Gardeners and farmers alike know which are harmful and which can be left in peace.

1 Privet Hawk caterpillar
2 Poplar Hawk eggs and young caterpillar
3 Pussmoth caterpillar
4 Emperor Moth caterpillar on Heather
5 Peacock caterpillar
5a Peacock chrysallis
6 Small Copper caterpillar on Lady's Smock

It is the butterflies and moths which really do repay our efforts to help them, for it is easy to encourage them into our garden; they are not difficult to feed as they prefer our favourite flowers to any others. The most beautiful and suprisingly 'tame' varieties are also the most common, but they are very vulnerable. Most depend upon warm sunny weather to enable them to fly, feed and mate during the few short weeks they live as winged insects; they are also liable to be caught by birds for food and by schoolboys and adults for their collections. Both butterflies and moths are becoming more scarce as their habitats are reduced and as herbicides and pesticides take a toll of their food plants and of their fellow insects.

There are less than sixty species of butterflies in Britain, and although you will not be able to tempt more than a quarter of them into your garden regularly, those which do visit you will be among the most colourful. The first primrose-yellow Brimstone in early Spring may fly a long way from the Buckthorn, upon which it lays its eggs, to visit our garden flowers. The Orange-tip follows shortly afterwards, looking for Lady's Smock and Jack-by-the-hedge, then the Blues and Small Coppers. The Peacocks, Red

Admirals, Commas, Small Tortoiseshells and also the Painted Ladies who fly in from the continent, are the butterflies of high summer.

Butterflies can see in colour and are attracted to certain shades. Small Tortoiseshells are said to prefer yellow flowers, and Brimstones will generally go to blue or purple ones. They can also detect scent at a considerable distance.

Just as you can select suitable and attractive wild flowers to grow in your garden, so too can you encourage the right butterflies and moths to stay and breed if you provide them with the correct food plants. None of the very beautiful and relatively common butterflies I have mentioned will harm any of your garden plants or vegetables, and you will gain great pleasure from watching them.

Once bitten with butterfly and moth mania, there is no cure. Butterfly gardening links the wild flora, which is the food of caterpillars, to the garden flowers which provide the nectar for the adult insect. Both must be carefully balanced, for it is no use providing plenty of the best succulent nettles for the eggs, and later for the larvae of Red Admirals, Peacocks and Tortoiseshells, if the butterflies promptly flit to the garden next door for their day-long flower feasts.

Provide the correct food and the best of British caterpillars will happily eat their way through it. Nettles come first on the menu, and once again we remind you to leave a few clumps in odd corners. It always impresses visitors if you can deliberately point out these spun-cocoon nurseries full of young caterpillars who chomp their way towards beautiful butterfly status as they demolish the nettles for you. So much better than apologising for not having removed such despised weeds. As well as our nettles, we have Lady's Smock—for the Orange-tips—growing in a mini-meadow amongst other caterpillar food such as small cruciferes, dandelions, violets, clovers and vetches, all of which are left uncut until the last moment.

Along the edge of the stream we have sallows and willowherb for Pussmoths and Elephant Hawkmoths. Primroses are for the Fritillaries who fly fast on elegant, russet-orange wings, never still for long, always in a hurry. We can expect to see plenty of Small Coppers which breed on sorrels and Common Blues which do so on the trefoils. Other Hawkmoths besides the Elephants can be encouraged if you grow the right trees for their larvae. If you have poplar, lime or privet, you will probably find the caterpillars which bear the same names emerging from their green-pearl eggs on the undersides of the leaves. On country walks over heather-covered moors, watch for the large emerald-green, gold-studded caterpillars of the Emperor Moth, look for Clouded Yellows in meadows and on marshy ground, study the sundews for the small Plume Moth larvae which have successfully learned to avoid the deadly clutches of these plants.

Flower Feasts
Provide a garden full of flowers and the butterflies will stay with you all summer long. Although they need little food once they have reached the butterfly phase, they cannot resist sipping nectar and sunbathing on the flowers, or on your shoulder if you are wearing their favourite colour. Plant

1 Orange-tip on Jack-by-the-hedge
2 Elephant Hawkmoth on Great Willowherb
3 Painted Lady on Viper's Bugloss
4 Common Blue on Birdsfoot Trefoil
5 Ringlet on Bramble

Michaelmas Daisies, Sweet Rocket and Lavender hedges for bees as well as butterflies. Grow pinks, honeysuckles, valerians and forgetmenots. Allow wild Red Campions, Ragged Robin, Wood Sage, knapweeds and Hemp Agrimony a spare corner or two. Chuck out those dull shrubs, those unscented, brash-coloured, overblown nectar-deficient modern flowers, and have a fragrant garden to the delight of bees, butterflies and yourselves. Visitors to our garden always say they know when they are near for they can detect its delicious scents far down the lane.

Watch Honeysuckle buds open in late evening, each new flower gleaming brightly and heavily scented, an open invitation to any passing Lime Hawkmoth. Plant Buddleias and watch countless butterflies basking on the flowers. Above all, plant *Sedum spectabile,* the Iceplant, which opens its flat-topped food counters in late summer, its pink flowers awash with winged insects; at times it will look like a plant of Small Tortoiseshell flowers, with bees and Silver Y moths queueing up for spaces at the feast.

Grow night-scented plants, particularly white ones which look so lovely in the late evening, to attract night-feeding moths. Watch them by torchlight and perhaps one day you may see a Convolvulus Hawkmoth during one of its infrequent visits to this country. You are more likely to glimpse the day-flying Humming-bird Hawkmoths which like common Valerian and Lady's Bedstraw. They are never still long enough to be seen properly but you can admire their wonderful darting flight and the speed of the wings, and remember with astonishment that this small insect

Honeysuckle and Lime Hawkmoth

crosses the Channel, often in large numbers, to visit our gardens.

Following Painted Lady butterflies around the herbaceous flowers is less difficult for they frequently stop to bask in the sunshine, and in the countryside around you will probably see them on thistles, wild mallows, Viper's Bugloss and Burdock. I am particularly fond of their soft tawny colours, like slightly faded silk, quite different from the sharp modern pattern of the Red Admirals which like to sit around on fallen apples in autumn, quite drunk on cider, and won't mind if you pick them up.

Look out for other insects on the wild flowers too. Hedge Parsley and various members of the Umbellifer family provide flat, white lace-covered tables of good food for beetles, flies, wasps, bees and ants as well as butterflies. Bees and flies, and even hornets, like the pink flowers of Flowering Rush which grows well in both natural and garden ponds. Blackberry flowers attract many Ringlets, Gatekeepers and Wall Browns, and if you have a Holly, or allow Ivy to grow up walls or trees as we do, look out for the Holly Blue butterfly.

If the farmers have left any Ragwort around their fields they may be covered with Cinnabar caterpillars, with black and gold stripes, which can quickly strip a plant almost bare of leaves. Woolly Bears, or Garden Tigers, will eat their way through many low-growing weeds such as dandelions, and can be found in many gardens, easily recognizable by their long-haired fur coats which can sometimes produce a rash upon the skin of those who handle them. They will help to clear docks and nettles and are not averse to eating garden plants.

Cinnabar caterpillars on Ragwort

Cinnabar moth

Small Tortoiseshell

Peacock

Food Plants for Animals and Birds

The majority of our wild mammals are insectivores, carnivores, grazers of grass or browsers of herbage and need little help, but a certain amount of control, from man.

We unwittingly have given a great deal of help, and certainly much encouragement, to a whole army of mice, voles and shrews, which was made evident by the large numbers that invaded our garden from the surrounding fields while it was being made. They stayed on and set up home in every bank and dry-stone wall throughout the garden. There is a warrenful of them under the meadow slope which we had already provided with a supply of expensive and obviously delectable food in the form of crocus bulbs. We no longer provide the mice with their annual banquet so they have turned their attention to other plants. Bank voles are active during the day and can be seen chewing the tops off our Martagon Lilies, which is unforgivable, or climbing rose bushes to snap off the hips, which is permissible. They do not appear to eat any of our Wild Daffodils, and we hope they will not attack any other species we are about to plant.

Apart from the mice, the only other animals which visit us regularly are moles and hedgehogs, which are not vegetarians, and grey squirrels which are after the hazelnuts, fir cones and acorns from the trees that border the far side of the stream. Occasionally a rabbit makes its way in from the fields and is not always welcome, but of dormice, which we would love to possess, there are no signs. They prefer a well-managed coppice of Hazel where their presence can easily be confirmed if you examine the eaten nuts. Dormice leave a small, neatly cut hole in each one, the edges always well sandpapered and not as rough as those nibbled by other mice.

Birds, however, do visit our garden in large numbers for food, shelter

1 *Goldfinch and thistle seed*
2 *Holly*
3 *Charlock seeds*
4 *Guelder Rose berries*
5 *Yew berries*
6 *Mistletoe berries*
7 *Acorn*
8 *Ivy seeds*
9 *Rowan berries*
10 *Rosehip*
11 *Cherries*
12 *Dormouse and hazelnut*
13 *Hawthorn berries*
14 *Crowberry*
15 *Silver Birch catkins*

and for nesting sites, as we supply them with everything they need—trees, shrubs, banks, berries, seeds, nestboxes, creeper-covered walls and Ivy-covered trees. Thrushes and Blackbirds take full advantage of the free food, eating every berry off the Rowans and Hollies before they look remotely ripe, but taking more time over the many Hawthorn berries along the lane hedge. Goldfinches eat the seeds of many small plants as well as the thistles, teasels, Burdock and Charlock in the fields. Greenfinches like much the same diet and include the poisonous berries of Mezereon, and live to tell the tale. Redpolls seldom visit us, but now that our Silver Birches are well grown, we hope their seed will entice these birds into the garden. All fruit buds are vulnerable when Bullfinches are around, but they will also eat the seeds of forgetmenots and other small plants.

It is worth remembering every autumn that all the wild-fruit harvest is important to birds, so please leave plenty for them. The more natural food they have, the better their chances of surviving the coldest spell. We throw windfall apples under hedgerows for Redwings and Fieldfares and marrow seeds for Pheasants. As well as providing birds with nesting sites and a night's lodging, Ivy produces large crops of berries which the Wood Pigeons particularly like. We have never found that Ivy harms our trees; it takes over only when a tree is dying of old age, allowing more light and room for the Ivy to grow to the top. It is far too valuable as a shelter for birds for us to remove it, although we do control it if it tries to smother smaller plants.

Apart from the bud-eating Bullfinches, the songbirds of Britain and the summer migrants do very little harm to the plant life of this country, for many live mainly on the abundant insect life, ridding the garden of aphids and all manner of pests. The remainder exists mainly on the renewable harvest of weed seeds and fruit, never destroying the entire plant, leaving no litter and giving a great deal of pleasure.

1 *Guelder Rose*
2 *Cherry*
3 *Beech mast*
4 *Acorn*
5 *Rosehip*
6 *Hawthorn*
7 *Pine cone eaten by squirrel*
8 *Apple and Red Admiral*
9 *Dormouse and hazelnuts*

PERFUMES AND PLEASANTRIES

With many different aspects of botany, it is possible to trace history back to the ancient Greeks and Romans, and this section on perfumes is no exception. Hippocrates, the Greek physician, considered the scent of a flower to be an important part of its medicinal properties. Pliny recorded more than sixty medicines based on the scent of Mint and Pennyroyal alone. Clove Scented Pink was taken by the Romans from Spain back to Rome where it was used to flavour wine. Pliny also tells us that Corn Mint stirs the appetite with its perfume and if it be eaten then 'milk will not sour in the stomach'.

The manufacture of various scented waters comes to us from many centuries ago. In hot climates, where they were used for refreshment against the heat, vats of water were covered with rose petals from which the essential oils separated and floated on the surface of the water from whence they were skimmed. Soon it was found that the resulting liquid could be concentrated by distillation. This is the basis of manufacture for many flower perfumes today.

Scented plants have always been used for strewing on the floors of houses and public buildings. Thomas à Becket ordered that the floor of the Hall at Canterbury be strewn with Sweet Flag and May Blossom so that those who came to see him and who could not find room on the benches provided could sit on the floor 'without dirtying their clothes'. They scented the Hall beautifully and camouflaged other less pleasant odours. Another way in which these ever-present odours were avoided was by the use of the Tussie-mussie. This was—and still is—a nosegay with a message. The improving of the air one breathed was the main object of carrying a Tussie but the warding off of infection was another important one. Each Tussie had its own message of love according to how it was arranged and which flowers it contained. A central flower, a rose or carnation for instance, was surrounded by concentric circles of other scented flowers and the more pungent herbs. Each circle was tied with wool before the next was added and the whole was finished off with a frill of lace or net, nowadays a paper or plastic doiley!

In earlier centuries, to clear a house of musty smells, the daily burning of aromatic seeds—many of them umbellifers—was one of the tasks of early morning. To retain sweetness throughout the house, flower scents were used, generally in the form of potpourris. Basically, a potpourri is a jar full of dried flower petals. To make one, pick a few handfuls of Wild Rose petals and dry them in a cupboard. We would advise adding a few petals from the garden if you have a good scented variety of rose. Mix the petals with some dried herbs; Marjoram and Rosemary make a lovely base and if Bog Myrtle can be added a delicious spicy flavour is given. Put the resulting mixture into a jar in layers, sprinkling a little salt between each. This will help to fix the scent so that it is given off slowly and will last much longer. The addition of finely cut, citrus-fruit skin gives a piquancy to the perfume. When not required, the lid should be kept on the jar, to be removed in the evenings when the potpourri can be placed by a fire to warm which will release its delicious perfume.

Shakespeare and many other poets have referred frequently to the scents of flowers. The violet was Shakespeare's favourite flower and is the one he mentions more than any other. In our opinion, every flower has our favourite scent as soon as we smell it. What better one is there than the first Primrose. We are lucky to have them flowering soon after Christmas in our garden and always look forward to their appearance. Then we walk through a wood with its floor covered in Bluebells and right away we have another favourite! So we go through the year, with different favourites as the seasons change. Lily of the Valley is another flower of the woodland which has a lovely perfume. Its spicy scent tells you it is near, growing in the warm damp litter of deciduous wood. And what more beautiful scent is there than that of the Honeysuckle growing in and over the hedgerow beside the road?

No sensation is better able to revive an old memory than a particular scent. A coconut at Christmas reminds us immediately of a walk over the cliffs in North Cornwall on a hot June day. Here the Gorse flowers in brilliant array, giving off its coconut scent and creating a memory worth recalling at any time. The scent of the leaves of Woodruff, when dried, is a reminder of new-mown hay all through the year. Put it in the linen cupboard for real freshness or press between the leaves of a favourite book. The Winter Heliotrope finishes our scented year—or does it begin the next? It is not a good plant to have in the garden, even a wild garden, because of its invasive habits, but to come across it in a hedge during a walk in the depth of winter is something we always enjoy.

As we have seen in Beginner's Botany, flower perfume and fertilization are directly related. By a complicated chemical process flowers give off their perfume at different times and even change its nature according to the time of day or the condition of the plant. By day, for example, the Pyramid Orchid has a clove-like scent which encourages butterflies. At night the scent changes to an unpleasant fox-like smell. On the other hand, the Fragrant Orchid has a delicious vanilla scent, particularly so after dark to encourage night-flying moths, but after their visit it turns to a rancid, unpleasant odour. Another example of changing perfume within the plant is that of the Hawthorn whose scent contains trimethylamine, a constituent chemical contained in the smell of putrefaction. On being fertilized by a midge, which is attracted by the smell, the chemical composition changes to make the scent pleasant to our nostrils.

Trimethylamine occurs frequently in flowers with unpleasant smells; Stinking Hellebore, which grows in deciduous woodland, contains it, as does Dog's Mercury, and both rely for fertilization on the midges attracted by the smell. Stinking Goosefoot has a greasy meal on the underside of its leaves, which gives off the stink of rotting fish because of the presence of trimethylamine; this is apt, because its habitat is mainly the salt marshes of some southern estuaries. After handling the plant, it is difficult to remove the smell, even by washing.

Very often a flower scent which is attractive at a distance, when well diluted with fresh air, in concentration can be described only as a stink! Some of the lilies grown in the garden have strong scents which are objectionable to many people but which others consider delightful. Close to, the influence of the chemical indole asserts itself, but at a distance this is sufficiently diluted to become acceptable.

Most poisonous plants have an unpleasant smell, as if to warn those for whom their poison is dangerous. There is only one evil-smelling umbellifer in Britain and that is Hemlock, a most poisonous plant in all its parts. Henbane is another highly poisonous plant which not only smells evil but is unpleasant even to the touch.

A flower gives off its scent through an essential oil which is located in minute cells within the leaf, petal or stem, and sometimes in the root. The oil is made up of various chemicals which determine the smell. Each perfume is an extremely delicate blend of these natural oils. The oils, and therefore the perfume, are released in one of two ways: because of damage to the wall of the cell by scratching or bruising; or when the cell walls are ruptured by pressure, for example, when a plant is trodden on. Nothing is new; there are on the market card pictures which, when scratched, will smell of the flower, fruit or whatever is illustrated—a gimmick which works on the same principle. The natural scent of flowers is part of the whole essence of life itself. It is the scent which attracts the insect for fertilization, as much as the colour of the flower.

When considering plant dyes, the first one that springs to mind is

1 Alder catkins
2 Acorn
3 Weld
4 Woad
5 Bilberry
6 Bracken shoots

Woad. The scene which it conjures up is inevitably that of the ancient Britons painting themselves with it and dyeing the crude cloth of the day. The last time Woad was put to any major use in Britain was for the dyeing of the material from which the original British police uniform was made in the early 19th century.

To obtain the dye from the plant is a long and complicated process which creates a terrible stink. Queen Elizabeth I even decreed that when she was on her travels no extraction of dye from Woad would be allowed anywhere along her route. Great quantities of the leaves of this plant of the Cabbage family were gathered and piled into neat round heaps, protected from the rain but in the open, and allowed to ferment. The smell of rotting cabbage leaves is well enough known to suggest how appalling the effect of

70

piles of fermenting leaves must have been. After fermentation, drying and grinding, the dye was eventually extracted. During the Second World War, thousands of tons of Stinging Nettles were harvested and the chlorophyll extracted to dye camouflage nets. This is another example of the value of this pestilent but excellent weed.

The dyeing of material, as a small cottage industry, can provide wool with beautiful shades of green, yellow and brown, but the great disadvantage of using purely natural dyes must be understood. They will not work on artificial fibres, and not one of them is 'fast'; all will fade in time, many to delicate shades more pleasant than their initial colour. To make vegetable dyes 'fast', it is necessary to use agents, called mordants; alum is a commonly used one which enriches and even changes some colours whilst fixing them.

Once the likelihood of fading is accepted, however, there is no reason why a limited amount of natural dyeing should not be done. A rough and ready way to make a dye is to use equal amounts of water and leaves, or other parts depending on the plant. Rinse first to clean them of stray matter, then boil and simmer until the resulting liquor looks about the right colour. It can be no more accurately gauged than that. Remembering the fading, it is obviously sensible to allow the liquor to go a darker shade than is really required. If possible, put the dyeing plant into a muslin bag, or old stocking, and submerge this in the water before adding the material to be coloured. Having boiled your material and obtained the colour you wish, rinse it out in hot water, following this immediately by another rinse in cold water before hanging the material up to dry.

Acorns and oak bark give a brown dye which darkens the longer it boils; the young shoots of alders will give a yellow-brown tone while male catkins from the same tree will dye woollens light green. Bilberries boiled as above will make a pink or purple dye according to the length of time it is boiled, but I can think of better things to do with Bilberries after all the bother of picking them! Use the whole plant of Weld, a weed of disturbed ground, to get a clear yellow dye, and the flowering tips of Heather to produce a more golden shade. A plant in plentiful supply is Bracken and it is the young shoots of this which give a pleasant light green. By breaking, not cutting them, the spread of this plant can be controlled so perhaps a supply of light-green pure woollens would be a good influence on the control of this graceful but excessively greedy plant.

Lichens have been used for hundreds of years in areas where they have been plentiful, such as the Outer Hebrides of Scotland, where the air is clean enough for them to thrive. The rock-borne lichen *Parmelia omphalodes* gives Harris Tweed its traditional shade of brown. These plants are generally under a great threat, so the use of synthetic dyes will make a valuable contribution to their survival.

WILD FLOWER GARDENING

If you pride yourself on having a tidy garden and regard any wild flower which appears in it as an unwanted weed, then you may well believe that this chapter is not for you, but if you grow Snowdrops and Lily of the Valley or Marsh Marigolds beside a pond, or the small hardy Cyclamen under some trees then you already qualify as a wild-flower gardener.

Wild flowers require as much care and understanding as their more robust garden relatives, and although a few can be relied upon to throttle your favourite Polyanthus before your very eyes and others to pine and die as soon as they can, many are well behaved and rewarding to grow. They are also most enjoyable to have in the garden, and that alone is sufficient justification for becoming a wild flower gardener.

In 1968 we looked at an inaccessible corner of our farm and decided to build our future home upon it. The site consisted of half an acre of meadowland which rapidly degenerated into a further acre of brambles, nettles and Bracken, the whole area having at one time been a rubbish tip.

Wild Snowdrops

Wild Cyclamen

It was always a problem corner, too steep in parts to cultivate, and where it levelled out the ground was inclined to be waterlogged. Many people (including ourselves sometimes) thought we were mad to choose this site, but it had great potential. There is a small stream twisting and turning through it in a series of lovely curves—which could not be designed by man—flowing over small waterfalls, There are mature oak, beech and ash trees along the boundary hedge and half a dozen more form a small wood in one corner. There are Primroses in profusion, various wild orchids and many plants of Bastard Balm which is so rare generally in Britain although locally common in parts of Cornwall. Today, with the slopes landscaped into curves and terraces separating lawns and flower beds, we have a garden which features all the best points that were there from the beginning. It successfully accommodates a new pond, Cornish stone walls, wandering paths, more trees and shrubs and a dozen larches which form another small wooded area. Around the house we have planted many colourful flowers but have chosen varieties with quieter shades where they meet the trees and where the garden flowers give way to the wild ones—including the Bastard Balm which still flourishes well.

There are many species of wild plants which can be cultivated. Some have familiar names though it is not always realized that they are, in fact, truly wild plants which have been adopted by gardeners. They include Love in a Mist, Dame's Violet, Sea Holly, periwinkle, Borage, Autumn Crocus, Monkshood, several members of the Cranesbill family and the beautifully scented shrub *Daphne mezereum*. There are many others which are only a step removed from the wild species and have been specially selected for colour and successfully bred for garden culture. For instance, the Cuckoo Flower, or Lady's Smock, can be bought in far less washed-out lilac colours than its native type and it also grows as a double-flowered variety. Primroses now come in all shades of the rainbow and although I still love the natural yellow form best we also grow the dusky pink ones which sometimes can be found wild in Cornwall and parts of Wales. They mix well with the other coloured primroses which are grown from seed. I do not like Cowslips in any other shade than their natural yellow, and although we have many times raised plants from seed they do not like our rather too acid soil.

The best way to increase wild plants in the garden is to search through catalogues of plants offered for sale by reputable nurseries. It is suprising how many British and European wild plants are now cultivated. One can also exchange cuttings with other gardeners or collect a seed capsule—or two at the most—while out for a walk in the country. Some of the most beautiful flowers can easily be raised from seed, and the Wild Pansy is certainly one wild flower which deserves a place in every garden and in every heart—it was not called Heartsease for nothing. We both love this flower and cannot pass it in the Highlands of Scotland or in the mountains of Europe without stopping to look long and deeply into its velvet face. Some are darkly purple as the night, while others are a mixture of violet and yellow, or all yellow. Buy seeds and you find that they spread their offspring far and wide around the garden and will appear in cracks between paving stones, on walls and in flower beds. They cross and mingle their colours in many different ways; they are never a nuisance and once you have them you will never wish to be without them. If our garden was reduced to the size of a flower pot I would choose this plant to put in it.

If you hear of a particular stretch of hedgerow or bank about to be removed, then take your field guide with you, ask permission to dig up plants suitable for the garden and bring back buckets full before they are buried under concrete. Many flowers under threat have been replanted in nearby habitats, with varying success, while others have been cared for in a few of the millions of gardens throughout the country which are potential nature reserves of the future. When a nearby pond to us was filled in by developers we were able to rescue some plants from under the blade of the bulldozer but, of course, not the hundreds of newts, frogs and water voles. That small willow-fringed, iris-flowered haunt of Grey Wagtails and dragonflies disappeared before our eyes, but at least the pond we have dug in our garden has in some measure replaced the one that was lost, for every local creature that swims, hops or likes to fly over water has discovered it and found it good.

The Meadow Garden
To call our slope of ground a meadow is pure affectation on our part, although I like to think 'affection' would be a more suitable word. It is not really large enough to be called anything at all, but it is a genuine piece of old English pasture which has not been ploughed for generations—if ever—and is full of old, English meadow flowers. There are buttercups and daisies, speedwells and Cuckoo Flowers, clovers and vetches, and the large Ox-eye Daisy which should be seen on a moonlit evening to appreciate its alternative name of Moondaisy, as it appears like small shining moons among the grass. We have sheltered the meadow on the north side with larches and added groups of Silver Birches underplanted with Wild Daffodils. The meadow itself is open to all the sunshine it can get, and there is ample room to sit in the middle, imagining it at least an acre in extent, and watch blue butterflies on the vetches and lose oneself completely among the meadow flowers.

Having established which flowers grow naturally in the meadow.

we gradually added new plants. Other plants arrived unasked and were welcome, such as the Early Purple Orchid and the lovely Pale Flax which hopped the fence from the adjoining field a year ago and we hope is here to stay; it is so delicate that its pale-blue petals drop off as soon as they

are touched. In a damp corner we grow Meadowsweet and the tall, sprawling Meadow Cranesbill with its blue-mauve dish-shaped flowers so delicately veined, and its relative the strange Dusky Cranesbill with small flowers which vary from plum-brown to black.

   You can buy packets of wild flower seeds and raise the seedlings in pots and pans to plant out into the meadow when they are large enough, and fill up spaces with as many early flowering bulbs as you can, such as Spring and Summer Snowflakes, small daffodils and Snakeshead Fritillaries. With bulbs, you must put from your mind all thoughts of having a really tidy field with short grass. In the first place you must be prepared to wait until late June or preferably July before cutting the grass, and even then it should be just lightly topped over, with a final, close cut in the autumn. The leaves of bulbs must be allowed to die naturally or they will not be able to rejuvenate the bulb for flowering next year. If—unlike us—you have no army of field mice and voles impatiently waiting for their annual picnic of crocus bulbs, you can plant dozens of the small winter and spring-flowering species which grow wild in parts of Europe and look so much more beautiful in a natural setting than the large-flowered, Dutch hybrid crocuses. We planted many of them but they merely provided us with fat sleek mice instead of flowers.

1 *Early Purple Orchid*
2 *Summer Snowflake*
3 *Spring Snowflake*
4 *Snakeshead Fritillary*
4a *Snakeshead Fritillary, white form*
5 *Wild Daffodil*

The Alpine Lawn
This is another rather grand name, but for want of a better one it is what we call the top of a spur of land in the garden above a curve in the stream. It is a miniature plateau on top of a miniature mountain. I can walk up the path leading to its summit and in half a minute I am transported to the Pyrenees. When we took possession of our plateau, there was a hundred years' deposit of beech and oak leaves from the nearby trees, through which had grown a lush crop of brambles, Bracken and nettles rooted in a dump of waste material. We cleared the weeds and sliced off the pointed

peak, as one would slice the top off an egg, to reveal the contents. We discovered that it contained mainly ash but also a treasure trove of Victorian bottles, which did nothing to improve the soil but gave us the incentive to dig deeply and thoroughly.

After adding peat and compost, we laid a carpet of prostrate plants and allowed them to join and mingle as they liked in a patchwork of colour and scents. In our original design there were no paths, and although many of the plants were chosen because they did not object to being walked on—such as Wild Thyme, Camomile and mints—the lawn became difficult to control, so we cleared areas and laid large pieces of Cornish stone to form winding paths around the remaining groups of plants, separating them into irregular-shaped islands which are easier to look after. The plants soon spread again and softened the edges of the stone slabs.

We added a few groups of small conifers and tall-growing heathers around the edges of the plateau and small shrubs down the sides of the mountain so that it became a secret garden within a garden, which always adds extra interest to a place. Our mountain can be reached in a few seconds from one part of the garden, but the new path which spirals around it starts from the lowest part of the valley and takes you in a wide sweep through the foothills and up to the summit, a perfect site from which to see the sun set between the two sloping fields at the head of the valley, which form part of our old farm. It sets behind a wood where the buzzards nest and beyond the steeply sloping field which, many years ago, used to turn creamy-white every June when a myriad of Greater Butterfly Orchids bloomed.

Between the carpeting plants we have small bulbs and alpine plants from various parts of Europe, all of which can be bought from nurseries. We also grow many of our native plants, including Mountain Avens—which is often shy of flowering in captivity but blooms well in our garden—and Alpine Lady's Mantle with its silver-edged silk-backed leaves which are more beautiful than its froth of yellow-green flowers. We have only one plant of Carline Thistle but this supplies me with enough flowers and to spare for winter decorations. The parasitic Thyme Broomrape appeared one year in a clump of Wild Thyme on the mountain top, so too did the Heath Spotted Orchid which grows wild in other parts of the garden and in the valley beyond, and both are spreading well. I cannot say the same for those two supremely beautiful native plants, Spring Gentian and Birdseye Primrose, both of which can be bought from alpine nurseries. In spite of the fact that they are perennial plants, they are never longlasting and tend to die out in gardens; although the latter is most obligingly prolific with its offspring if left to its own devices, the gentian is more difficult and we have to keep a watchful eye upon the plants or they just disappear from sight.

Primrose   *Wood-sorrel*

Woodland

I am at heart a frustrated forest owner. I would like to have thirty acres of woodland carpeted with flowers and full of birds and animals, but I still consider that I am lucky indeed to have a small corner of larch and another with oak, ash and alders bordering the stream which is approached by a long path between beech trees and various shrubs. This path is edged with celandines and violets which need little encouragement for they flourish with great pleasure, and also with primroses which we occasionally divide and replant. In the areas between the trees we have a small glade full of Snowdrops, some drifts of daffodils, Green and Stinking Hellebores, Solomon's Seal, Lily of the Valley and beautiful ferns. We also have far too much Yellow Archangel which tends to smother out the other plants and needs severely cutting back. Round the boles of the largest trees we have planted clumps of wild Cyclamen—always a delight to behold for their silver-splashed leaves are as beautiful as their pink or white flowers which, to me, look as though they are poised for flight a few inches above the plant. Wild Honeysuckle scrambles up over the Hawthorns and Hazels which separate the wood from the field beyond. Wood-sorrel and Wood Anemones are beginning to spread into the parts which we have cleared of nettles, and Foxgloves appear here and everywhere throughout the garden. We have one small area of wild Bluebells growing between two large oaks on a bank which slopes steeply down to the stream's edge. They have been there as long as I can remember and have never spread beyond those two trees, but there are sufficient of them to scent the whole garden.

   If you have only one or two small groups of trees—or even a single specimen on the edge of a lawn—you can grow several beautiful woodlanders in the shade they cast. It is not generally known that the best way to grow Silver Birches is to plant three at a time, no more than eighteen inches apart, to form a triangle. They take up very little room, grow rapidly and each tends to bend outwards towards the top. No tree is more beautiful or graceful. We like the ordinary wild ones which grow in this country and have several groups, and are particularly fond of the more weeping type *Betula pendula*. Under small groups of birches you can grow Winter Aconite and Cyclamen, early flowering crocuses and many other bulbs and plants.

My love of trees began in childhood. When I left the Isle of Wight at the age of twelve I found myself shut in by suburban Surrey. I was given a small patch at the far end of our long narrow garden and allowed to choose the plants I would like to grow. All I wanted was a wild Silver Birch tree. I allowed daisies and tall grass to grow all around it and this patch became my escape from suburbia and my tree my forest.

The Water Garden
The plants which naturally grow by or in water are some of the most beautiful wild flowers of this country. Many have relatively large blooms, such as the Yellow Iris and White Water-lily; others are prolific with their flowers, including the Marsh Marigold which in the spring looks lovely reflected in the pool. The majority of water plants are easy to buy and are also very amenable, settling down happily if you have a pond or a boggy area in your garden. We have both, and sometimes too much of the latter if

Flowering Rush

Yellow Iris

Water Mint

we have a typical Cornish winter which can be warm and wet or cold and wet, but, whatever the temperature, fifty-four inches of rain a year is a lot of wet.

Fed by bubbling springs after a rainy spell, the low-lying patch of garden below our mountain was permanently boggy, with the water unable to drain away because of the saucer shape. So we lowered it still further until we eventually had a large pond, which was roughly pear-shaped, with a small island in the middle full of Marsh Marigolds and some of the lovely wild irises from Japan which have flowers the size of a tea plate. Our island looked delightful, and we were not the only ones who approved, for a mouse promptly decided to make it her maternity home. She ferried dead grass across in her mouth to make her nest—to which she added pieces of our young iris leaves—and we watched her repeat the journey many times, swimming backwards and forwards from mainland to island—a distance of about two yards. All we could see of her was a small furry nose held somewhat desperately skywards as she paddled with furious speed, leaving behind her a V-shaped ripple in the water. We often wondered why she bothered because a warm, dry home among the many plants around the edge of the pond would surely have been preferable to a bedroom furnished with sodden grass on a small and still muddy island. Judging from the high success rate of the breeding programme of all her countless relatives in our garden, there were no predators around to harass her. Perhaps she was a loner, and which of us would not like to own an island? We did not witness the resulting family's departure to the mainland and often wondered if they took to water like the proverbial duck. Perhaps they were so used to the arrival of a soaking wet mother at mealtimes that they fondly imagined they were water voles and needed no persuasion to swim ashore.

While we were excavating our own pond, the other one nearby, which we loved, was being relentlessly filled in for development so we made a final journey to rescue one Water-plantain, an Arrowhead and some Marsh Marigolds before the bulldozer destroyed them for ever. We felt great satisfaction in doing so and in planting them in the shallow area of our pool together with the Water Violets which we had bought and which look like miniature Candelabra Primulas with their soft mauve whorls of flowers. Bogbean is another plant which grows in the same shallow depth, its pink-backed buds opening to reveal white petals covered in glistening spun-sugar threads. Both can grow successfully in garden ponds, like the Flowering Rush which unfortunately is apt to produce a lot of leaves and not enough of its rose-pink blooms. Globe Flowers among the Marsh Marigolds, Purple Loosestrife and Meadowsweet all look particularly lovely on the banks of pools and streams, and none of them is shy of flowering.

Many other moisture-loving plants can be purchased, but choose with care for some can ramp and spread too quickly at the expense of other more choice plants. The wild water-lily, for instance, requires a large lake rather than a pond so smaller garden forms are preferable. Yellow Irises can be very invasive so we are content with only one clump in the garden, leaving the rest to grow naturally in the field beyond, discouraging them from poking under our dividing fence. The wild irises from farther afield than Europe are really the best ones to grow. The purple *Iris laevigata* and the huge clematis-flowered *Iris kaempferi* from Japan are my favourites for they are beautiful, free-flowering and last for many years. The plants I raised from seed ten years ago show no sign of departing nor have they outgrown their allotted space. The yellow Monkey Flower and its red-spotted relative, Blood-drop Emlets, are both aliens which have become established in the wild and have settled happily near water. They are not very longlasting plants and seed themselves almost too readily around the garden, but they are colourful and we leave most of them in peace among the forgetmenots and the sweet-smelling Water Mints. Beware, however, of the delightful-sounding Fairy Moss, a wildling from South America. Twenty years ago we introduced a piece no bigger than the half-crown it had cost us into a vast but shallow pond we had on the farm. The catalogue described it as a delightful floating mosslike plant, its tiny leaves—bedecked and bejewelled with diamond-like drops of water—turning scarlet in autumn before being killed by the winter frosts. The catalogue suggested that some pieces should be overwintered in a bucket in the greenhouse and refloated next spring. By the first autumn that charming little fairy was already showing signs of going quite berserk, and obviously our Cornish frosts were not sufficiently cold to deter it—or them—for when spring came round again the signs of renewed vigour and growth were alarming. After two years there was no sign of any water even after prodding the heaving mass of spongy moss which was increasing layer upon layer. True to its word, it changed colour each autumn but the whole 'waterless' pond looked as though it consisted of raw minced beef—even a stone flung into its midst failed to sink. The cows looked gloomily at this large dish of raw meat and wandered on to drink from the stream that flowed into it. They could no longer stand about in the water looking rural and pretty and they obviously resented it. Eventually we stopped up the flow from the stream and allowed the invader to die a slow and evil-smelling death as it dried out. In two years our half-crown's worth of moss had multiplied into a million-pound load of the stuff, but I would not give one leaf of it to anyone with a pond situated south of the Arctic Circle. Needless to say, it has not been introduced into our new pond.

Once you have water in your garden, many species of dragonflies will probably visit you. One year we had a positive explosion of these beautiful insects, from the fat powder-blue 'darters' and the large swift-flying 'hawkers' to the myriads of fluttering damselflies which covered the pond with a metallic sheen of blue and red while they hovered and dipped and laid their eggs into the still water. They basked in the sun on flowers and leaves, on warm stones surrounding the pond and on us if we paused for a few moments to watch them. A plague of dragonflies is something I would willingly put up with every year.

You will find that the numbers and variety of birds will also increase if you have a pool. They will come to drink and to bathe in the shallows of even the smallest pond. We have a Kingfisher which regularly visits us, no doubt hoping for a repeat performance of the feast we unintentionally gave him a few years ago when we put a couple of dozen goldfish in the pond for our enjoyment. All we did, however, was to provide the Kingfisher with an excellent and productive two days' fishing and ourselves with a perfect view of this brilliant bird as it dived like a blue dart from the willow tree into the pond below. It kindly left us two fish, probably because they were too large for it to swallow, but they remained for only a short while before they too disappeared, leaving the imprints of a Heron's feet in the mud of the pond to tell their fate. I am glad, however, that it was these two birds who took our fish rather than the family of mink who gambolled their way up our stream and into the pool a few weeks later, for they are vicious killers of fish and poultry and not to be encouraged in the garden. Another experienced swimmer is the grass snake—for several years we have had a pair living under a large cushion of Thrift which grows on top of a warm retaining wall near the pond. Often we have seen them curled up together basking in the sun on top of their cushion, with an occasional lizard asleep beside them. Whenever they feel too restricted, they drop their transparent skins like discarded stockings on the lawn—some of them perfect in every detail with scales and eye sockets clearly marked. Grass snakes are supposed to be active during the day, and ours probably live such a life of ease and luxury that they hardly have to move away from their larder, stocked as it is with a super-abundance of tadpoles, newts, frogs and small trout, yet we have never seen them in the water collecting their meals. Grey Wagtails, with their sulphur-yellow breasts and long tails, visit us regularly and nest beneath a waterfall not far up the valley; a Dipper can often be seen sitting on a spray-splashed rock singing loudly and clearly above the noise of the water. We have had a brief visit from Moorhens and wild ducks and in one particularly cold spell the frosty weather drove a Snipe, two Woodcock and one lovely Green Sandpiper from their moorland pools down to our pond where they stayed for most of the day.

Patios
Plants which are particularly suitable for growing in containers include many wild herbs which look very decorative, are easy to grow and are also useful as flavourings to add to hotpots, sauces and stuffings. They include the well known Thymes, Winter Savory, Marjoram, Lemon Balm—so pleasant with fish—and Chives. Besides the common mints, there are others which taste of apple and even pineapple. All are best controlled by growing in pots or in bottomless buckets sunk into the ground, which prevent them from taking over the entire herb garden. Any type of container can be used for herbs; we have an odd collection of earthenware and plastic flower pots, ornate urns, tubs, troughs and crocks and also some huge and ancient earthenware forcing jars for rhubarb which we inherited with the farm. Turned upside down, they make lovely tall containers for plants.

As many of the herbs have to be cut before they bloom, I like to grow a few edible flowers between them to add some colour. Borage is a most attractive plant with its royal-blue flowers, the leaves of which are used to flavour drinks and, when chopped finely, add a taste of cucumber to salads. The flowers can be candied, like violets, and used to decorate cakes. Even the old-fashioned marigold can be grown among herbs in tubs or beds, as the petals, though somewhat tough, are sometimes chopped into salads or used instead of saffron to colour rice.

We have two areas which we have paved with stone, one of which is circular and cut into the sloping ground so that the front is level with the lawn and the back is three feet below the rising ground around it. We have made a long stone-faced seat against the back wall and so created a pleasant outdoor studio for the summer months. We left several small gaps between some of the Cornish stone slabs where we planted some of those obliging

1 Fennel
2 Borage
3 Tansy
4 Wild Thyme
5 Chives
6 Marjoram

aromatic herbs, such as Wild Thyme and Camomile, which do not object too violently to being trampled on by small grandchildren at our annual barbecues. One patch of Thrift—a plant which grows to vast proportions in our garden unlike its windswept relatives on the cliffs of Cornwall—found its own way into one of the pockets and has spread over the cool stones until it is now three feet across and so thick that it easily bears the weight of several grandchildren who use it as a cushion. Other plants of Thrift regularly appear on our garden paths, and we always leave a few until we find our way is barred and we either have to make a detour around them or jump over.

Cornish granite troughs, once so commonly found and even discarded on farms, are now at a premium, for they have become more popular as containers for rock plants than for their original purpose as containers of pig food. Discarded stoneware kitchen sinks, however, are more easily procurable and can be made to look quite presentable if coated with adhesive and then daubed thickly and roughly with a mixture of peat and cement to cover the sides and top edges—a coating which will last several years. The sinks are most suitable for plants which are slightly fussy about their habitats or are in danger of being pushed out of their beds by more energetic companions. The plughole acts as an excellent drain; a large stone should be placed on top of it to allow water to seep away. Next a layer of small stones and then the sink can be filled up with any good compost to suit the particular plants you wish to grow. A top layer of stone chippings or grit will ensure that any alpine plants which object to wet necks will live in comfort for the rest of their days. Perhaps in fifty years time the covering will be carefully removed so that these sinks can be restored to their original use in the fashionable 'olde worlde' kitchens of the future.

We have two such sinks on our second paved area which is immediately outside the kitchen door and was designed to be decorative as well as functional. We built a low wall, topped with paving stones around part of it, which acts as a pleasant sitting-out bench for snack lunches where we only have to reach out an arm to pick fresh thyme or Chives to flavour our salad. It also acts as a retaining wall for the raised beds behind it, and a restraining one for all those galloping herbs which are planted there and are for ever trying to get out. During the early summer, Fennel, Dill, Tansy and Sage, Rosemary and Basil run riot, and I am grateful for their restricting playpen until I have cut and dried them and order is again restored. In the two sinks we have small bellflowers and Mountain Everlasting which hang over the edge, also Wild Pansies which have no right to be there but are always appearing—anyone who has been looked at fairly and squarely in the face by a Wild Pansy just cannot be hardhearted enough to remove it.

European Favourites

There are many delightful flowers of mainland Europe which do not grow wild in Britain; fortunately many of them are now in cultivation and most of them can be relied upon to bloom in our gardens. They add colour and mix harmoniously with our native or cultivated flowers. Even plants which normally grow on dry, cold or snowy ledges high up in limestone mountains settle down happily in our warm, wet, acid-soil garden in south Cornwall. The conditions we offer could not be more different from those which nature provided for them.

All the plants I mention can be bought from nurseries, and there are many selected forms and named varieties from which to choose, although we prefer whenever possible to grow those species which have not been altered in any way, not because they are any better but because they form a necessary part of our collection of wild flowers and are always on hand if I want to paint them. We are particularly fond of the Blue Anemone (*Anemone apennina*) which flowers in early spring under our trees and mixes well with wild, white Wood Anemones and Wood-sorrel. It has spread over the years and blooms profusely even in the most shady parts. The colour of the flower is bluebell-blue, soft, misty and quite beautiful, and the ferny foliage is no less attractive. A flower of much the same colour is the wild Alpine Clematis (*Clematis alpina*) which scrambles over rocks and shrubs in its native habitats among the mountains and will behave much the same way in the garden. We like to see it draped over a

Martagon Lily

Alpine Clematis

Dog's Tooth Violet

Alpine Snowbell

Blue Anemone

Trumpet Gentian

Hepatica

85

hedge or wall, and it also looks beautiful growing up a pillar or through a climbing rose. Another flower which can be found growing in rocky places, among grass and in woods on the limestone mountains of Europe is the blue Hepatica *(Hepatica nobilis, H. triloba* or *Anemone hepatica)*. It can also be found with pink and occasionally white flowers. Although it is rather shy of flowering in our garden, it is a delightful plant with ace-of-club-shaped leaves, but I think it would do rather better if we moved it into the more damp and shady spots of the wood.

Ramondas *(Ramonda myconi)*, from the Pyrenees, have mauve-violet flowers held above very crinkled and rather coarse leaves which form rosettes. It is said to be of paramount importance to plant them on their sides in a crevice in a vertical rock face, in full shade, so that water can run off and not settle in the middle of the rosette. I took great care to plant my first Ramondas on their sides but they promptly died. A few years ago I hastily pushed a plant—which had been sent to me to paint for *The Alpine Flowers of Britain and Europe*—into a shady sink, flat on its back, which I know well was totally wrong, and it has flowered and flourished ever since.

Gentians are known to most people, and it is as exciting to see them flowering on the mountains as in the garden where some species are not too difficult to grow. The large Trumpet Gentian *(Gentiana acaulis)* has the habit of flowering well in some gardens but not in others; there seems very little reason for, and certainly no answer to, this problem, but it is well worth trying.

The snowbells are all beautiful,

Bearded Bellflower

Campanula cochlearifolia

particularly so when seen flowering so freely among melting snows high up in the mountains. They cannot always be relied upon to grow well in gardens, but our plants of the Alpine Snowbell *(Soldanella alpina)* have spread like weeds throughout the small pockets where we planted them and give us a generous display of leaves, but the lovely mauve flowers with deeply cut fringes are few and far between. They are worth growing nevertheless but would probably succeed far better in pans in a cold glasshouse. There are over 150 bellflowers—if you include all the subspecies—growing wild in Europe, as well as all the rampions and the two species of lobelia which also belong to the Bellflower family but do not outwardly resemble them. Most of them can be relied on to behave well and flower profusely, although great care has to be taken with some of the tiny and very rare ones.

Whether we are in the mountains or on our alpine lawn, we enjoy the sight of the small *Campanula cochlearifolia*—a very long name for a very tiny plant, but it is the one I use because its English name of Fairy's Thimble is over-sentimental, but I have to admit that it does truly describe those tiny delicate blue bells hanging from thin wiry stems over rosettes of small rounded leaves. Another campanula which delights us and which I like to paint is the Bearded Bellflower *(C. barbata)*; the leaves are rather coarse and the whole plant is larger than the other species, but each bell is packed with gossamer hairs which also fringe the margins of the five points of the bell, as eyelashes edge an eyelid.

There are also many bulbs of Europe which are readily available from firms in this country. We have planted a group of Yellow Turk's-cap *(Lilium pyrenaicum)*, mainly because they add to our collection of wild bulbs, for I cannot call them spectacular or even very beautiful and their scent is overpowering at close quarters. The pink Martagon Lily *(Lilium martagon)* I like very much—and so do our bank voles. In spite of their addiction for the tender, growing tips, these lilies flower year after year and show no sign of weakening. The Dog's Tooth Violet *(Erythronium dens-canis)* is another member of the Lily family which is easy to grow. The name is very inappropriate for there is nothing violet-like about its relatively large, pink, star-shaped flowers.

There are many more of our European favourites in the garden. The list of plants which can be bought is endless and the choice so varied and interesting that we occasionally run out of space. We have learnt over the years that many alpine plants which are advertised are too difficult to grow out-of-doors, and we are now far more careful about which we select. We would rather see a colourful display of common ones than a few sickly, unhappy varieties which should have been left in their native habitat.

PLAYTHINGS AND PASTIMES

The Pursuits of Childhood
The flowers which had a great influence upon me when I was a small child retain their magic to this day. Not one can surpass the Primrose as far as I am concerned. Other flowers may be the true harbingers of spring, flickering briefly into bloom here and there or, like the Snowdrops, covering the ground with their cold white flowers which reflect the colour of winter more than spring. Although I look for signs of spring as soon as the shortest day has passed and find them in the lengthening catkins on the Hazel and the changing song of the Great Tit, it is the Primrose which really proclaims that spring has arrived. Why do I choose it as my favourite flower? There are many more beautiful but few so breathtakingly lovely, many more highly scented but few so refreshing, and there are hundreds more brilliantly coloured but none so clear and incomparable, but, most of all, I choose it because each year it brings with it a childhood memory—an awareness of a different world that existed to be explored and was within my reach yet too far away for more than a fleeting glimpse each spring. It was a wood I called the 'Primrose Place', which left such a profound influence upon me that for the rest of my life Primroses, rivers and trees have been of the greatest importance. When we chose our small corner for the site of our new house, I was totally convinced that no other place would do because it had a stream, enough trees to make me feel as if I was living in a wood and more than enough Primroses to cover every shady bank within it.

  As a child I lived on the Isle of Wight and it was my birthday treat to be taken to the 'Primrose Place', hidden deep in the interior of the island, a car-ride away from our seaside house and totally different from anywhere else within walking distance. It was far from the normal sounds of sea and gulls; full of silence, bird song and cawing rooks nesting in the trees above; and it was carpeted with Primroses—long-stemmed and lush—right down to the stream at the bottom of a small wooded valley. It was a world away from the chalk downs and wind-dwarfed flowers I normally saw.

Buttercups are another childhood memory; no doubt I had a flower held under my chin to see if I liked butter, just as I have performed this traditional act with my own children and they with theirs. Who knows, perhaps in future, if we all become too cholesterol-minded and butter too expensive, we may have to rename this flower, and small chins will reflect the colour of 'Polyunsaturatedfatcups'! Such rituals continue; time is still told by blowing dandelion clocks, and the state of young love revealed as daisy petals are removed one by one. The same country games and songs which feature flowers are played and sung in school playgrounds as generation follows generation.

The natural progression from butter-testing and time-prediction is to the making of necklaces of rosehips, followed by conker battles and the fashioning of many, small, rather dubiously shaped animals from natural objects, for example, fir-cone hedgehogs, acorn men, conker creatures and pussy-willow cats. The last named did not figure in my own childish attempts at animal impersonation. I had not heard of them until I illustrated Richard Mabey's book *Plants with a Purpose* and discovered the sticky business of fastening pussy-willow bodies on to paper and then adding Hazel-catkin tails. As a child, however, I did make small, fluffy, grey-coloured baby owls by sticking numerous pussy-willow 'bodies' on to black card on which the outline of an owl was marked. The result looked remarkably like the feathers of the young bird and was delightful to stroke. The eyes were big, black, shining buttons fastened on with thread and tied at the back of the card. The final touch was to stick on a bright gold paper moon and a piece of bark to resemble a branch on which my owl perched with non-existent feet. I also made all the other animals I have mentioned—I had families of fir-cone hedgehogs, from large ones to tiny babies, around my room and to me they looked just like the real thing, with glitterwax noses and beady, berry eyes. No doubt they looked just like mutilated fir cones to everyone else. I met poppy dolls, also for the first time, when I illustrated Richard Mabey's book. These little ballerinas are somewhat fleeting playthings, for their petals do not last long after they have been tied down with cotton to form the waist. A piece of stalk is pushed through for arms and features are inked on to the seed capsule to complete the little figures.

Other games of childhood are still played despite television and plastic toys: guns are made from plantain seedheads; goosegrass and burrs are attached to clothes and to hair, peashooters are made from hollow stems of Hogweed. But no longer can we encourage children to pick bunches of flowers to turn into Cowslip balls.

A pastime which has recently gained popularity among both children and adults is the making of dried flower pictures, although I think grasses and leaves are better than flowers, particularly for children. If pressed, arranged in pleasing designs and then lightly glued on to suitable cards or material, they last well when framed and look most attractive. The same idea can be used for greetings cards and wall-plaques, by covering with clear adhesive film instead of glass. They look particularly well if a dark colour is chosen for the background as this shows up the pale dried leaves and grasses to the best effect.

Children can enter the floral art world at a young age by exhibiting in the classes which are often included at local flower shows. I feel they should be encouraged to do so and be allowed to express their own natural feelings for flowers. Many of these classes call for wild flower arrangements, and I wish it could be stressed that only common ones should be used; many times I have winced in horror on seeing quite rare orchids pushed in among buttercups.

Before we move on, there is a plaything which Richard Mabey mentions in his book whose description reads like a horror story—a 'Children's Necklace for the Teeth', a 17th-century type of comforter. Roots of the poisonous Henbane, Orpine and Vervain were cut into beads and strung together into a necklace which was then soaked in red wine until saturated. Finally, red coral and powdered paeony root were rubbed into the beads until they became dry. The necklace was placed around the child's neck so that it could suck the beads and leave its mother in peace. Too much of this sort of comforter would, I think, have left the mother with no child at all and both of them in peace for ever!

A Disarray of Flowers
From the pursuits and playthings of childhood, we progress to the popular art of flower arranging by adults. This may be anything from a casual pastime for the amateur to the full-time occupation of the professional arranger whose sophisticated creations have little or nothing to connect them with the simple bunches of wild flowers which children exhibit at local shows.

From the outset I must admit that I do not like many of the modern flower arrangements. Having made such a sweeping statement, I must now qualify it by adding that this is partly due to a personal dislike of the word 'arrangement' when associated with the word 'flower'. My dictionary defines the word 'arrange' as 'to set in a rank or row, to put in order', and for me this conjures up visions of contrived, contorted, stiff and unnatural arrangements which are too perfect. Few people will agree with me wholeheartedly and my criticism may sound harsh to many, for it is based on a purely personal dislike of the formal, the symmetrical and the straight line, whether in flower arranging or in garden design. In no way do I criticize the undoubted skills of all the arrangers, nor do I always dislike all their creations. It is merely that I prefer a jam jar filled with a disarray of Dandelions, a pitcher of Queen Anne's Lace or a branch of Horse Chestnut in a copper jug to any complicated composition.

A jug full of buttercups, bright and fresh as a summer day, would never win a prize because it would be too untidy: nothing must ever be out of place in the show-bench exhibit. Like smart new coiffures, they are trimmed, curled, pinned, sprayed and supported by devices which grip like gintraps. Not for these experts does an entire bowlful of daisies suddenly erupt on to the table below, nor does a branch of Hazel in a vase tip over when no one is near it. This is the sort of thing which happens to those of us who put our flowers into containers without supports and who do not have the expertise of the trained arranger.

Where flower festivals are concerned, I have no word of criticism but only of praise. I particularly love those held in and on behalf of old churches. The inhibitions, formalities and rules of the show benches are forgotten and flowers and fancies fly free. It is like a painter of miniatures suddenly undertaking a vast mural. The inventive designs, colour schemes and sheer brilliance of the work are often beyond praise. Windowsills burgeon with blooms which seem to capture and reflect the colours of the stained glass behind them. Fonts flow over with flowers which drip like fountains to the floor. Flowers swathe columns with colour or flank the altar with pure white perfection, and the perfume is strong and sweet throughout. Jacob's coat of many colours, made entirely in ribbons of differently shaded flowers, was a masterpiece we admired in our church several years ago. In such a perfect setting of old pillars and plain stone walls, nothing seems too large or even too flamboyant; all are beautiful to behold.

It is difficult to say at what stage in history flowers were first arranged in vases to beautify the home, for there is very little evidence handed down to us of such ephemeral things until we see them actually painted on canvas during the Renaissance period. Vases there were in plenty but they generally contained wine for humans rather than water for flowers! Just as flowers were beginning to appear in gardens in ever-increasing numbers and varieties in the 15th and 16th centuries, so too were they being featured in art, gradually breaking the ties which bound them to their spiritual significance and their practical uses. They now blossomed in gardens and in art for their beauty alone. Paintings by Dutch and Flemish artists overflowed with flowers such as tulips, roses and carnations, all mixed up with birds and butterflies, birds' nests full of eggs, grapes and peaches, all so obviously arranged merely to look beautiful and for no other reason. They now formed the most important part of the painting and were no longer used as mere props.

It was not until the 17th century, however, that vases specifically for holding cut flowers were produced in great quantity, and not until the Victorian era did flower arranging for the home become an art. Apart from child bearing, it seems to have been one of the few occupations left for a genteel Victorian lady, for she had butlers, cooks, servants and nannies; she had gardeners to grow her flowers and gardeners' boys to help her cut and carry them. Now the roles are reversed for the one pair of housewifely hands which does all the work of the below-stairs staff rarely has a moment off to 'do the flowers'.

The flower arrangements of early Victorian times were often stiff, formal and overpowering in ornate and heavy vases, but towards the end of the 19th century a gradual change to the natural look was taking place, not only in flower arranging but in many other spheres. More informal gardens were planned, less heavy decoration within the house became the vogue. No small part in this change was played by William Morris, born in 1834, poet, artist, designer of household decoration, artistic furnishings and furniture, publisher of magnificent and much-sought-after books; a man of many talents who brought a breath of fresh air and lightness into the heavy Victorian scene. Gertrude Jekyll, who followed him, waved her magic wand over gardens in the early part of this century and introduced simplicity into their design and informality into the planting of flowers and shrubs within them.

Flower arranging reached its zenith in the 20th century when Constance Spry—famous also as a teacher of haute cuisine—made a name for herself as the foremost, and for me the only, painter of floral art, not on canvas but in the vase. Her creations had a freshness, spontaneity and style never before equalled but often afterwards copied. She brought flower arranging to the notice of women in this country, who suddenly discovered that they too could join in and learn to master the art. Show benches hitherto filled with carrots and turnips and all manner of garden produce, including cut flowers, had to make room for the new floral arrangements which now strayed from traditional vases into teapots, thimbles, wine glasses, black-painted baking tins, large baskets or tiny shells; anything that could hold water was used with alacrity. Later, the introduction of blocks of water-retaining materials into which flower stems could be pushed, revolutionized the floral arranger's world. Flowers even found themselves having to bloom upside down as well as sideways. Blocks were cut into various shapes, and it became simple to produce pyramids, balls or upsweeping crescents. This equipment enabled vases to be dispensed with altogether and arrangements appeared to bloom on slabs of wood or the twisted root of a piece of driftwood.

Ideas and flowers ran riot. Humdrum lives blossomed as people discovered that they had a flair for the new floral art form. Flower groups were started in towns and villages as floral fever spread across the country. A great deal of pleasure was given to those who performed with flowers and to those who saw the final results.

Fashions changed and these lavish arrangements gave way to more restricted styles as the flowers which had to be bought became more expensive. Only a few were needed if a plethora of stage props were included. Seashores were combed for driftwood and shells; woods were searched for twisted branches, fungi and lichens. No curling Honeysuckle stem was overlooked, no acorn-cupped branch passed by. Anything and everything which grew, or which nature had discarded, was pressed into service and into containers. Various methods of drying flowers and grasses were tried and the varieties found to keep successfully were soon appearing in many arrangements. All the harvest of the countryside was gathered in, including berries, dried grasses and empty seed heads from all kinds of flowers, thus enabling the arrangements to spread from short-term summer ones to long-lasting autumn and everlasting winter ones.

Most wild flowers last well in water, but I very rarely use any except the most common and rampant amongst them. I find the majority of wild flowers too small to make much impact, too fiddly to arrange or too rare to collect. I prefer to leave them for others to enjoy, and as I am lucky enough to have a garden full of flowers I make full use of these instead.

Some wild plants, however, are irresistible. No garden blooms of brilliant colour can outdo a vase full of the bursting pink-shaded leaf buds of a sycamore or early forced Hazel, Pussy Willow or Silver Birch catkins. Young beech leaves are always favourites. We are fortunate to have all these in our garden, and we pick them with great care, using secateurs. Primroses grow in large numbers along our shady bank beyond the stream and a flower or two picked from each bunch does no harm. Later in the year Cow Parsley, its other name of Queen Anne's Lace as irresistible as its flowers, grows in such frothy profusion in the lanes that a few stems pushed with little ceremony into a tall white vase make a lovely sight. I also like to add a few Red Campions which flower every month of the year in Cornwall and are common along every lane, mixing well with bluebells and stitchworts to give a ribbon of our national colours. There are plenty of Ox-eye Daisies too, and these look beautiful with buttercups. I never mind picking a few stems of wild Hops, Bryony, Wild Clematis or plain Ivy, all of which threaten to take over their territories, and I like them to trail down from a vase to add interest.

From May onwards I cannot resist collecting grasses as soon as they come into flower. I either dry them upside down in small bunches or stand them up in vases without any water. I find either method will work. They mix well with many flowers in summer arrangements and in all autumn ones. On a country walk I look for Rye and Couch, Bents and Meadow Grasses, Timothy, Cocksfoot, Wood Millet and the beautiful Quaking-grasses, and above all, when we travel on the continent where it is commonly found, I like to collect Harestail Grass for it is as soft as sable fur, as fluffy as swan's-down and the colour of pale honey. You can buy seeds of this and many other lovely ornamental grasses, including Large Quaking-grass which is easy to grow. Sow patches of them in your garden and pick the grasses on a dry day when they are just in flower and then hang them up. Leave a few to seed themselves around the garden and you will never be short of winter decorations.

Some wild flowers can be dried successfully, in the same way as the garden ones, by hanging them up in small bunches in an airy place—Sea-lavender, Tansy, Lady's Bedstraw and Lady's Mantle (even lovelier when it is fresh), all of which I grow—but I prefer the wild harvest of berries and seeds to any dried flower for autumn and winter decoration. I like to shake the ripe seeds of campions on to the hedge before I take them home and then examine the empty seed containers which are shaped like deep golden-brown goblets, their rims turned back into ten tight curls. Nipplewort is a very common plant and its small delicate egg-shaped capsules grow on attractively branched stems.

I keep several large vases, without water, in my studio and add new

Beech

Harestail Grass

Red Campion seed pods

Large Quaking-grass

Common Quaking-grass

seed heads as I pick them. These include Wild Radish, the somewhat unkempt but attractive Black Mustard, Foxgloves—after their seeds have dropped—knapweeds, sorrel and figwort (which I really think is far nicer dead than alive) and all manner of others; they are useful subjects for my paintings and later help to decorate the house. Umbellifers are best picked fairly early in the season otherwise all their seeds will drop off, but I never mind if they are just seedless skeletons for I think they are attractive anyway. All willowherbs produce lovely seed capsules and the Rosebay is common enough to yield a few stems. Some people pick them long before they are ready to burst and spray them with lacquer. I like them when the golden tangle of curled empty capsules is twisting this way and that up the stems. The other small species of willowherbs are just as decorative and after their seeds have wafted away—doubtless all over our garden—the whole stem dries and keeps very well.

Wild Clematis, known as Old Man's Beard and also by the lovely name of Traveller's Joy, provides the best seed heads I know for shape and soft background colour. Gathered while still greeny-gold and shining, they can be sprayed with lacquer to hold them or they can be gathered later when grey-bearded. I do not bother to lacquer them at any stage; I find they will keep well on their long trailing stems, with only occasional hairs from their beards to sweep up. They can also be treated with glycerine while still green and after a week in this they will keep successfully for even longer. Stinking Iris can often be found growing wild near the sea in Cornwall and also thrives in our garden. Its flowers are faded, insignificant and frequently overlooked, but no one could miss the brilliant orange seeds which show up so well when the brown pods burst open. These too can be sprayed which helps to preserve them.

Other seed heads to be found in our garden are from the English and Spanish Bluebells; both are very decorative, as also are the various poppies, including the Welsh Poppy whose seed heads remind me of very tiny Victorian street lamps. Fritillaries—too rare to pick in the wild—grow in the garden in sufficient numbers to spare a few seed heads; so also does Love in a Mist with its inflated pods. A Mediterranean plant found occasionally growing wild both in this country and in France, this annual has become popular with gardeners and is easily grown from seed. The lovely everlasting flower of Carline Thistle, with its gold strawlike petals, should be picked when wide open on a sunny day, and will stay like that for as long as you want to keep it in a dried condition. We have had a plant of this thistle in the garden for many years; it is no trouble to look after and its flowers are always much in demand. Teasels are easy to manage when picked as they need no drying if you leave them on the plant until late in the year, by which time the finches will have eaten their valuable oily seeds. We grow, especially for cutting, the red-twigged Dogwood, various pussy willows and the thorny, wild Burnet Rose (grown from a sucker) which provides many dark purple-black hips, while the Dog Rose in the lane gives us the red ones. I like to mix the two in a shallow bowl full of yellow leaves from our Rugosa Roses and seed heads from Old Man's Beard.

Spindle-berries, all cerise and orange, and Wild Privet berries in black cone-shaped heads are lovely, but great care should be taken with these—and many other berries—if used in arrangements, for they are poisonous and should be avoided if young children are about. Blackberries while still green and red can be substituted and will ripen on the branch. Elderberries can be used too, but both will stain the carpet if the berries drop off. I prefer to leave them for the birds—after the wine bottles and the jelly pots have been filled.

A few leaves can be picked at any time of the year; or you can wait until they drop and then choose lovely, shaped ones such as Mountain Ash, Sweet Chestnut or Field Maple. Press them between sheets of blotting paper or newspaper, lightly iron them if you like, and when they are quite dry arrange them in bowls, accompanied by berries and seed heads; you can even wire or glue them back on to branches for taller arrangements. Beech leaves for keeping should be picked while still green, before any hint of gold appears, and then preserved in glycerine, which is quite simple to do. Just mix one part of glycerine to two parts of boiling water, crush the ends of the stems and stand the branches upright in a jug containing two inches of the still-hot liquid. Leave them for two to three weeks and then arrange them in a dry vase. They will last for as long as you want them to. Hornbeam, maple and other soft leaves can be treated successfully by the same method, as can those of some garden trees including the Eucalyptus. The remaining liquid can be bottled and used many times over.

Some flowers will keep their colour well if dried in silica gel. Forgetmenots, gentians—from the garden I hasten to add—Green Hellebores, Love in a Mist, buttercups and daisies will all respond to this method, but handle them with great care as they become very brittle. I am not particularly fond of these ghost-like reminders of summer in my own home, although I have seen some very attractive arrangements of this kind. I prefer to use fresh flowers, when available, until autumn produces enough berries to add to my collection of seeds and pressed leaves. This is my personal viewpoint, and it is probably just as well that few people will agree with my ideas on flower 'disarrangements', for a riot of Ragwort, a tangle of Teasels or a positive jungle of Traveller's Joy in every home might well turn even these common plants into rarities. Careful and restrained picking of a few wild flowers here and there will do no harm, provided they are very common species throughout the country, but know your flowers before you pick them. A patch of some 200 plants of Heath Lobelia grow in one small field we know, and if you chanced upon it you could easily make the mistake of imagining this plant to be common everywhere. But the Heath Lobelia is exceedingly rare elsewhere, and such endangered species must not be touched nor should their habitat be trampled upon in order to get a closer look at the flowers. The feet of numerous, keen naturalists seeking rarities do as much damage to such plants as those of tourists who walk over them without seeing them.

Leave wild flowers in their natural surroundings, which is out of doors and not in the home. Picking some of them may not do much harm but it will not do any good either, so choose carefully and exercise restraint. Fill your vases with garden varieties and collect the numerous empty seed heads and grasses which can easily be spared around the countryside. They look just as beautiful as expensive flowers and last a great deal longer which is a boon for busy people. If you like gold and silver arrangements at Christmas, remove some of the oldest, dried pieces from your vase, or any you are tired of looking at, spread them on newspaper, preferably out of doors, and spray them—leaves, seed heads, grasses and all. Immediately they are transformed, and for a short spell will glow in dark corners like gilded lilies, before being thrown on the bonfire along with the discarded holly and the old Christmas tree.

Field Bindweed

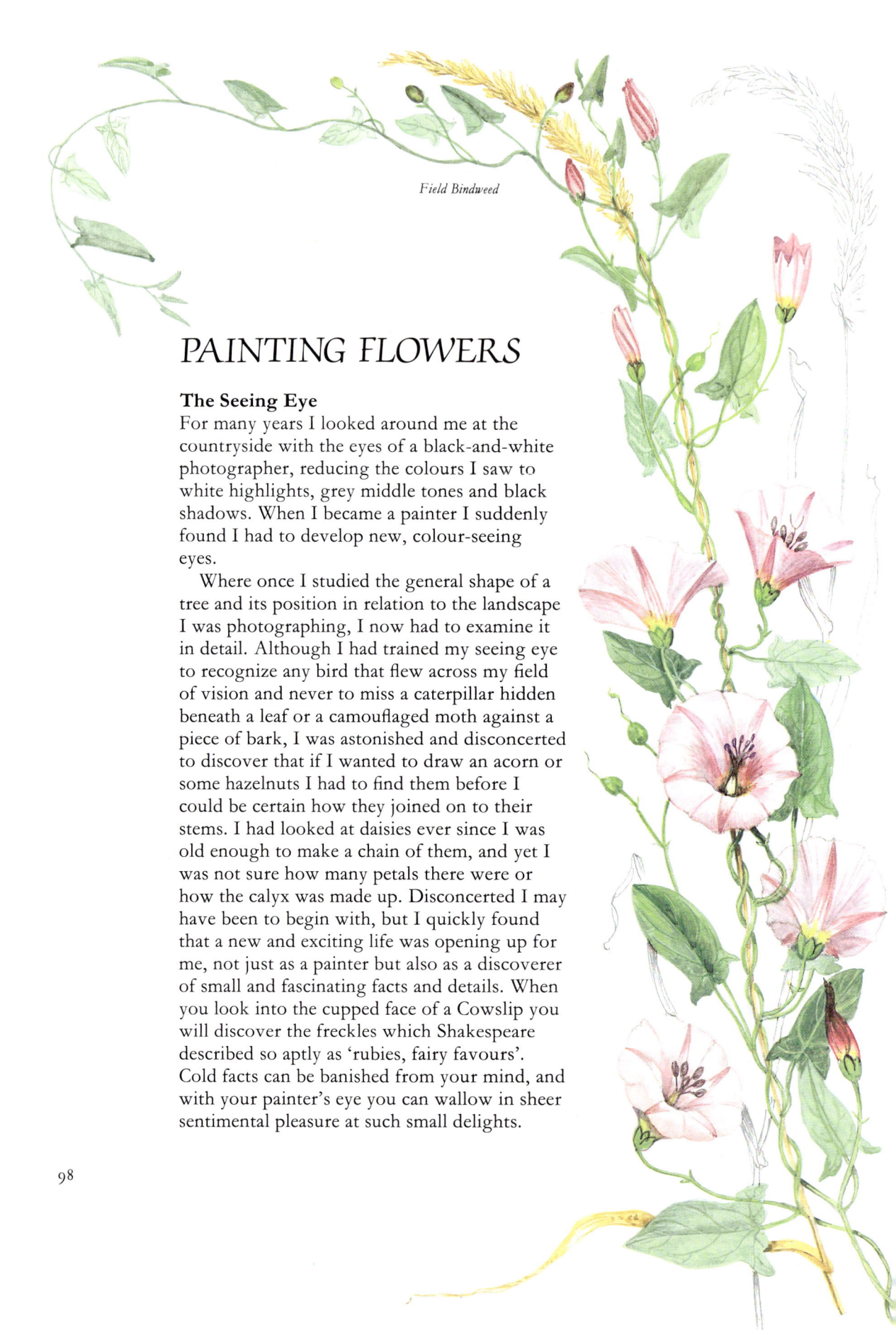

PAINTING FLOWERS

The Seeing Eye

For many years I looked around me at the countryside with the eyes of a black-and-white photographer, reducing the colours I saw to white highlights, grey middle tones and black shadows. When I became a painter I suddenly found I had to develop new, colour-seeing eyes.

Where once I studied the general shape of a tree and its position in relation to the landscape I was photographing, I now had to examine it in detail. Although I had trained my seeing eye to recognize any bird that flew across my field of vision and never to miss a caterpillar hidden beneath a leaf or a camouflaged moth against a piece of bark, I was astonished and disconcerted to discover that if I wanted to draw an acorn or some hazelnuts I had to find them before I could be certain how they joined on to their stems. I had looked at daisies ever since I was old enough to make a chain of them, and yet I was not sure how many petals there were or how the calyx was made up. Disconcerted I may have been to begin with, but I quickly found that a new and exciting life was opening up for me, not just as a painter but also as a discoverer of small and fascinating facts and details. When you look into the cupped face of a Cowslip you will discover the freckles which Shakespeare described so aptly as 'rubies, fairy favours'. Cold facts can be banished from your mind, and with your painter's eye you can wallow in sheer sentimental pleasure at such small delights.

Colour Sense
I find the colour scheme of the countryside around me remarkable in its perfection and in the way everything harmonizes. The background of greens and browns is the perfect choice to show up the flowers which contrast and clash, mix and match in extraordinary ways but are never unpleasant, unlike so many man-made colour groupings I have seen in some gardens. The flowers I associate with spring are cool coloured, white and lemon, soft blues and mauve. The first beech leaves are paper thin and of the clearest apple-green. Larches begin to show colour when small tufts of shrill green appear, but by the time their leaves have grown longer the colour is cool and quiet. All these soft shades fit in with our landscape and with the season of the year. Pale-blue skies and grey rain clouds, soft sunlight, earth browns and spring greens suit our country. Flower colours brighten as the summer advances but so do the skies, and the leaves darken to act as foils for the pinks and magentas, the purples and sharper yellows which are common colours amongst the summer flowers. I quarrel slightly with nature for producing so many magenta flowers—it is not my favourite colour—but never with her wisdom in leaving out most of the reds and hot-orange shades which would look too tropical in our countryside.

Only three flowers in Britain are of such a clear red tone that you might think they would clash with the predominant colour scheme of cerise-pinks and magenta-purples, but the first and the most brilliantly coloured flower is almost banished from much of the cornlands, the second is so tiny that you will have to kneel down to look at it properly, and the third is an uncommon, introduced species.

The first are members of the Poppy family, ranging from pure orange-scarlet to scarlet-crimson, lovely to sketch at all stages of growth from the tightly packed buds to the seed pods. They can be found on waste ground and disturbed areas or on the borders of cornfields but are banned from entering them so that you have to cross the Channel to see them as they once were in Britain, spreading like a scarlet rash through the golden corn, or running like fire along the roadside, mixing with cool-mauve Creeping Bellflowers and tall green grasses, and with occasional Cornflowers amongst them to provide a startlingly beautiful colour scheme.

The second of our red flowers is the Scarlet Pimpernel, looking as though the sun has faded its flowers somewhat, which is not suprising for it lies on the ground with its small star faces so intent upon sun worship that they close up whenever a cloud passes above them. A magnifying glass is needed to appreciate properly the finely cut petals and the clashing purple eye of the flower.

Finally, the alien Pheasant's-eye with its crimson-red flowers with black patches is not unlike a miniature poppy with feathery foliage.

100

Stems from
different
plants

Papaver rhoeas
Cornwall
Aug 1978

Pheasant's-eye

Adonis annua x1

Petal x2

Underside of leaf showing purple punctate x1

Seed capsule x3

Scarlet Pimpernel

Anagallis arvensis x1

You may be lucky enough to find it here and there in the extreme south and east of England, but it is far more common on the Continent.

It is in autumn that the colour scheme changes so remarkably. Then we find the brighter, tropical shades among the berries—orange and red, plum and black—but by then the leaves are becoming gold, russet and copper-brown, never the brilliant red of Canadian Maples but suiting our countryside, the soft lights and paler sunshine of autumn. At this time of the year, look for the Spindle-tree and see what in my opinion is the most daring mixture of all the natural colour schemes in its ripening cerise-pink-covered orange berries.

Spindle-tree berry

Ox-eye Daisies

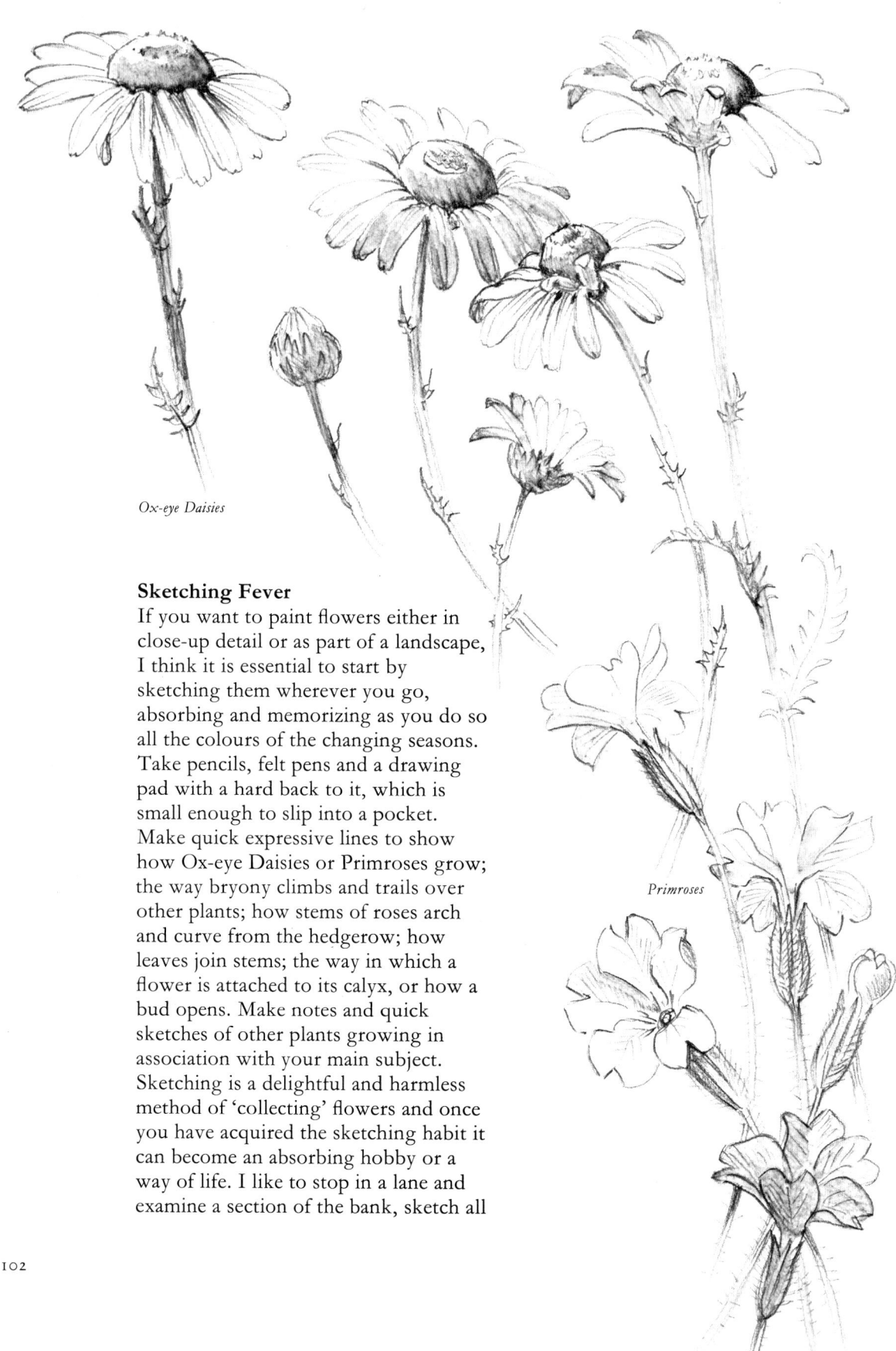

Primroses

Sketching Fever

If you want to paint flowers either in close-up detail or as part of a landscape, I think it is essential to start by sketching them wherever you go, absorbing and memorizing as you do so all the colours of the changing seasons. Take pencils, felt pens and a drawing pad with a hard back to it, which is small enough to slip into a pocket. Make quick expressive lines to show how Ox-eye Daisies or Primroses grow; the way bryony climbs and trails over other plants; how stems of roses arch and curve from the hedgerow; how leaves join stems; the way in which a flower is attached to its calyx, or how a bud opens. Make notes and quick sketches of other plants growing in association with your main subject. Sketching is a delightful and harmless method of 'collecting' flowers and once you have acquired the sketching habit it can become an absorbing hobby or a way of life. I like to stop in a lane and examine a section of the bank, sketch all the flowers, grasses, seed pods and insects within that small area. A rapid drawing done in the field shows much more life than a carefully arranged subject in a vase at home.

In the light of experience, I now realize there is no substitute for sketching from a growing specimen, not just once but as often as possible, at different seasons of the year, from bud to seed pod, and in different habitats, growing tall and lush in a sheltered valley or stunted on a wind-swept hillside. It is worth noting also that colour varies according to the type of soil and the altitude at which a particular plant is growing. This can be seen when comparing the same species from similar habitats but at different altitudes or on different soils.

I take my sketchbook with me in trains, in the saddlebag of my bike, in the haversack on my husband's back or packed into my home-made holdall in our motorized caravan studio. This holdall is simply made of a stiff material with a main pocket on one side sufficiently large to hold a lightweight plywood board and a sketch pad of similar size. In the other half of the holdall I have smaller pockets for paints, slots for pencils and pens, a zip-fastened pocket for small objects such as a rubber and a pencil sharpener. A ruler and some kind of measuring device, such as dividers, are most useful. The board keeps the holdall firm and is a valuable working support.

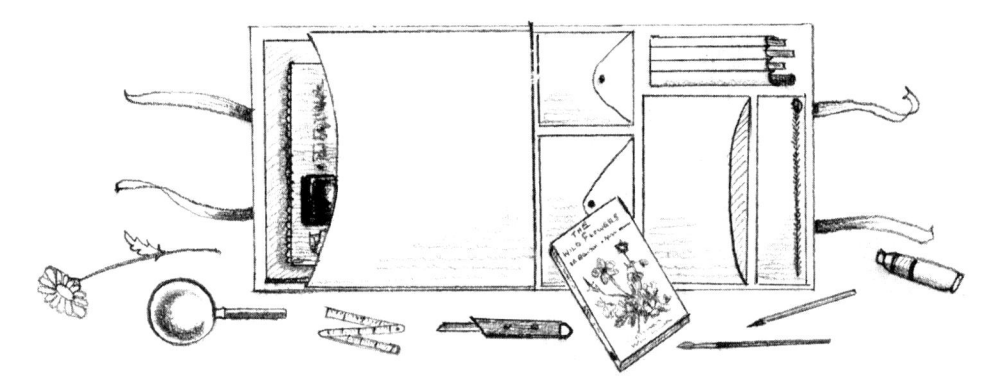

I am therefore always equipped to sketch anything, anywhere: a white bindweed twisting up a wire fence on a railway siding; a Yellow Horned-poppy of fawn-gold silk on some quiet beach, with long, curving seed pods, its buds about to doff their blue-green, prickly caps; or maybe the smallest pansy you are ever likely to see, with the longest name, *Viola kitaibeliana,* the Dwarf Pansy. To sketch this, you will have to lie down and use a magnifying glass for it avoids the Atlantic gales by growing only an inch high. Even in winter there is much to draw: Hazel catkins already growing on bare twigs, seed heads of umbellifers bedecked with frost, and dead grasses tied together with cobwebs, all damp and jewelled on a river bank.

Perspective, Perception and Perseverance

The perspective of flowers and the way in which they are joined to the calyx must be studied if you are going to draw them accurately. Examine them from all angles and practise first by drawing a series of discs (figure 1), the first one almost edge-on, the last one fullface. Within each of these discs draw a smaller one at the same angle—these are the mouths of the corolla. After this you can add the tube-shaped calyx of a dianthus (figure 2), remembering that as you tip the flower towards you the calyx will turn away and become foreshortened. Finally, mark in the petals, five evenly

Fig. 1
Discs

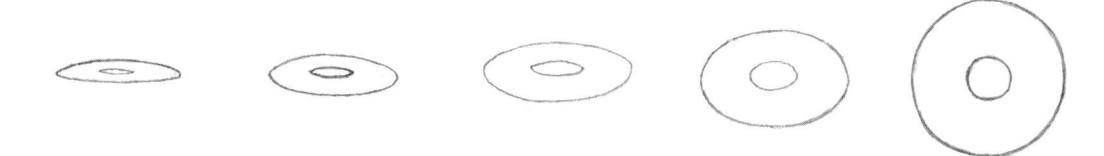

spaced ones for a dianthus (figure 3A) or a primrose (figure 3B). Using the same outline as before, draw the flower from the back view, showing the

Fig. 2
Discs and calyx

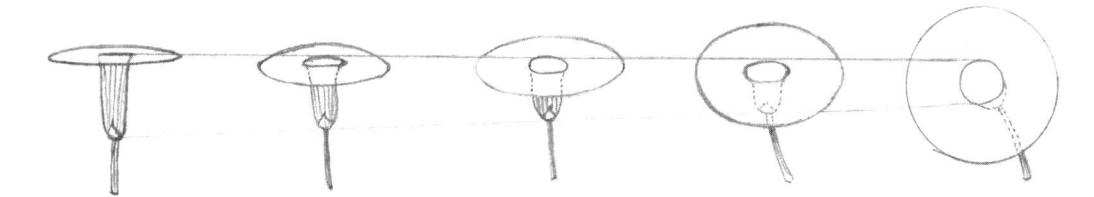

calyx accurately (figures 3C and D). Never make the mistake of drawing the flower fullface and impossibly attached to its calyx (figure 3E).

Fig. 3
The petals

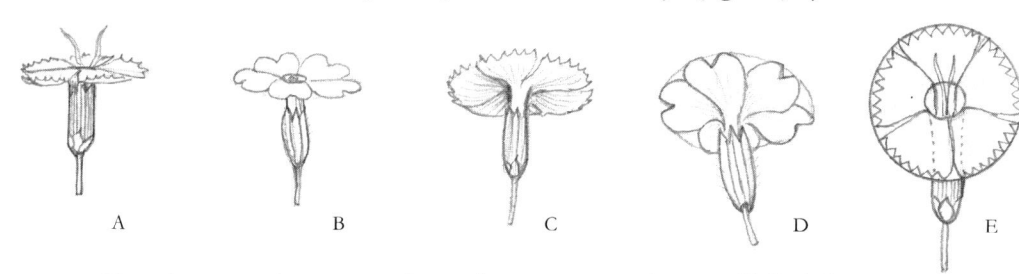

A B C D E

Examine, perceive, memorize and persevere, and you will find the mechanical part of painting becomes easier. You will then be able to store in the back of your mind all that you have learnt, and with your improved technique begin to enjoy free sketching in the field. A few quick lines are often far more expressive and natural than slow, highly detailed drawings. Concentrate on an easy style, good composition, on colour and botanical accuracy, and, above all, enjoy yourself.

Leaves are very often neglected by beginners. Pushed in at the last minute, their midribs are often dislocated or even fractured in an effort to make them look pretty. The central rib should be drawn first (figure 4A), then the outline of the leaf (figure 4B). Here I have repeated this shape twice more, once looking at the front of a leaf and then from the back; the outline is precisely the same. Always carry the line of the central rib in a smooth curve and think of the leaf as being transparent so that each line joins the others in a natural way. Practise drawing leaves from the side and at varying angles until you know exactly how they bend and curl, and always note how they are attached to the stalk and the stalk to the main stem.

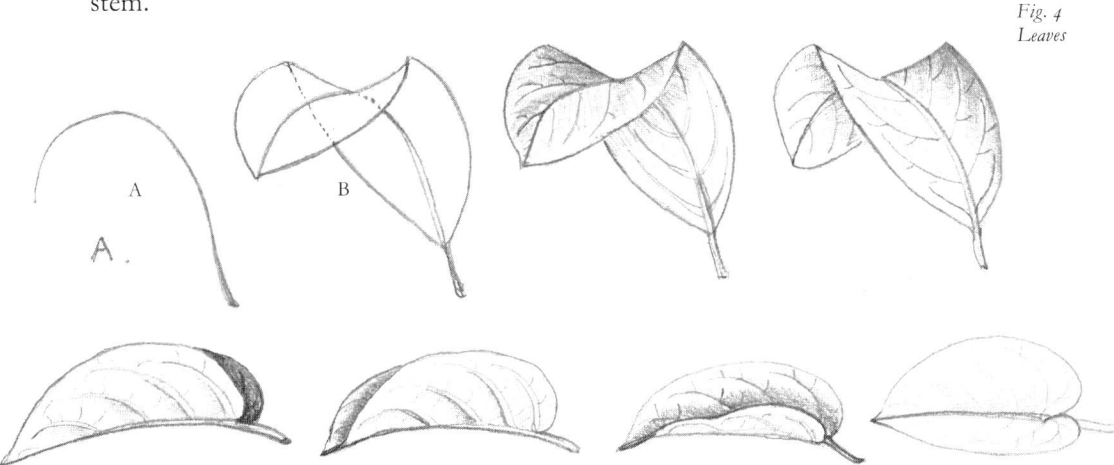

*Fig. 4
Leaves*

Sketch very lightly, using HB, H or F grades of pencil for the outline before painting over with the colour. If you are working indoors with cut flowers, start with the flowers in case they begin to wilt. I use a very smooth-surfaced painting board or paper if I want the detail to show up sharply and clearly. I think it is best to experiment with all surfaces of paper and many grades of pencil until you find the combination that suits you. Brushes must be of the highest quality and as fine as you personally prefer, though I think a good point to the brush is more important than its thickness. I use artist's watercolours in either pans or tubes. Although many colours fade a little over the years, others are permanent and should be used in preference to the fugitive ones. For book illustration I am free to use any type of paint, and if I cannot find the shade I want among watercolours—particularly cerise and magenta—then I sometimes use inks or gouache. Compose your plant in a natural way on the paper. Above all, if nature never intended a stem to grow in a graceful S-bend or a leaf to develop an undulating outline, do not think you can improve upon her design—or your painting—by inventing such things in the hope of adding extra prettiness to, say, a plain hawksbeard. Never try to make a flower look more beautiful than it is, for surely you will fail.

Great Bindweed
(Calystegia sylvatica)

RECORDING AND PHOTOGRAPHING FLOWERS

The recording of flowers is an essential part of our work, but for others, to whom it is not so professionally vital, it can become a rewarding pastime. We find it an enjoyable way of taking our grandchildren for walks—there are always eager hands to help and testing questions to be answered.

There is a tremendous amount to be learnt merely by observing plants and insects, and by writing down the results the various stages of growth of a plant can be built up month by month into an interesting and absorbing picture. In our case this is an invaluable source of reference. For instance, we may need to know how advanced a Hazel catkin is in February, or even November (the fact that catkins are already formed on the bare branches in autumn surprises many people), and our record system can tell us.

Before deciding on which recording method to use, examine your assets as these will help to determine the best one for you. Can you draw or paint? Have you a camera or would you prefer a collection of pressed specimens with descriptions? We use all these methods as each one plays an important part in our work.

A good field guide is essential. We recommend the Collins books, *The Wild*

Flowers of Britain and Northern Europe for identification of flowers up to altitudes of about 1,250 feet and *The Alpine Flowers of Britain and Europe* for flowers above the altitude. Use these books as indices for your system (the botanical order in which they are arranged is the one we use), and note in them what record you have of each flower. Is it a photograph or a drawing? Is it a leaf, flower or seed? Nothing is gained by just ticking off in the book's index which plant you have seen. By recording what you have, you ensure that you take your book with you and that you do not duplicate your efforts. Note down only those records with which you are satisfied. If your photograph is not perfect because a gust of wind moved the plant at the critical moment, do not list it—get another one later and make sure that you do not have the same misfortune.

Having organized your system, the next piece of equipment you will need is a small magnifying glass so that you can look into a flower and see what an incredible creation even the simplest one is.

If you are intending to pick flowers, remember the protected species in Britain (listed on page 117) and do not touch them. Pick only the common ones, but, however widespread the plant, not the last one of a particular patch. Remember, too, that in National Parks no flower may be picked at all. If your interest spreads abroad, bear in mind that in Europe flowers are protected very much more vigorously and that no plant with any root attached may be brought into this country without a licence.

Before starting on your first project, have your equipment ready at home. Interesting botanical collections can be gathered into the large scrapbooks sold by most stationers. A very handy and more flexible way of keeping things tidy and in order is the use of index cards. They should be of a convenient size and stored in a box or filing cabinet either in strictly alphabetical order or in the same order as the plants are arranged in your field guide. We have over two thousand cards so far; each is headed with the details of the plant—it shows the scientific, family and common names and when, where and by which of us it was recorded. We include colour references by matching the living plant to the Royal Horticultural Society Colour Chart, and each of our cards has a pressed specimen of the flower, seed head and leaves from various parts of the plant. A drawing and the reference numbers of photographs are also included. The photographs show details in close-up of habitat, associated plants and anything else we consider relevant. Keeping just a few cards takes a surprising amount of time, as there is always plenty to write on each one. Our pressed specimens are sent to us from botanical gardens all over Europe and from wild areas only where they are common. Some of our rarest flowers in Britain grow in profusion in other places where the flora is not under such strain. It is an essential part of our work to preserve specimens so we have as complete a record of each one as possible, should it be needed to illustrate another publication.

We prefer not to encourage the pressing of flowers, but if it is to be seriously done a few notes will be of help. Very often most of them are wasted—if flowers are picked to be pressed then it should be done properly. You should have several presses. Ours are made of two pieces of plywood (five ply), measuring about twelve inches square, and a length of wide upholstery tape ties the two pieces together. A supply of blotting paper and old newspapers cut just smaller than the press will suffice for the 'bread' in the 'sandwich'. Place the specimens between two pieces of blotting paper and then add three or four sheets of newspaper as padding on either side. If the plant has a thick stem, it sometimes helps to slice it lengthways; this needs quite a bit of practice but it is a great help later on when mounting the specimen. When laying your plant on the blotting paper, arrange the leaves in as natural a position as possible. Add the plywood boards top and bottom, and tie the tape round tightly. For the first few days the press should be examined, the blotting paper changed if damp, and the flower checked for position. This is when any leaves which may have become folded over or creased should be smoothed out because they will not unfold later. To identify the specimen, tie on a small label as soon as you collect it. The time which a flower has to spend in the press varies greatly and is a matter of judgement, trial and error.

When the plant is ready, remove it from the press and mount it on your card. Use small strips of narrow, transparent, self-adhesive tape to stick the specimen down, taping over the stem in several places and over the ends of the leaves. As time passes your specimens will become brittle and will have to be treated with considerable care. We use an adhesive film to cover a specimen completely. Your collection should be kept in a warm, dryish atmosphere. The world's greatest collection of pressed flowers is kept in the Herbarium at the Royal Botanical Gardens at Kew in London, where the temperature and humidity are both controlled within very narrow limits. Some of the specimens are over a hundred years old and remarkably well preserved.

Plants will spare a few leaves at most times so pick a basal leaf and trace around it at the bottom of your card. Do the same for those from higher up on the stem, noting the texture of the leaf, how it joins the stem and whether there is another one opposite it. Leaves are important in identification and notes can be made even when the plant is not in flower.

Photographing Flowers

The camera has brought a new dimension to recording flowers. Not only can extremely close detail be photographed but also the whole plant can be seen with other plants with which it is associated and in its proper habitat. It has been said that the camera replaces the vasculum, or collector's box. The good use of a camera can produce as excellent a botanical collection as any other method. The results are stored easily, take up little room and, if well indexed, need never get lost.

The first items to consider are which camera and which lenses to use. Much depends on how much you want to spend, so discuss your needs with a good photographic dealer. In our experience, however, a single-lens reflex camera is most useful—it enables you to see exactly what you are going to photograph and is also easily portable. By its nature it is simple to use. By turning the focusing ring on the lens, the image on the lens screen is brought into focus and you will see your subject in the detail you wish to record. When the image is in sharp focus in your eyepiece then you may be sure that your photograph will be too. Most single-lens reflex cameras take other lenses for specific purposes. The ideal one is the micro lens which will focus down to about five inches. A lens with a focal length of two inches is probably as good as any for habitat shots. To get the best close-up detail, extension tubes are useful. Here again, a discussion with your dealer will be helpful. If you already have a twin-lens reflex or a plate camera, do not change. The bigger the negative, the better the detail, and many of the best botanical photographers use large-size cameras.

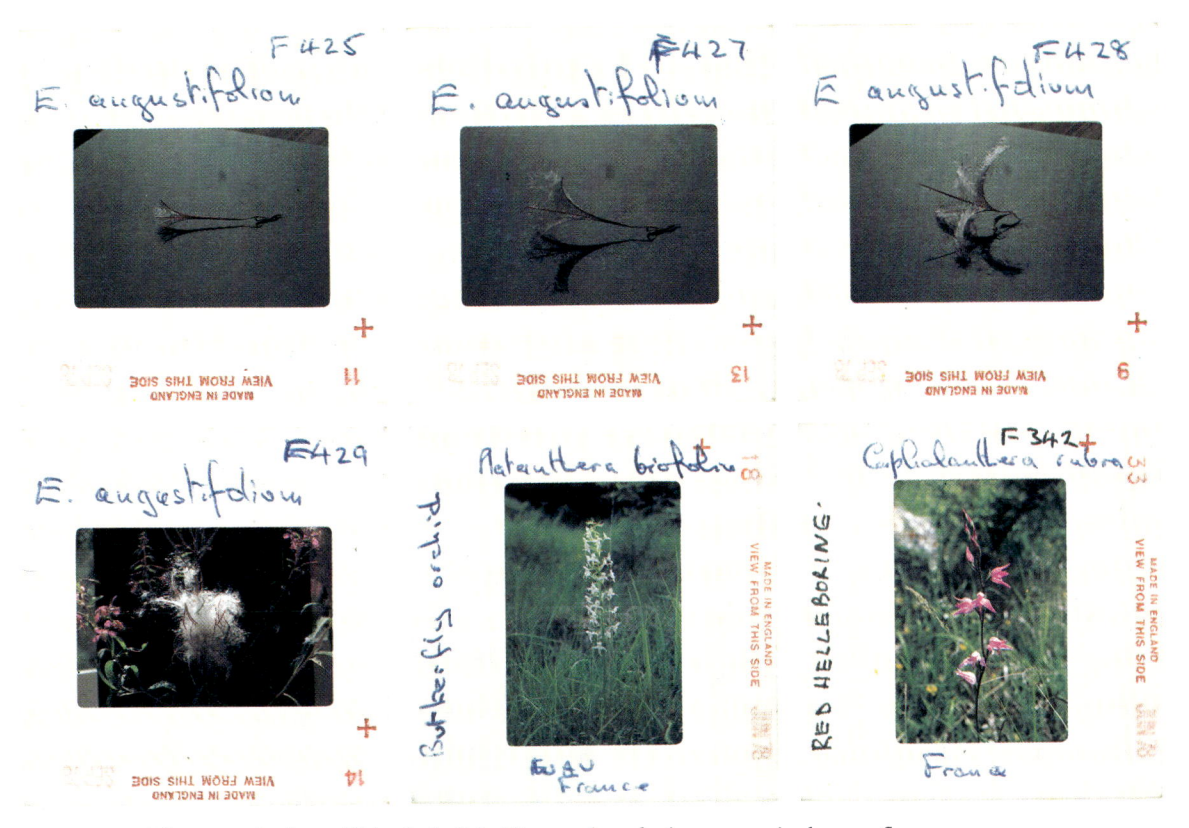

The most useful pieces of equipment are a tripod and a short extension release cable. Although we have some good record shots taken at 1/60th without a tripod, they were taken while standing on flat, firm ground. Photographing flowers *in situ,* the best way to take them, involves getting into some extraordinary positions in no way conducive to a steady hand.

Films are made to react to light at different speeds, with the speeds given as ASA or DIN numbers. In black-and-white photography, with 35mm negatives being enlarged many times, good definition is vital. The slower the film, the finer the grain and the better the definition. For botanical photography, a faster film may be easier to use, and for that reason alone may be best. We use a film speed of 25 ASA and find it most satisfactory.

The question of the correct aperture, or stop, to be used depends on whether you are photographing a small part of the flower in detail or the whole plant. If it is to be a close-up, then a small aperture is essential—say *f*16 or *f*22. Use your tripod and watch out for sudden gusts of wind! The closer you get to an object, the smaller the depth of focus becomes. A small aperture will give you sufficient depth to get the flower from the edge of the nearest petal to the farthest one, all needle sharp. When photographing the whole plant, you can use a larger aperture as much more will then be in focus. If you want the plant to stand out sharply from the background, use the largest aperture and the background hedge, wall or hill will become softer and less obtrusive. Practise using different stops at various distances, making notes as you go; trial and error are the best teachers.

Be careful about the colour of the background. Too much contrast in light and shade can be annoying. It may be necessary to do some 'gardening' to remove any unwanted stalks or grass. Do this carefully. Be prepared to get down to your subject, but be careful where you kneel or lie—there are other plants about.

Sometimes you will find that the sun is just wrong, the wind is blowing and a shower of rain is imminent! This need not ruin your chances. Two pieces of white card will help greatly with any lighting problems by reflecting light to where you want it. Wind and rain are best coped with by using a colourless, transparent umbrella at a convenient angle over your subject.

Be prepared to seize your opportunities. The Rosebay Willowherb (*Epilobium angustifolium*) on page 111 was photographed on a patch of waste ground near our home. We brought back some seed capsules for our record cards, and suddenly saw one of them opening up. As always, the camera was ready to record the event.

A PLACE FOR FLOWERS

Conservation

As mankind's knowledge has grown and developed, so too has his appreciation of and interest in wild plants. But it is this same interest which has led to the urgent, present need for conservation.

The flora of Britain and Europe was largely unrecorded in the Middle Ages, but we know sufficient to be able to visualize it as it was then. There have been many losses but also many new plants have been recorded since those days. Now, the need to protect our wild plants is more important than ever before. In spite of some clearing for agriculture, indigenous trees still clothed large tracts of countryside whereas today Britain, with the exception of Iceland, has the smallest tree cover in Europe. Where lichens and ferns grew freely, now they festoon trees and rocks only in favoured places, generally in the western half of Britain, clear of sulphur-belching chimneys and exhaust pipes. Flowers which were once plentiful and were sold in city streets now rate as endangered species. People lived their lives with a plentiful supply of land and flowers around them, and it is understandable that they could not envisage any scarcity, so we should not say 'if only they hadn't'. Today it can justifiably be said, 'if only they wouldn't'.

In nature there are reasons for all things, but these are either not understood or are ignored by those who have no regard for wildlife. Two things dominate life of any form—food and reproduction. It is the insect seeking its food which enables the flower to reproduce itself, thus establishing the joining link in the chain of life. It is called the food chain, and it demonstrates the complete interdependence of all wildlife, with the worm or the primitive amoeba as important as the daisy or man himself.

A fascinating example of interdependence is that of the Large Blue Butterfly and its relationship with ants. The butterfly lays her eggs on a plant of Wild Thyme where they hatch and feed on the flowers. After moulting their skin three times, the grubs reach the stage at which they leave the plant. They wander about in the short turf, seemingly aimlessly, until an ant from a nearby nest happens along. As ants are very inquisitive insects, it explores this grub by massaging it with its antennae. This excites the grub and it exudes a sweet fluid which attracts the ant still further. The ant then carries the grub to its nest where it is installed and fed on ant larvae on which it thrives. Eventually the grub pupates and awaits the summer. On time, the butterfly emerges, pumps its wings to expand them and flies off to seek a mate. After mating, eggs are laid on a plant of Thyme. The circle is complete and the butterfly dies within a few days. In 1979 this lovely creature became extinct in Britain, an event caused by the increasing scarcity of Wild Thyme, smothered by coarse grasses no longer grazed by sheep or rabbits. Yet although not directly connected to sheep or rabbits, it was the Large Blue Butterfly which suffered.

For thousands of years plants have been a factor in man's evolution and civilization. They feature in religious life, in legends and myths. They have

Large Blue Butterfly and Wild Thyme

Obituary of a Blue

On 12th September 1979, the Nature Conservancy Council announced that the Large Blue Butterfly should, from that date, be considered extinct in Britain. For a few years a small colony was kept in captivity after the wild specimens had died out. No fertile eggs were laid in 1979.
It still flourishes in other parts of the world where there is less strain on its habitat, but there is no longer a British Large Blue. It must be deleted from the schedule of the Wild Creatures and Wild Plants Act 1975—a reminder that extinction is forever.

been used to protect us from evil spirits and to cure illness. We have spun and woven them for cloth, twisted them for rope and cord. We cut, cook and distil them for their flavour and perfume. We paint, photograph and enjoy them. They are part of our responsibility for the rest of life upon earth, and what have we done with that responsibility? What are we doing to it now?

The picture is not a pretty one. We pour thousands of tons of poison—mainly sulphur dioxide and lead—into the air every day; we make our rivers into chemical closets; and we drain our wetlands and fill them with concrete and rubbish. Constantly, new names are having to be added to the list of extinct species. For thousands of years we have ill-used our dominion over wildlife.

It was during the Roman occupation that many of the oak forests which covered Britain were cut down for charcoal and the ground cleared for agriculture. Farming—basic but sound—spread across the land, plant life began to change throughout the areas grazed by sheep and cattle. Habitats were destroyed as the natural pattern of nature was disturbed. After the Romans, the Saxons carried on the policy of forest clearance, and it was the Normans who made the first move towards conservation by passing laws to protect the main Royal Forests from the axe. They did so simply to safeguard the wildlife the forests contained to ensure good hunting, but for whatever reason, we must be grateful to them for our great woodland areas. Land was plentiful, and in the main was used for hunting. Gradually this changed as estate management improved and the stock carried increased in numbers and quality. By the middle of the 14th century sheep outnumbered man in Britain by six to one, and as livestock increased so did the need to grow crops for winter feed. Good land in lowland areas was drained to grow the roots which then formed the major part of winter fodder, and wet lowland has been under pressure ever since.

In the hunting estates new techniques were being developed and applied. The most important of these was the introduction of the close season to protect the young and allow beasts to breed. Nevertheless, the wolf and the wild boar, two of the prime objects of sport, due to overhunting and the clearance of many forests, became extinct, the wolf in 1500 in England and in 1740 in Scotland, the wild boar in the 17th century. Soon walls and fences were built around the big estates to keep the hunted animals in and people out. The first reserves were created—and the first poachers appeared—no doubt!

We are still stripping the land of its tree cover. At the present rate of destruction, aided by Dutch Elm disease, the future of a well-forested Britain fades away. A major tree-planting policy is vital in all areas immediately, with a tightening up of tree preservation on land being developed. Some startling figures from the Council for Nature are worth quoting. In 1978 in Britain one Elm tree succumbed to Dutch Elm disease every fifteen seconds of every day. Almost more disturbing in many ways is the fact that in every minute of every day about eight yards of hedgerow, complete with their wildlife, are removed. Although generally not more than three centuries old, the hedgerow system is one of our most important wildlife assets and is protected less than any other. In a few cases preservation orders have been placed on trees in hedgerows but not with any great effect. They are allowed to die or, because the penalty is so ridiculously low and replacement impossible, they are cut down with the rest. It is said that the deserts of the world, like the Sahara and those in the Middle East, were created by overgrazing. New deserts are being created now by the felling and clearing of tropical rain forests. The protecting cover of the trees is taken from the land and the valuable litter is burnt, leaving the soil to the mercy of the heavy rainfall and the resulting erosion.

This is not the place to list only our follies as guardians of wildlife, but also to try to strike a note of optimism. The dangers we face are being recognized and efforts are being made to keep our wildlife in a healthy state. Our modern methods and lifestyle have a continual impact and cause strain on the environment; conservation must be practical. On the fringe of every movement, creed or campaign are extremes and it is so with conservation. There is a large and vociferous body everywhere which does not accept that nature, including man, is in a state of continual evolution and which insists that a negative attitude is the only one. It does not agree with any development and says that nature must be allowed to take her course. This attitude feeds the other extreme with its total disregard of any conservation, those who seem to be incapable of realizing that life is a co-operation between man and nature—that is what positive conservation is all about.

Nature is trying to establish what is called climax vegetation, while we, as much as any other force, are constantly trying to stop it. Each stage towards a climax is a succession—a delicate balance achieved as the vegetation evolves towards the next stage. What conservation, in a positive way, tries to do is to hold nature in a state of suspense so that the balance is maintained; this is what makes the management of nature reserves such an extremely difficult job.

Flowers and the Law

There are national and local nature reserves managed by organizations like the Society for the Promotion of Nature Conservation, and the forty-one County Naturalists' Trusts within its orbit, and the Government Agency, the Nature Conservancy Council, working through its regional offices. A Wild Flower Working Party made up of members of County Trusts and the Botanical Society of the British Isles worked to promote legislation for the protection of wild flowers. In 1975 the Conservation of Wild Creatures and Wild Plants Act received the Royal Assent, making illegal the picking of any flower on the list of protected plants or the uprooting of any wild plant without the consent of the landowner, whether on the list or not. The list is reviewed every five years, and the original 1975 list is shown below. It covers eighteen flowering plants and three ferns.

Entirely through the lack of man's presence, natural reserves are appearing throughout Europe on the verges of motorways. Some authorities are still doing a great deal of harm by spraying and cutting banks and verges to make them tidy but fortunately others have a much more realistic attitude and are allowing some very valuable sites to develop. Good relationships are being built up between conservationists and these authorities, enabling interesting rarer hedgerow flowers to be protected and plants from threatened areas to be transplanted to motorway banks and similar sites, but this is not a task to be undertaken lightly or without the co-operation of all the authorities concerned. To leap into action without agreement would be illegal and against the 1975 Conservation Act.

Only by education will the wildlife be protected for future generations, but personal action by individuals is also vital to allow plants to flourish. The picking of wild flowers, whilst not to be encouraged, can do less harm than is sometimes thought, provided some flowers are left to set their seed for next year. The pleasure felt by a child gathering a bunch of common spring flowers need not be denied; it is the unnecessary and wasteful picking that is to be deplored. Many times we have seen bunches of wilting flowers waiting in cars to be taken home to sit dejectedly in vases, only to be thrown away within a couple of days. Our plea is, don't pick flowers just for the sake of it; try to leave them where they are for their continued existence and their enjoyment by others.

The Protected Plants

Alpine Gentian · *Gentiana nivalis*
Alpine Sow-thistle · *Cicerbita alpina*
Alpine Woodsia · *Woodsia alpina*
Cheddar Pink · *Dianthus gratianopolitanus*
Diapensia · *Diapensia lapponica*
Drooping Saxifrage · *Saxifraga cernua*
Ghost Orchid · *Epipogium aphyllum*
Killarney Fern · *Trichomanes speciosum*
Lady's Slipper Orchid · *Cypripedium calceolus*
Mezereon · *Daphne mezereum*
Military Orchid · *Orchis militaris*
Monkey Orchid · *Orchis simia*
Mountain Heath · *Phyllodoce caerulea*
Oblong Woodsia · *Woodsia ilvensis*
Red Helleborine · *Cephalanthera rubra*
Snowdon Lily · *Lloydia serotina*
Spiked Speedwell · *Veronica spicata*
Spring Gentian · *Gentiana verna*
Teesdale Sandwort · *Minuartia stricta*
Tufted Saxifrage · *Saxifraga cespitosa*
Wild Gladiolus · *Gladiolus illyricus*

THE PROTECTED FLOWERS

By placing the eighteen species of wild flowers in Britain, considered to be in the greatest danger of extinction, under the protection of the law, it is hoped that some of them will be able to maintain—and possibly to increase—their numbers and even spread to other areas. For a few, however, this protection may have come too late.

The present list of endangered plants is not the end of the story. At least seventeen other species have declined so rapidly during the last twenty years that they too may soon have to be added. These include many flowers of arable land, such as Corn Cockle, Spiked and Round-headed Rampion, Least Lettuce, Fragrant Evening Primrose and Field Cow-wheat. Then there is the strangely beautiful Snakeshead Fritillary which was widespread and common in damp meadows during the last century but which has disappeared from many of its old habitats as they have been drained and ploughed until it now occupies only twenty sites in the Thames Valley. There are probably well over 300 species in longer-term danger; a survey conducted ten years ago established that they had vanished from two-thirds of the sites in which they had been recorded over the last 300 years and that the rate at which they were disappearing was rapidly accelerating.

We do have seven species still growing in sufficient numbers not to be included in the British list but which are now declining so rapidly across the Channel that they have had to be added to a similar list issued in Europe by the International Union for Conservation of Nature and Natural Resources. These flowers include Corn Parsley, Spring Gentian and Isle of Man Cabbage. With the decline of these species in Europe, it is highly important that we should guard them well here.

The fact that so much of our native flora has been living in small and ever-diminishing groups isolated from contact with its continental counterparts for thousands of years, has resulted in many British plants showing unique characteristics. According to most botanists, this is a fatal barrier to the introduction of similar species from abroad. Our strains must be kept pure to the bitter end, and for some that cannot be far off.

Several of our rarities are now so reduced in numbers that they appear to have become self-sterile and therefore self-destructive. Lady's Slipper Orchid is probably the most talked-of case. The only Cypripedium orchid to grow wild in Britain, with a tropical, flamboyant beauty, it is now under guard in one small habitat. It is ironical to think that it was botanists' hands full of freshly dug-up specimens from its original twenty locations that helped to reduce its numbers to a single sterile plant.

Let us look first at the protected flowers found in our mountains, half the British list. Never abundant, their remoteness once safeguarded them from human interference. Now nowhere is too remote for man, and flowers can no longer bloom in safe isolation.

An easily overlooked plant with tiny white flowers on thin stems, not particularly beautiful, but one which requires special conditions if it is to continue to survive, is **Teesdale Sandwort** *(Minuartia stricta)* over whose innocent head a fierce verbal war was waged during the building of the Upper Teesdale Dam in Cumbria. The site chosen for the dam was the only place in Britain where this small flower grows. Vehicles crossing its habitat would surely have destroyed it. Eventually, the conservationists won and the plants were physically protected while the dam was built around them. them.

Drooping Saxifrage *(Saxifraga cernua)*, in spite of its delicate appearance, can withstand the rigours of winter in our mountains. It is found only in a very few places in northern and western Scotland where it clings to life in damp pockets and crevices on mountainsides. It seldom sets any seed and very often does not even flower. However, it produces small red bulbils at the base of the leaves, which fall off in the autumn and lie dormant under the snow until spring arrives, when those which have found a suitable pocket may grow.

Tufted Saxifrage *(Saxifraga cespitosa)* grows in very inhospitable places, such as the Arctic and in parts of Scandinavia. The only other

1 Snowdon Lily
2 Spring Gentian
3 Alpine Gentian
4 Mountain Heath
5 Tufted Saxifrage
6 Drooping Saxifrage
7 Teesdale Sandwort
8 Diapensia

sites in Europe where it survives are on the mountains of Wales and Scotland. It is probably the rarest member of the Saxifrage family and in Britain is found on exposed north-facing mountainsides above 3,000 feet, surviving the storms and bitter winds of winter. There may only be about a hundred plants left in this country and its newly granted protection is very important to its chances of survival. It grows in quite dense cushions; new leaves appear among the dead ones and form fresh tufts from the centre of which the short stems rise, each producing one or two flowers. Unlike Drooping Saxifrage, it is often covered in blooms.

Mountain Heath *(Phyllodoce caerulea)*, a member of the Heather family, is another of our rare plants growing in only two or three sites in the Scottish Highlands. Outside Britain it may be found in the Arctic and in a few locations in the Alps and Pyrenees. It too is shy of flowering so seldom sets any seed; it is mainly increased by runners. It is always in danger because it is a low-growing shrub, and although its main site in Britain is fairly extensive it is being increasingly trampled on by the ever-growing band of hillwalkers. The flowers, when they appear in June and July, are purplish-pink tinged with blue. They are typical heather-like bells, fairly large and in clusters of one to six, each with five calyx teeth.

Spring Gentian *(Gentiana verna)* is one of our most beautiful plants, a true alpine flower, and because of this it has always been greatly sought after by gardeners and has suffered much at their hands. It is not a very long-lasting plant but can easily be bought from alpine nurserymen. Seeds can be purchased and with a little care and patience any gardener can grow these flowers and collect his own seed to ensure a succession of plants. There never has been any excuse for stealing this lovely species from the few British sites in which it grows and now that it is protected by law it must be left in peace. This flower, above all others, turns small patches of our country into real alpine meadows—the relatively large, intensely blue flowers rise singly on short stems above tiny rosettes of leaves. The plants form small groups, often covered in blooms, among the hillsides and mountains in the north of Britain and western Ireland.

Alpine Gentian *(Gentiana nivalis)* is also very beautiful and very rare, growing in only ten localities on the mountains of Scotland. It varies greatly in height—some may be tiny, others growing to as much as four inches in sheltered places. Its flowers are about half the size of the Spring Gentian's but are the same intense blue. Because it is an annual it has to germinate, grow, flower and produce seed in a very short space of time, so each year the weather plays an important part in its survival. In a good year there may be quite a number of them, each one covered with up to twenty flowers which—as on other members of this family—open only when the sun shines.

Diapensia *(Diapensia lapponica)* is the only member of its family growing in Europe, and was discovered in 1951 for the first time also growing in one or two localities in Scotland. Outside this country, its range is circumpolar, extending as far south in Europe as Scandinavia, through North America to Greenland, in north Eurasia, and even as far south as Korea. It makes up for its great rarity in Britain by growing into large cushions, a few feet across in some places, covered with hundreds, possibly thousands, of creamy white flowers, in May and June. As with the common Mossy Saxifrage, grown in gardens, the centre of the cushion tends to die out after flowering and fresh, small rosettes form. These in turn fan outwards into new and ever-increasing cushions so that they cover the barren rocks of their chosen habitat quite quickly. Luckily, these places are fairly remote and in difficult situations above altitudes of 2,500 feet. It is hoped that they will be left alone and allowed to spread at will.

The well-known Scottish naturalist, the late Seton Gordon, volunteered to show us a plant when I was illustrating *The Wild Flowers of Britain and Northern Europe*. At the age of well over ninety, he still climbed mountains and was once dismayed to find a maximum-minimum thermometer pushed into a crevice beside the most easily accessible plant of Diapensia. He greatly feared it had been put there by some collector to record the conditions most suitable for growing this species, with the object of cultivation.

Diapensia is one of the few flowers which has not been given a vernacular name in Britain, perhaps it has not been with us long enough. Let us hope it will remain for many years and eventually become a more common plant.

Snowdon Lily *(Lloydia serotina)* is another plant of the mountains which is freqently to be found elsewhere in Europe but is very scarce in Britain. As its name implies, it is restricted to the mountains of North Wales where it was first discovered over 300 years ago. Once it could be found in several locations in the Snowdon range, but these have now dwindled to about five, with only a few plants remaining in each one. This is mainly due to the passage of so many walkers and climbers who have literally trodden the plants to death in their former habitats. When we think of lilies, we tend to think of tall-stemmed, large and beautiful flowers. This lily, although a member of that family, is a tiny plant with solitary, white, purple-veined flowers, slightly cup-shaped and growing on thin stems with narrow grasslike leaves.

Alpine Sow-thistle *(Cicerbita alpina)*, illustrated overleaf, is a tall robust plant, often reaching a height of six feet, and is therefore not easily overlooked. It is common in the mountains of Europe but rare and decreasing in Britain because of collectors and the ravages of grazing deer. It has a spike of mauve-blue daisy-like flowers.

1 Alpine Sow-thistle
2 Wild Gladiolus
3 Cheddar Pink
4 Spiked Speedwell
5 Mezereon

Wild Gladiolus (*Gladiolus illyricus*) comes from the Mediterranean. Its exotic beauty is the main cause of its decline for flower pickers find it irresistible. It grows as tall as the overblown garden forms but has daintier flowers of a brilliant pink with a splash of cream on the lower petals. Similar forms occur as garden escapes.

Cheddar Pink (*Dianthus gratianopolitanus*) is a short, tufted plant which grows in Somerset on the limestone cliffs of the gorge after which it was named. So many of the plants were dug up or trodden on by tourists that it had to be protected. It is naturalized in a few other places but everywhere it is very rare.

The beautiful, **Spiked Speedwell** (*Veronica spicata*), once common in the meadows of East Anglia, has now nearly disappeared through the ploughing up of its habitats. We have seen a few plants, perhaps the last, in a cage in a nature reserve.

Mezereon (*Daphne mezereum*) suffers because of its beauty. It is a winter-flowering shrub whose intense fragrance attracted collectors. It is found only in limestone areas where the clearing of woods in which it grew has also contributed to its decline. There is some controversy about whether it needs to be so vigorously protected as it is found in twenty sites. Since it once had seventy, it is still rare so we are pleased to see it legally protected.

The remaining protected flowers are all orchids, members of a family which has always suffered at the hand of man, and although only five are listed at present, many others are endangered.

Red Helleborine (*Cephalanthera rubra*) is a flower of such a pure and brilliant cerise-pink that it is not easily overlooked and has become another victim of pickers unable to resist it. It is shy of flowering in Britain and is now confined to a small area of woodland in the Cotswolds. We will always remember in a wood in France coming across a glade full of these plants, glowing pink in the sunshine. It was a sight so full of pure pleasure that it left us with feelings of regret that such a scene does not occur here.

Ghost Orchid *(Epipogium aphyllum)* is a small, pale, almost transparent yellowish plant, a mere three or four inches tall, without leaves and lacking all chlorophyll, which grows in the deep shade of beech woods and flowers only spasmodically. It sometimes stays dormant for several years until a particularly wet spring causes it to send up a flowering stem. It lives entirely on decayed matter in the soil and is found in small numbers in a few places in southeastern England. It is also found in parts of Europe and beyond, even in the Himalayas, but never in large numbers.

Lady's Slipper Orchid *(Cypripedium calceolus)*, once common enough to be sold to travellers on the coach roads of northern England, has dwindled so disastrously since that it is now the rarest of Britain's rare flowers. Not so long ago, it was known to be growing in over twenty sites, but it was ruthlessly hunted by collectors obsessed by the desire to have a plant of their own. In spite of the fact that it had been known for a long time that its days would be numbered if thefts continued, one site after another was stripped of its plants, until now only one plant remains, carefully guarded by botanists who are unable to increase its numbers. The pollen from one flower will no longer fertilize another on the same

Lady's Slipper Orchid

Red Helleborine

Ghost Orchid

Military Orchid

Monkey Orchid

plant, and the meristem method of propagation, which works so well for most orchids, will not for the *Cypripediums*. Everything has been done that reasonably can be to discover if any of the stolen plants still survive, with no success. It is doubtful if any specimens will now come to light, if any survive at all. The illustration for this book had to be painted from a European specimen. In outward appearance it is the same as our native one, but I felt no pleasure in drawing it, only sadness that we may never again see this species growing in Britain.

The **Military Orchid** *(Orchis militaris)* is a beautiful soft-mauve and pink orchid with dark spots. It is not uncommon in Europe—indeed we have seen long ribbons of them growing along the verges of some French lanes—but so rare in Britain that for twenty-five years it was thought to be extinct. In 1947 it was rediscovered in its old haunt in Buckinghamshire and later in a new site in East Anglia where a raised walkway has been erected to enable the public to see this almost-lost species blooming within its cage which, unlike those in zoos, is not there to prevent the wild creature from getting out, but to stop the human ones from getting in.

Monkey Orchid *(Orchis simia)* was frequently found in the Chilterns a hundred and fifty years ago when it was certainly not the rarity it is today. Its decline has been caused by the ploughing up of its chalk-down habitat and—as usual—the greed of collectors. There are now only a few well-guarded plants left, and even abroad it is sadly dwindling in numbers. It is unique among our orchids in that the top flowers of each spike usually open first.

HABITATS FOR FLOWERS

A habitat is more than just the home of a plant, it is the actual locality in which a plant will naturally grow and reproduce itself, coupled with the conditions around the locality. Many things not directly connected to a plant may influence its natural growth. A change in the water table, for instance, due to drainage some distance away, will sadly affect many wetland plants.

Every habitat has its flora and every flower is suited to a particular habitat. Influences affecting various habitats, called environmental influences, can be summarized as alkaline or acid, wet or dry, high altitude or low, barren or fertile. Each of these may influence the growth of a plant and may occur together or separately.

We have stressed earlier how nature is constantly changing and developing. This is equally the case within the various habitats. The very growth and death of plant life causes changes, just as they may also be brought about by factors outside the actual locality. Such changes are slow and may not be noticed from one year to another, unless there is regular detailed study of individual habitats.

There is a recognized system of classification of habitats used and recommended by the Nature Conservancy Council and the County Naturalists Trusts. The main classifications are Woodland, Grass and Heathland, Wetland, Coastal, Artificial and Subterranean. Each one is again subdivided so that a particular habitat may be described as 'Woodland, deciduous, beech'. It sounds rather like the call of an old Army quartermaster, but it is a most efficient and simple system and it enables a great many habitats to be described in a similar way by a great many different naturalists.

Scientists tell us that many millions of years ago, life moved out from the sea and on to dry land, so that seems a good starting point for our look at some habitats. The sea is salt, on the face of it presenting us with the first problem, but nature has solved it by devising a system whereby plants avoid too high an intake of salt. By a complicated process called osmosis, the rate of absorption of salt water and nutrients through the root system is controlled. Plants tolerant of salt water, called halophytes, have a lower rate of absorption thus enabling them to cope with the salt. Halophytes will do well in freshwater conditions but freshwater plants wilt and die quickly in salt water due to their much greater rate of absorption.

1 Buckshorn Plantain
2 Sea Bindweed
3 Sea Spurge

Sandy and Shingle Beaches

On sandy beaches above the high tide marks, plants have to be tough to withstand not only bitter winds laden with salt but also burning heat and rapid evaporation in the summer, making it necessary to grow long taproots in order to find cool moisture. Sea Kale and Sea Radish grow in these areas in association with Sea Plantain, Buckshorn Plantain and Sea Bindweed. Sea Mayweed and Sea Spurge grow at the top of the beach in the sand.

It is not possible to list all plants which can be found on the seashore; often an unusual one will appear, brought in perhaps by winds or even by the sea. Various types of knotgrass, some oraches, Prickly Saltwort, Sea Sandwort, Sea Campion, Scurvy-grass, Sea Rocket, Oyster Plant and Sea

Wormwood are also to be found on sandy seashores. Several of these also occur on shingle beaches where conditions may seem even more harsh, but where there is actually a suprising amount of moisture. The daily heating and cooling of stones in moist conditions generate a considerable amount of surface condensation of which shingle plants make full use. Yellow Horned-poppy grows in all the coastal regions of Europe where shingle conditions occur. Here we also find Curled Dock, the first of the family of docks, Biting Stonecrop, the lovely Sea Pea, the prostrate form of Bittersweet and Sea Holly with its beautiful blue leaves and flowers.

Sand Dunes

On the seaward side of sand dunes there is not much chance of finding a rich flora because the conditions are most hostile. However, in the steadying presence of Marram Grass, Sea Bindweed will get a hold and grow, as will Common Storksbill. Dunes are built up and maintained by the continual blowing of dry sand over their seaward slopes. Polished stones and driftwood show how harsh is this environment, and how dry. It is on the landward side, stabilized by vegetation, that we find a more interesting flora. Near the beach, several annuals grow close to rabbit holes and above their warrens, making use of such nutrients as there are in rabbit droppings on the disturbed ground. However, because of the excessively dry sand, these plants have to fulfil their lives within a very short time. Early Forgetmenot—a very small species which grows only an inch tall in these places—is typical, as are mouse-ears, especially Little Mouse-ear

1 Common Centaury
2 Rest-harrow
3 Early Forgetmenot
4 Common Storksbill
5 Sheepsbit Scabious

with its white-edged bracts. In partially fixed dunes you should find Silverweed, Rest-harrow, Birdsfoot Trefoil, White Clover, Lady's Bedstraw and Mouse-ear Hawkweed. The Common Storksbill, which grows inland up to seven inches tall, is a ground-hugging little plant on the dunes. This low habit of growth is a characteristic of most dune plants and should be remembered when you are trying to identify them. We have seen in a dune habitat Common Storksbill growing in company with the smallest viola in Britain, Dwarf Pansy, and with the equally minute Early Forgetmenot.

Eventually, as dunes become more established the flora becomes more varied and vigorous. As dunes grow older so the lime content is reduced, because the rain drains away rapidly and leaches out the calcium. Acid-tolerant plants become more frequent, so look for Sheep's Sorrel, Tormentil, Heath Milkwort, Dog Violet, Heath Bedstraw and Sheepsbit Scabious. You may also find Centaury, Wild Thyme, Eyebright, Spear and Creeping Thistles and Red-veined Dandelion. The spiny Burnet Rose also grows here.

These fixed dunes with their increasing acidity are on their way to becoming heathland. I have mentioned the moisture draining quickly from the sand and this, of course, has to go somewhere. On occasions it can be seen in low-lying parts of the dunes, probably down to the original level of the basic soil, where it forms wet areas called dune slacks. These wet lands in the midst of the sand provide very interesting flowers. Creeping Willow is the dominant and most characteristic plant of the slacks. Its numerous leaves, which drop each year, add to the humus and encourage the establishment in many parts of Europe of such plants as Round-leaved Wintergreen which grows in association with Yellow Birdsnest, Yellow Iris and Dune Helleborine.

Sea Cliffs
The flora of sea cliffs varies greatly. Although the face of the cliff is often in the teeth of the wind, the salt content is not as high as it is on beaches and among dunes. Neither does this habitat contain abrasive sand, so the turf-hugging plants are able to put their heads down, hang on in the winter and cope with their tough environment. Among the more usual plants to be found on cliff faces by the sea are Sea-beet, Sea Campion, Scurvy-grass and Rock Samphire—a very common plant along the south and west coasts of Britain and the north and west coasts of France—Thrift, which is an almost universal favourite, Rock Sea-lavender, Sea Mayweed and Golden Samphire. Only common locally and therefore not to be touched are Wild Cabbage, Sea Radish, Tree Mallow, Scots Lovage, and Sea Wormwood. As we get to the top of the cliff, so the flora varies again. Biting Stonecrop and Thyme make their appearance in bare

places and in short turf. Rock Sea Spurrey grows between stones and rocks in company with English Stonecrop. In parts of the south and west coasts of Britain and along the French coast facing the English Channel, you will occasionally find pale-blue patches of Spring Squill or the darker-blue Autumn Squill. They are not common throughout the country, in spite of growing in large, localized colonies, so our plea is to leave them where they are. The Bluebell grows well on certain sea cliffs, particularly in the southwest. Sea Mouse-ear, Sea Purslane, Kidney Vetch, Birdsfoot Trefoil and Common Storksbill are widespread. Fennel, Alexanders and other members of the Carrot family grow just off the tops where the growth is dominated by Gorse and some scrub. High, rugged cliffs tend generally to be acid—the exceptions being limestone and chalk cliffs.

1 Rock Samphire
2 Rock Sea Spurrey
3 Spring Squill
4 Golden Samphire
5 Thrift

Estuaries, Mudbanks and Salt Marshes

Estuaries are formed by the slowing down of water carrying soil particles from inland, or by the slowing down of sea water in its flow and ebb. At times when these two forces meet, the water becomes stationary, allowing the sediment to fall to the bottom, slowly establishing mudbanks. Between the tides along all the coasts of Europe, salt marshes grow and develop from these mudbanks. Slowly they rise until they are above the high-water mark and only occasionally do they receive a topping up of deposit. Small seeds or small halophytic plants come ashore where they will grow and make more banks. The more plants there are, the slower the movement of the water and the thicker the deposit. The outer parts are covered by sea water twice a day so have a very small selection of flowers. In time, the silt will build up so that for over 50 per cent of the time the plants are comparatively dry.

1 Sea-lavender
2 Sea Aster
3 Glasswort

    The outer regions of mudbanks might well be referred to as the Glasswort zone, for this is the tough, salt-tolerant, dominant plant which is very often the only one there, until it is joined, in areas where the ebb and flow of the tide are not so swift, by Annual Seablite. Sea Aster is the next plant to become established and, as we move inland from the most exposed areas, it gradually becomes the dominant species. Sea-lavender appears in late summer to cover the marshes with its mauve-coloured sheet; this marks the middle level of salt marsh—here the ground is firm enough to bear grazing animals which do no harm to the lavender. Soon the less salt-tolerant plants begin to show themselves; the first of these is Thrift which grows in the middle level of the salt marsh as a ground-hugging little plant, its small pink flowers becoming paperlike when they have shed their seeds.

Rivers and Fenland

In fresh water, the flow, depth and acidity of the water are the governing factors. Flowers are to be found on the banks of rivers or where the flow is not too rapid. Water Dock, Common Meadow-rue, Himalayan Balsam, St John's Wort, Purple Loosestrife, Marsh Woundwort, Arrowhead and Flowering Rush grow on the banks. Amongst the taller plants and rushes you may find crowfoots, forgetmenots, Gipsywort, Monkey Flower, Brooklime and Butterbur, and making its presence known by its scent will be Water Mint. In faster flowing rivers are plants which are specialists in hanging on underwater. They anchor themselves to the bottom, their small flowers reaching to the surface among their trailing leaves. Spiked Water Milfoil has small pink or red flowers, while Fennel Pondweed grows entirely underwater. Where the water flows gently or is nearly still, as in a canal, then the flora is much more varied. An abundant growth of water weeds covers the bottom, a few of which send their flowers to the surface on straight erect stems. Water Violet is one of these—with finely pinnate leaves growing up to but not above the surface, so as not to detract from the simple, pale-lilac flowers arranged in whorls around a slender stem. Just to confuse, it is not a true violet but a member of the Primrose family. In more open spaces grow Water-lilies, free-floating Frogbits and Amphibious Bistort. In small ponds liable to dry out, Water Crowfoot is able to survive.

Another water habitat of great interest is fenland, where it is possible to see the first signs of a succession from marshland to dry oak woodland. In still areas, reeds grow closely to form beds which develop and deepen to create a floating habitat. The great volume of dead vegetation clinging to the base of the reed beds contributes to this build-up.

Generally it is the Alder which first colonizes these areas and which soon becomes dominant, to give a state called 'alder carr' in which will grow Marsh Pea, Fen Violet and Milk Parsley, the food plant of the beautiful Swallowtail butterfly. Grass of Parnassus, Marsh Cinquefoil, Common Comfrey, Early Marsh Orchid and Marsh Helleborine make the wet alder carr a fascinating place to study flowers, but one in which it is dangerous to walk unless you know where you are treading. This is still an almost floating habitat; the ground may look solid, but if you go through the crust you could sink to the shoulders or further. In areas where the reed has been cut—and this is a necessary part of the good management of such

1 *Grass of Parnassus*
2 *Marsh Violet*
3 *Arrowhead*
4 *Water Violet*
5 *Water Forgetmenot*

areas—and the trees thinned out, Ragged Robin, Marsh Marigold, Lady's Smock, Meadowsweet and the spreading Yellow Iris all flourish. Where the Alder remains, the Hop scrambles up and over the branches, to hang down again once it has reached the top or if it has lost its grip.

Slowly the succession goes on, water draining away and trees moving in until dry oak woodland has been reached. There are many examples of this succession and the best documented one we know, from open water to dry oak woods, is at the Broadland Conservation Centre at Ranworth in Norfolk, which is owned and run by the Norfolk Naturalists' Trust.

1 Ox-eye Daisy
2 Meadow Buttercup
3 Dandelion seed head
4 Burnt Orchid
5 Bee Orchid

Grassland

The grassland areas of Europe are mainly cultivated, but many of the older meadows have their own natural flora which varies tremendously. In France we have seen agricultural grassland with a richer wild flora than many of the most favoured wild places in Britain, with Pyramid Orchids, Meadow Clary, Yellow Rattle, bellflowers and poppies. These areas were obviously not grazed but cut once, or maybe twice, for hay making. The usual run of agricultural grassland will be well limed and fertilized with chemicals and will contain only Red or White Clover according to the needs of the farmer. In old permanent pastures on neutral soil in lowland areas we would expect to find Common Sorrel, buttercups, Ox-eye Daisy and Dandelion. In some areas Early Purple, Green-winged and Butterfly Orchids, together with Autumn Lady's Tresses, would grace the grassland with their presence. These flowers grow in Britain but only in wild grassland areas, rarely in the old permanent meadows which are rapidly changing because of the use of chemical fertilizers. When limestone or chalk underlies the grassland, spectacular changes in the flora take place. Gentians grow and are worth searching for—but only to look at—especially Early Gentian in July followed by the rare Chiltern Gentian and Marsh Felwort in August. Dropwort, Birdsfoot Trefoil, Hairy Violet, Common Rock-rose, Cowslip, Yellow-wort and Small Scabious add many shades and colours to the scene. In areas where they are not under pressure from collectors and farming methods, orchids do particularly well in this type of habitat. Long grass encourages the growth of Common St John's Wort, Dark Mullein and Greater Knapweed, and orchids will battle their way up to the light. Acid grassland has little to commend it botanically; the little Tormentil, Heath Bedstraw and Harebell are typical of an acid grassland on which coarser grasses and sedges grow.

Artificial Habitats—Town and Wasteland

Towns and wastelands often have a suprisingly interesting flora. Waste places include many areas in the centres of most large towns—demolished buildings, odd corners of car parks and places which many years ago were

1 Ribwort Plantain
2 Rosebay Willowherb
3 Ivy-leaved Toadflax
4 Dandelion

little front gardens, lovingly tended. Rosebay Willowherb will take root and grow in a crack in a wall followed by Oxford Ragwort; Groundsel will grow from a blocked gutter and a plantain will setttle down in a crack in a path to be walked on by innumerable feet (in Old English it was called 'weg-breade' because it grew the full width of the path). Wall-rocket, bittercresses, Whitlow-grass and Shepherd's Purse grow in nooks and crannies whilst Hedge Mustard, Yellow Rocket and Horseradish take over larger areas where there is a reasonable depth of soil for their roots. The inevitable Curled Dock, Fat Hen, Golden-rod, Mugwort, Yarrow and Coltsfoot grow with Dandelion and Burdock wherever there is room, whilst the lovely little Ivy-leaved Toadflax clothes the wall with its tiny bunny-nose flowers. In this sort of habitat, particularly in dock areas, some strange and exotic flowers may turn up, their seeds having arrived on some imported vehicle or crate.

Natural growth quickly appears wherever plants can get a foothold in an artificial habitat, as is well illustrated by the following example.

Road builders and estate developers filled in a lovely old pond we used to visit, thus destroying a fine, rich wetland habitat. Water voles had frequented the pond, a rare duckweed floated on its surface and many large dragonflies flew over it and in and out of the surrounding willows. A stream which had fed the pond from farther up the valley was canalized on a bed between walls of concrete. Now the stream flows through corrugated concrete tunnels under the road, between concrete banks and down concrete steps to fall into the main stream. An asbestos-clad building occupies the site of the erstwhile pond and, being larger, overflows into what once was the hamlet's football pitch. Sterile concrete covered with fast-flowing water only a couple of inches deep would seem to be an insuperable barrier and no place for wildlife. Several generations of Dippers have come and gone since their waterfall was flattened, but at last one has found that the stream is worth visiting and we have frequently seen the bird and heard its lovely song. Soil leached out of the bed of the stream from farther up the valley has settled into low parts in the concrete. We now have Watercress growing and Common Duckweed settling in the still waters within the compass of the Watercress stems. Other water weeds are colonizing the stream, making additional calm areas for the spread of more plants. Grass is hanging down the banks and will soon flower and seed itself, thus returning man's concrete to nature's clothes. Last year a Grey Wagtail joined the Dipper. Within this small industrial estate a very pleasant flora is developing, softening the corners and bringing it all to life once again. The water voles will probably find the place too far removed from their natural abode, and there is no sign as yet of the rare duckweed. We dread a visit by some authority intent upon making the place tidy and have no enthusiasm whatsoever for those who bury the countryside in concrete and tarmac or throw their rubbish into the stream, but it is heartening when nature reclaims her habitats.

Hedgerows

On the outskirts of towns, grass verges and hedges have a tremendous potential even in built-up areas for they can reflect the flora of the fields behind them, or what used to grow there. Unfortunately, some local authorities like to keep their hedges 'tidy', and even where they are allowed to grow, they seem to be used as a source of free timber for burning and as a rubbish tip. To take wood from a hedge is all part of good management, but it must be done by an expert.

It has been said that the verges and banks of our motorways are the longest nature reserve in the country, perhaps because we cannot stop to look at the flowers and dig them up. A survey taken a few years ago on a 180-mile stretch of motorway showed that some 385 species of wild flowers were growing, including Yellow Vetchling, Purging Flax, Pepper Saxifrage, Creeping Jenny and Dark Mullein.

As a result of the Enclosure Acts of the 17th century, farmland was divided up and had to be marked by boundaries, the style of which varied from region to region. In the north of Britain drystone walls were built, while in the south thorn or beech hedges were used. Some hedges are curved at one end or the other; this curve was dictated by the turning circle of a team of oxen pulling a plough; by building the hedges with the correct curve there was no waste ground. Trees and thorns were planted to make these boundary hedges stockproof, and maintenance operations provided country folk with a legitimate source of firewood. If left alone to grow, the hedges would have become tall and spindly, allowing bullocks to walk through without difficulty, so they had to be kept trimmed and laid, to thicken the growth at ground level and up to about four feet. In time, a rich flora developed within this growth. Gradually, Bramble, Honeysuckle and Old Man's Beard crept in and up the trees and shrubs. Often damp at the base, with grass dominant, the habitat now supports stitchworts, Herb Robert, violets, Primroses, vetches, Lords and Ladies and various umbellifers.

1 Oxlip
2 Yellow Birdsnest
3 Dog's Mercury
4 Moschatel
5 Herb Paris
6 Ivy
7 Foxglove

Woodland

There are basically two types of woodland—deciduous and coniferous. Many coniferous woods are dark and sterile places; some deciduous woods have a very small selection of flowers while others allow a very wide variety. Apart from the soil, the most important factors controlling the flora of a wood are light and, to a certain extent, the type of litter provided by fallen leaves.

Different species of oak grow on different types of soil and, whilst sharing some flowers, each has its own specialities. Pedunculate Oak prefers moist heavy loams and is often associated with a shrub layer of Hazel. Durmast Oak prefers the lighter, sandy, acid soils. In early spring, before the leaves open and draw a curtain over the floor of a wood, the flowers are at their best. The first to be found in the damper woods of Pedunculate Oak are the yellow faces of Winter Aconite, but these are less common than Lesser Celandine or Dog's Mercury. Soon Wood Anemone will flower in the lighter areas around the rides and open glades. Green and Stinking Hellebores and Wood Spurge grow in these parts and into the edge of the wood, with Early and Common Dog Violets, Primrose and forgetmenots making it a veritable garden. To find all these in one place would be most rewarding but it is more likely that local conditions will favour one and not others. Described by a visitor from the Continent as Britain's answer to the beauty of the Alpine meadows, the Bluebell grows in sheets in many drier areas of oak woods. An unusual flower growing in these oak woods and one which is often overlooked is Moschatel, with its four square faces like a Town Clock, one of its several local names.

Common in all but a very few habitats, and certainly plentiful in all deciduous woodlands, are members of the Willowherb family which thrive, hybridize and generally colour the rides. Foxgloves will compete for attention and will grow to considerable size in a damp wood. Durmast Oak woods have many of the above, but in addition Heather and Bilberry may well be found on the edge and in open spaces within. Wood Sage and Golden-rod will flower in the drier and more acid areas—particularly the former. For us, a favourite flower of these woods is St John's Wort, especially Woodland St John's Wort which tells you there is no lime present in the soil, but if lime is present then Hairy St John's Wort takes its place. On lime, oak trees will mix with beech, and the woods will share a common flora which includes Herb Bennet, Water Avens, Nettle-leaved Bellflower and Herb Paris, with its four symmetrical leaves at right angles seemingly supporting its yellow-green flower and its one black berry.

There are two main types of beech wood—one consists of the well-known 'hangers' which grow on steep limestone banks, the other, the 'plateau' beech wood, grows on level calcareous, or chalky, ground where there is a great depth of soil and therefore a greater potential for growth. Among the 'hangers' there is little to see because the slope of the ground generally means shallow soil leached of its nutrients, what is left being taken up by the trees. With a thick canopy of leaves, the beech wood precludes much growth of small flowers. Under these conditions, saprophytic, or fungus-dependent, plants, such as Birdsnest Orchid, thrive. In plateau beech woods, Spurge Laurel—beautiful but poisonous—and its sister plant Mezereon—even more beautiful and also poisonous with a really lovely perfume—are two shrubs well worth searching for. Helleborines grow where there is sufficient sunlight penetrating the canopy. In the dry, sunny areas Dog's Mercury, Sanicle and Ivy soon take a hold and in summer Wild Strawberry and its associate Barren Strawberry will appear with Sweet Woodruff.

The ash is a tree which frequently shares ground with both beech and oak but occasionally will flourish on its own. It is common throughout Britain and Continental Europe and is often planted. Dog's Mercury, Lesser Celandine, Ground Ivy and Moschatel grow happily within its boundaries. In some areas, Lily of the Valley scents the wood with its delicious perfume. Growing with these we would expect to find Bloody

Cranesbill and Ramsons, that potently scented wild garlic, in conjunction with Bluebell.

Birch and pine woods grow in similar habitats and each has its particular flora. In sandy soil, producing acid heathland out of woodland, grows another saprophytic plant, Coral-root Orchid, and Creeping Lady's Tresses, an orchid also partly dependent on a fungus. Wintergreen, both the Common and Intermediate species, grow in these woods, being of the same family as the heaths. Totally unrelated to either of the plants which make up its name is Chickweed Wintergreen, which is in fact a member of the Primrose family. Twinflower, which delicately lightens areas of some pine woods, is frequent in Scandinavia but scarcer in Britain.

1 Cranberry
2 Bog Asphodel
3 Harebell
4 Bog Rosemary
5 Bog Orchid

Heathland and Moorland

There are two possible ways in which heathland can be created. Coastal heaths evolved from fixed sand dunes with the calcium leached out, and support heather and other low shrubby plants. Then there are inland heaths, well away from the coast, which grow similar flowers but evolved, it has been suggested, as the result of the destruction of forests and the consequent damage suffered by the unprotected soil. Three types of heather are dominant on most heathland and common throughout Europe, Common and Bell Heather and Cross-leaved Heath. Growing with them are two species of gorse—Common and Dwarf. In some parts of Britain and Europe, a few other low shrubby plants will compete with the heather, such as Bilberry; and in northern and eastern areas, Cowberry and Cranberry. Away from the smothering habit of heather, Sheep's Sorrel, Tormentil, Heath Milkwort, Heath Bedstraw and Common Cow-wheat thrive, with Harebell and Heath Spotted Orchid growing in more open places. Fire is a frequent hazard of heathland and spreads rapidly where Gorse grows. Quickly burning off the tips of the heather is beneficial to the plant to a limited extent, but it is without doubt disastrous to animal wildlife and less tough plants. Bracken is an invader which is always ready to take over and colonize heathland laid bare by fire.

It has been said that a high altitude heathland becomes moorland, but this is too much of a generalization. Moorland, based upon peat, is usually acid and is not often as dry as heath. Such ground absorbs vast quantities of water and holds it within its basic foundation of peat moss until it becomes over-saturated. Then flooding may occur—with the disastrous results we saw at Lynmouth in North Devon during the 1950s when Exmoor's sponge became overfull. Moorland is not always a natural habitat but can be brought about by clearance and maintained by management, either by burning heather, to provide the right condition for grouse shooting, or by grazing with sheep and cattle which increases the areas in which grass is dominant. Apart from shrubby plants, the flora primarily consists of various species of grasses and some sedge, with a few wintergreens and twayblades. It is in the wetter areas that the more interesting flowers grow. Sphagnum Moss forms the sponge which holds it all together, with little flags flying from the tops of Cotton-grass stems, Bog Rosemary, Cranberry—beloved by the Americans on Thanksgiving but suffering greatly from man's mania for drainage—Bog Pimpernel, Bog Asphodel, Bog Pondweed and the beautiful Common Butterwort, which makes the most of the conditions, whilst various sundews await their meal of midges. Over the typical smell of a moorland bog will come a delicious spicy fragrance denoting the presence of Bog Myrtle, or Sweet Gale as it is sometimes called. Bog Orchid is rare and difficult to find but a great bonus when seen.

Changes in moorland flora can indicate the ways in which man can affect nature. To keep in existence one of their nature reserves, the Cornwall Naturalists' Trust has had to deal with not only the problems caused by a dropping water table because of drainage some time ago, but also a consequent rapid increase in Gorse, which threatened the survival of other plants, as well as the wide-reaching effects of chemical fertilizers. The reserve is no longer the acid bogland it was originally, but it is still important and recovering fast, although a constant watch will have to be maintained

1 *Starry Saxifrage*
2 *Yellow Saxifrage*
3 *Mountain Avens*
4 *Alpine Lady's Mantle*

Mountains

Man's influence is seen everywhere, but least of all in one of our favourite places, the mountains, where man has done comparatively little damage to the environment. These massive eruptions of bygone millenia and their vast open spaces with the constant sound of rushing water are magical places to us. Harsh and beautiful, they always remind me that we are here for such a very short time and that we are very small indeed.

When climbing up from high moorland to mountains, we pass through foothills. In the highest moorland or foothill regions a very lovely type of flora is to be found. Alpine Bistort, Moss Campion, Saxifrages such as Purple, Starry and Yellow grow on the way up, with Mountain Avens, Alpine Lady's Mantle, Alpine Cinquefoil and Mountain Pansy, but it is unfortunate that above this in Britain there is little to be seen botanically, apart from the rare and protected species which are dealt with in Protected Flowers. To enjoy mountain flowers at their best, it is necessary to visit the Alps or the Pyrenees or other major mountain regions.

It would be quite impossible to list all the flowers in all the habitats we have mentioned, as this is not intended to be a field guide to the habitats of Britain and Europe. If, however, your appetite has been whetted and you wish to visit and admire the flowers, then we have succeeded in one of our objects.

PORTRAITS OF WILD FLOWERS

Harebell

PORTRAITS OF WILD FLOWERS

In the following pages we present portraits of some of the flowers which we have found during our travels and which have interested us particularly during our months of research. Some names have fascinating derivations, and the uses, both medicinal and culinary, to which some plants have been put reflect the past and are little histories in themselves.

Some flowers are beautiful and delicate, others striking and colourful. The varieties of shade, texture, shape and habit are infinite and intricate and make each and every one a delightful subject to paint. Many seeds are included as their shapes are often helpful when trying to identify a plant after it has finished flowering. Our portraits are, however, based on a wider view than as a guide to identification —they are chosen simply because we like them.

The order of classification we have followed is the same as in the two field guides, *The Wild Flowers of Britain and Northern Europe* and *The Alpine Flowers of Britain and Europe,* which include detailed identification notes on all and more than we have chosen here. The plants whose names are given in bold type within the text are illustrated.

Water-pepper

Persicaria

Male flowers

Hop

Pellitory of the Wall

Mature hops

Knotgrass

The Hemp, Nettle, Dock, Purslane and Goosefoot families

Found in hedges and damp woodland, **Hop** *(Humulus lupulus)* grows by twining up its supports in a clockwise direction. The female flowers, used to flavour beer, appear from July to September. The male flowers bloom at the same time on separate plants. The Hop has been cultivated since the 9th century when it was introduced from Holland. It is a member of the Hemp family (Cannabaceae) whose only other representative in Britain is *Cannabis sativa*, also known as Hemp, which was grown in great quantities in the 18th and 19th centuries for its fibre.

Pellitory of the Wall *(Parietaria judaica)*, as its name implies, grows in walls and rocky banks in western Europe. The insignificant flowers appear from June to October on reddish stems. In medieval times it was used medicinally, as were other members of the Nettle family (Urticaceae).

Persicaria *(Polygonum persicaria)* is one of the first weeds to colonize newly reclaimed lowlands. It is a member of the Dock family (Polygonaceae). Known also as Redshank, it flowers from June to October. The black blotches on the leaves are said to be the marks of the blood of Christ, or alternatively, the fingermarks of the Devil when he cast it aside as Useless (yet another name) because he mistook it for **Water-pepper** *(P. hydropiper)*. This plant grows in damp meadows, wet mud and shallow water, flowering from July to September. It has a peppery taste and care should be taken not to touch the eyes after handling it. **Knotgrass** *(P. aviculare)* sprawls on bare ground and seashores and flowers from June to September. William Turner called it 'Swyne gyrs' because it was fed to pigs to improve their appetite.

Fairly recent newcomers to Europe are the two purslanes (Portulacaceae). **Pink Purslane** *(Montia sibirica)* was first recorded in 1838 in damp woodlands and on stream banks. It flowers from April to July, as does its relative **Spring Beauty** *(M. perfoliata)*, also known as the Buttonhole Flower and first found in 1837. Its flowers are supported by the leaves which completely surround the stem. It grows on light acid soil.

In spite of both its names, **Sea Purslane** *(Halimione portulacoides)* is in fact a member of the Goosefoot family (Chenopodiaceae). A halophyte, it grows within the tidal reaches of salt marshes.

Pink Purslane

Spring Beauty

Sea Purslane

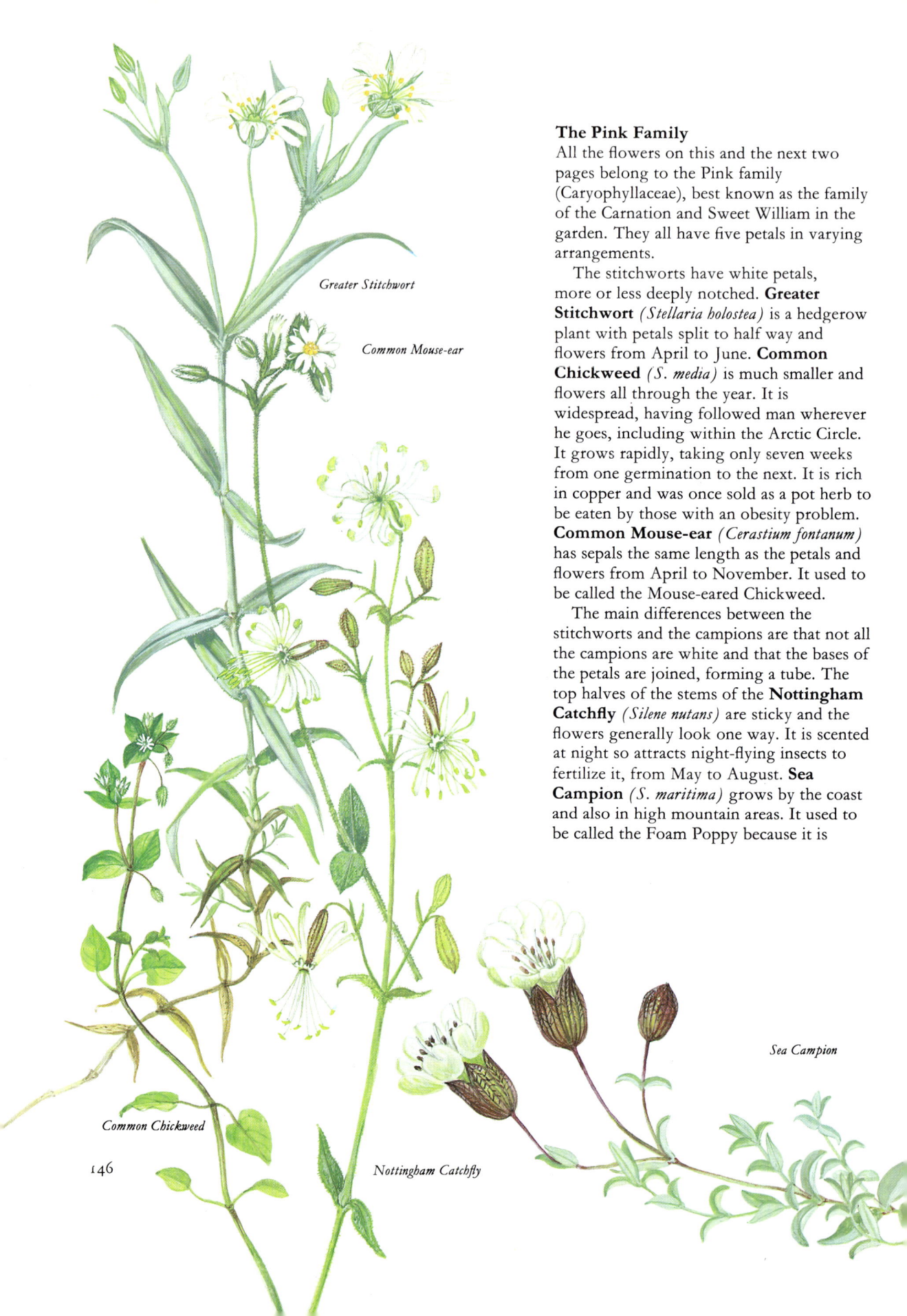

The Pink Family
All the flowers on this and the next two pages belong to the Pink family (Caryophyllaceae), best known as the family of the Carnation and Sweet William in the garden. They all have five petals in varying arrangements.

The stitchworts have white petals, more or less deeply notched. **Greater Stitchwort** (*Stellaria holostea*) is a hedgerow plant with petals split to half way and flowers from April to June. **Common Chickweed** (*S. media*) is much smaller and flowers all through the year. It is widespread, having followed man wherever he goes, including within the Arctic Circle. It grows rapidly, taking only seven weeks from one germination to the next. It is rich in copper and was once sold as a pot herb to be eaten by those with an obesity problem. **Common Mouse-ear** (*Cerastium fontanum*) has sepals the same length as the petals and flowers from April to November. It used to be called the Mouse-eared Chickweed.

The main differences between the stitchworts and the campions are that not all the campions are white and that the bases of the petals are joined, forming a tube. The top halves of the stems of the **Nottingham Catchfly** (*Silene nutans*) are sticky and the flowers generally look one way. It is scented at night so attracts night-flying insects to fertilize it, from May to August. **Sea Campion** (*S. maritima*) grows by the coast and also in high mountain areas. It used to be called the Foam Poppy because it is favoured by insects of the family Cercopidae, which are responsible for producing cuckoo-spit. The grub lives within the foam as protection against predators. The plant flowers from May to September, at the same time as **White Campion** *(S. alba)* which is sweetly scented at night thus attracting moths, especially the Elephant Hawkmoth. Its seed capsule has ten upright teeth, whereas **Red Campion** *(S. dioica)* has teeth which are tightly rolled back. These two plants hybridize in damp hedges and woodlands to produce a pale-pink form. The **Bladder Campion** *(S. vulgaris)*, so called after the inflated tube at the base of the flower, prefers dry grassland. It blooms from May to September, producing a seed capsule with six teeth. In contrast, the seed capsule of the **Soapwort** *(Saponaria officinalis)* is a long thin tube, giving the effect of the flowers growing on stalks. It is generally a garden throw-out, being invasive and obstinate, and flowers in waste ground from June to September—a month earlier than **Ragged Robin** *(Lychnis floscuculi)* whose five petals are so deeply cut that they appear to be ten in number. This delightful plant is found in damp and marshy ground.

Ragged Robin

Soapwort

White Campion female flower

White Campion male flower

Red Campion

Bladder Campion

The name Dianthus is said to be derived from the ancient Greek words for 'flower of the gods'—*Dios anthos*—and we can see every justification for it on this page.

Deptford Pink *(Dianthus armeria)* is an annual whereas all the others are perennial. It flowers from June to August in dry sandy places and is a rare native in Britain, unlike the **Wild Pink** *(D. plumarius)* which may be seen on the walls of old Norman Castles, confirming the suggestion that it was introduced to Britain when the castles were built of imported stone. In medieval times it was the symbol of true love.

The **Clove Scented Pink** *(D. caryophyllus)* is almost certainly the 'gillyflower' of Shakespeare's time. The name was anglicized from the Old French *girofle* meaning 'love flower'. Both Clove and Wild Pinks are fragrant and were crossed and bred to produce the highly scented garden carnation.

Maiden Pink *(D. deltoides)* is not fragrant. It was so named by John Gerard in the 16th century because he thought it was a 'virgin like pinke' with a blush to match. All these pinks flower from June to August and grow best in a limey, light soil. The rare Cheddar Pink *(D. gratianopolitanus)* is illustrated on page 122 among the Protected Flowers.

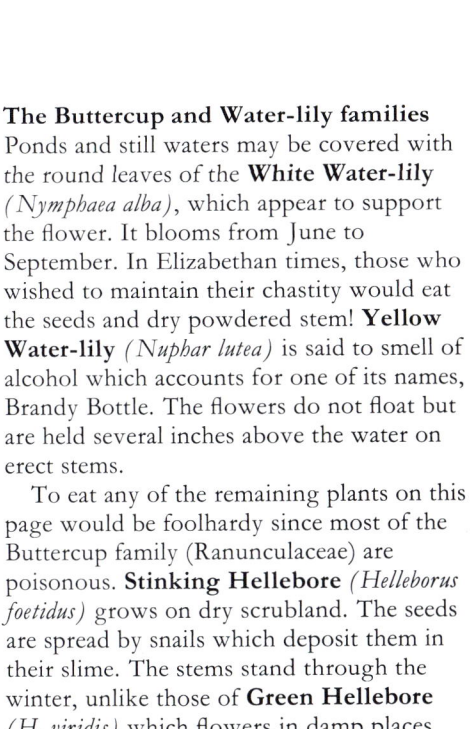

The Buttercup and Water-lily families

Ponds and still waters may be covered with the round leaves of the **White Water-lily** *(Nymphaea alba)*, which appear to support the flower. It blooms from June to September. In Elizabethan times, those who wished to maintain their chastity would eat the seeds and dry powdered stem! **Yellow Water-lily** *(Nuphar lutea)* is said to smell of alcohol which accounts for one of its names, Brandy Bottle. The flowers do not float but are held several inches above the water on erect stems.

To eat any of the remaining plants on this page would be foolhardy since most of the Buttercup family (Ranunculaceae) are poisonous. **Stinking Hellebore** *(Helleborus foetidus)* grows on dry scrubland. The seeds are spread by snails which deposit them in their slime. The stems stand through the winter, unlike those of **Green Hellebore** *(H. viridis)* which flowers in damp places and woods and then withers away. It is rather rare, whereas **Winter Aconite** *(Eranthis hyemalis)* is more plentiful and one of the earliest harbingers of spring with its ruff of lobed leaves. Introduced from southern Europe about four hundred years ago, it is grown extensively in gardens.

Green Hellebore

Stinking Hellebore

Yellow Water-lily

White Water-lily

Winter Aconite

Globe Flower

Marsh Marigold

Lesser Spearwort

Common Water Crowfoot

Globe Flower *(Trollius europaeus)* grows in damp pastures, often in mountains. We have seen and admired it growing amongst violas in high meadows in the Pyrenees. In the 16th century it was known by its old English name of 'locker gowan', meaning 'closed flower'. Far older than this though is the **Marsh Marigold** *(Caltha palustris)* which grew in Britain before the last Ice Age. Also known as Kingcup, it was cultivated by John Parkinson in his garden in the double form, but he left the single form to grow 'in its proper place', as he said. We have both forms by our pond.

Also to be found in or near water is **Lesser Spearwort** *(Ranunculus flammula)* which flowers from June to October and was used medicinally in the Middle Ages as a blistering agent, as many of this family were. It is native to Britain, as is **Common Water Crowfoot** *(R. aquatilis)* which grows in slow-moving water up to a depth of three feet. Its floating leaves are toothed, and those which are submerged are branched.

Meadow Buttercup

Creeping Buttercup

Bulbous Buttercup

Lesser Celandine

Three species of buttercup help to make up the yellow flora of our old meadows. **Creeping Buttercup** *(R. repens)* is common in wet grassland, and is capable of growing twenty-five runners in a season, covering forty square feet. Favouring chalky grassland is the **Meadow Buttercup** *(R. acris)* which has been recorded growing at an altitude of 4,000 feet in Scotland. Not all buttercups are in wet grassland. The **Bulbous Buttercup** *(R. bulbosus)* is a weed of dry grass and fixed dunes. Its bulbous root and down-turned sepals are the main clues to identification. One of the first flowers to appear in damp woodlands and on waste ground is **Lesser Celandine** *(R. ficaria)*. It dies away completely in May when it has finished flowering, so is one of the weeds we accept and control in our garden as best we can. The roots to the corms are very brittle, making it difficult to dig this plant out.

Old Man's Beard

Columbine

Monkshood

Pasque Flower

Traveller's Joy

Wood Anemone

The plants illustrated here are those least like the usual image of flowers of the Buttercup family

Traveller's Joy *(Clematis vitalba)* was so called by John Gerard who found it growing beside the road when he was on his travels. Its flowers are small, fragrant and delicate and are seen from July to September. They are followed by the seed head which gives the plant its winter name of **Old Man's Beard**. In this form it can take over a hedge completely. Lengths of its stem used to be smoked by gypsies, and this is reflected in its vernacular names throughout Europe, like Gipsie's Bacca in Britain, *Bois à fumer* in France, *Smookhout* in Holland and *Rauchholz* in Germany.

Quite different is **Columbine** *(Aquilegia vulgaris)* which is often a garden escape. Both the English and scientific names refer to the birdlike qualities of the petals. *Aquila* is Latin for 'eagle' and refers to the claw-like spurs on the flowers, but more peaceful is the English name derived from the Latin word *columba* for 'doves'. The flower was said to resemble a group of five doves, and a glance at the illustration here shows why. Columbine blooms from May to July and is poisonous.

Also poisonous is **Monkshood** *(Aconitum napellus)*, the 'juice' from which was once used to poison the spears and other hunting weapons of the Greeks and Romans. A variant of Monkshood is Wolfsbane *(A. vulparia)*, so called because its poison was used in baiting wolf traps.

Pulsatillas and anemones have no petals but only brightly coloured sepals. The now rare **Pasque Flower** *(Pulsatilla vulgaris)* grows on dry grassy slopes and flowers from March to May. It has only one flower on each stem, like the **Wood Anemone** *(Anemone nemorosa)* which will grow in any but the most acid or waterlogged ground. Its natural habitat is deciduous woodland where it flowers from March to May.

Common Poppy

Welsh Poppy

Long-headed Poppy

Prickly Poppy

Rough Poppy

Common Fumitory

The Fumitory and Poppy families
A low-growing, straggling plant with smoke-blue foliage, **Common Fumitory** *(Fumaria officinalis)* was called in the Middle Ages *Fumus terrae*, 'smoke of the earth'—the smoke of the burning plant was said to cast out evil spirits. A weed of cultivated ground, it flowers from April to October. Its juice is an irritant, so care is needed after handling the plant.

In flamboyant contrast are the poppies. Ceres, the Roman goddess of agriculture, awoke so refreshed from a sleep induced by a poppy that she decreed that the poppy should always grow with corn, but seed-screening and spraying have put a stop to that. All poppies have four petals, some overlapping, others separate, like those of **Prickly Poppy** *(Papaver argemone)*, generally the first to flower in Britain, from May to July. The pod is long, narrow and bristly, while the much larger **Long-headed Poppy** *(P. dubium)* has a hairless pod and deeply overlapping petals when it flowers, from June to August. It is a plant of arable and disturbed ground as is the **Rough Poppy** *(P. hybridum)*. Rare in Britain, it blooms from June to August and has round pods with dense bristles. The **Common Poppy** *(P. rhoeas)*, with a long hairless pod, is better known as the Flanders Poppy which grew profusely in the war zones of the First World War. It flowers from June to October. An edible oil is made from the seed and also one for mixing oil paints. Matthias de l'Obel, the Flemish botanist, found the **Welsh Poppy** *(Meconopsis cambrica)* growing in Wales in the 16th century. It flowers from June to August, producing a long, narrow pod, small when compared to that of the **Yellow Horned-poppy** *(Glaucium flavum)* which grows on shingle and coarse sand beaches along most European coastlines. The sap is orange and has an unpleasant smell. In medieval times it was used to reduce bruising.

Yellow Horned-poppy

Wild Cabbage

The Cabbage and Stonecrop families
The Cabbage family (Cruciferae) is one of the most important. Many vegetables are bred from wild species, as are several garden flowers. In sailing ships, the problem of scurvy used to be lessened by eating **Common Scurvy-grass** *(Cochlearia officinalis)* rich in vitamin C. A halophyte, it grows in salt marshes and also on shady cliffs where it is the first crucifer to bloom, in April.

Found at the back of beaches is **Sea Rocket** *(Cakile maritima)*. The flowers, seen from June to August, vary from white to pink. It tolerates shifting sand by growing long creeping roots which also help to stabilize the dunes. Different in habitat and habit of growth is **Hedge Mustard** *(Sisymbrium officinale)*, often flowering from May to September. Its spreading upper branches and seed pods close to the stem make it instantly recognizable.

Sprouts, cabbage, cauliflower and sprouting broccoli all come from the **Wild Cabbage** *(Brassica oleracea)* which grows on rocky cliffs in southern Britain and northern France and was first cultivated by the ancient Greeks.

Large Bittercress *(Cardamine amara)* flowers in

Hedge Mustard

Sea Rocket

Common Scurvy-grass

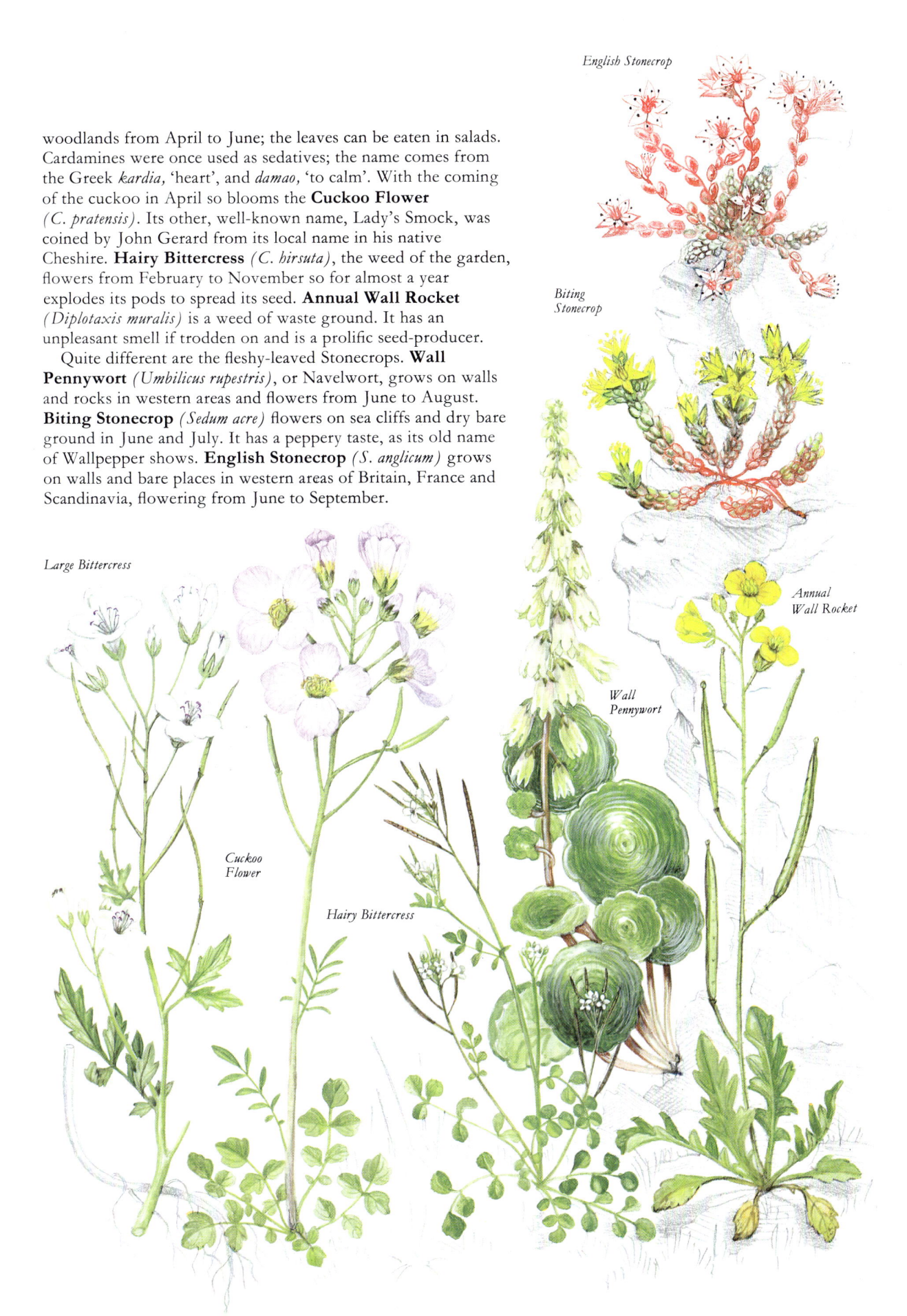

woodlands from April to June; the leaves can be eaten in salads. Cardamines were once used as sedatives; the name comes from the Greek *kardia*, 'heart', and *damao*, 'to calm'. With the coming of the cuckoo in April so blooms the **Cuckoo Flower** *(C. pratensis)*. Its other, well-known name, Lady's Smock, was coined by John Gerard from its local name in his native Cheshire. **Hairy Bittercress** *(C. hirsuta)*, the weed of the garden, flowers from February to November so for almost a year explodes its pods to spread its seed. **Annual Wall Rocket** *(Diplotaxis muralis)* is a weed of waste ground. It has an unpleasant smell if trodden on and is a prolific seed-producer.

Quite different are the fleshy-leaved Stonecrops. **Wall Pennywort** *(Umbilicus rupestris)*, or Navelwort, grows on walls and rocks in western areas and flowers from June to August. **Biting Stonecrop** *(Sedum acre)* flowers on sea cliffs and dry bare ground in June and July. It has a peppery taste, as its old name of Wallpepper shows. **English Stonecrop** *(S. anglicum)* grows on walls and bare places in western areas of Britain, France and Scandinavia, flowering from June to September.

The Rose family

On these pages are the first members of the Rose family to which belongs probably the best-known flower in the world. The family is very varied and includes many flowers unlike the rose itself.

The fragrance of **Meadowsweet** *(Filipendula ulmaria)* is one of the loveliest scents in the countryside in September. It grows, from two to four feet, in wet meadows, but this in fact has little to do with its name. It was once used for sweetening mead, or 'meodu' in Old English, and it is said that a pleasant drink can be made from the flowers. It was used as a strewing herb and as a decoration at weddings, hence the alternative name, Bridewort. It was used to cure malaria in the days when that scourge was rampant in Europe.

To cure snakebites and ease pain **Agrimony** *(Agrimonia eupatoria)* was recommended by both Dioscorides and Pliny. It grows in dry grassy places throughout Europe and on hedges and banks in limey areas. It has the smell of apricots and flowers from June to August.

The scientific name for **Herb Bennet** *(Geum urbanum)* shows it is scented, since *Geum* is a Latinized form of the Greek word *geuo*, 'agreeable flower'. The root is also scented and was used to freshen clothes cupboards and to repel moths. Legend has it that the powerful scent repelled the Devil, which led to its being hung up in houses for that very purpose, and it became known as the Blessed Herb or *Herba Benedicta*. It grows in dry woodland edges and occasionally hybridizes with its unlike cousin **Water Avens** *(G. rivale)*, producing extremely vigorous plants. Water Avens was first recorded in 1633 by Thomas Johnson, a London botanist and apothecary.

John Gerard found **Marsh Cinquefoil** *(Potentilla palustris)* growing near some ponds in the Colchester area and took some plants back to his garden where they 'flourish and prosper well', he said. They grow in wet limefree places.

'Cinquefoil' means literally 'five leaves' and Dioscorides called **Creeping Cinquefoil** *(P. reptans) Pentaphyllon* which was Latinized to *Potentilla,* also meaning 'five leaves'. It grows from a taproot of up to a foot in depth and spreads in damp shady places by means of runners. In sunny drier places, reproduction is by seed.

Tormentil *(P. erecta)* grows on acid heathland up to an altitude of 2,000 feet. In olden days colic was cured by drinking milk in which the roots of Tormentil had been boiled. In the Hebrides it was also used as a tanning agent for fishing nets.

The white flowers of the **Barren Strawberry** *(P. sterilis)* have led some people to confuse it with the **Wild Strawberry** *(Fragaria vesca),* but the petals of the former are notched while those of the latter are not. Although the latter is not the plant from which the large domestic strawberry was bred (its ancestors came from North America), the fruit is small and delicious. It grows in woods and hedgerows throughout Europe and flowers from April until June when the fruit is ready to eat.

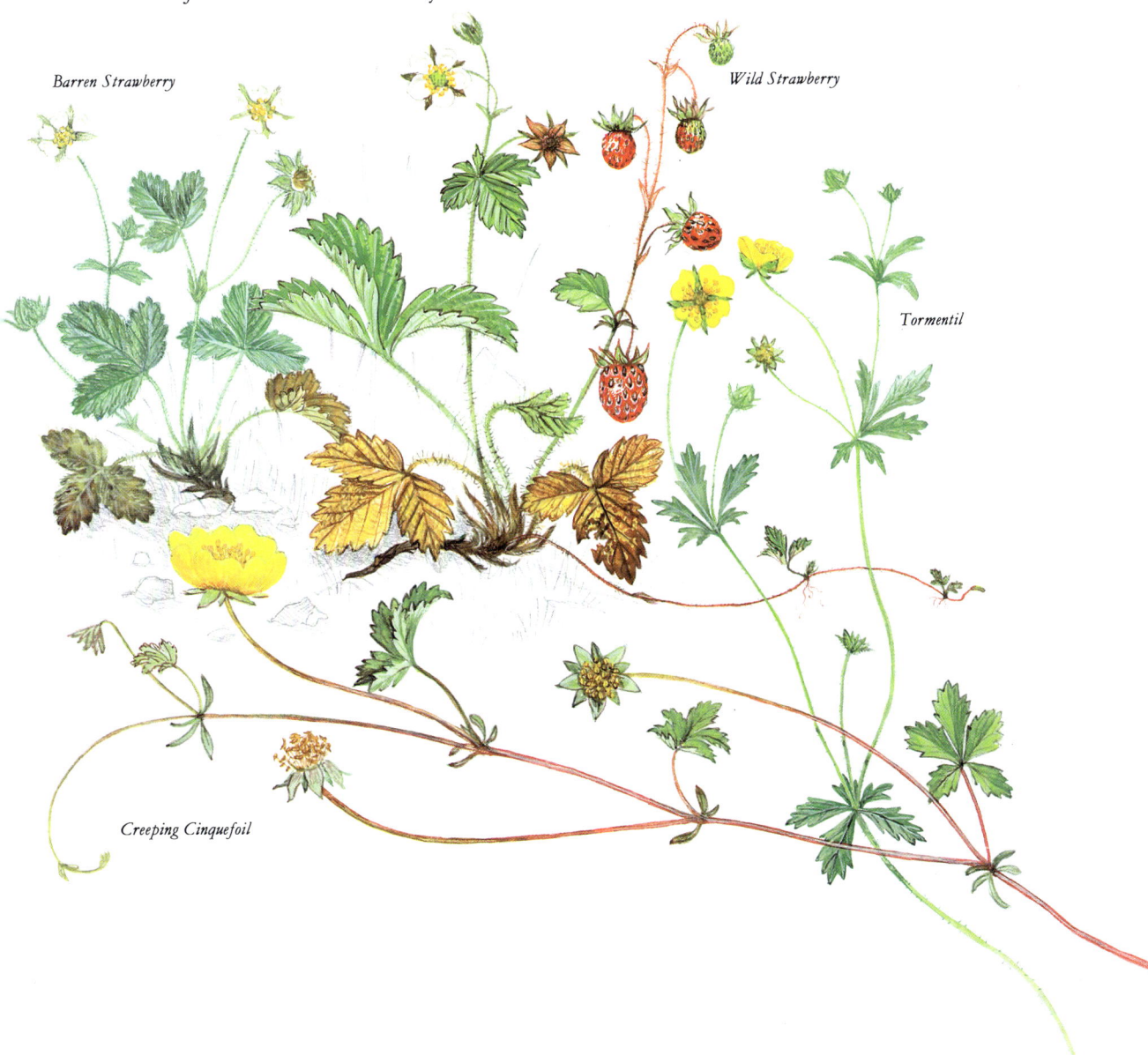

Barren Strawberry

Wild Strawberry

Tormentil

Creeping Cinquefoil

Dog Rose

 Roses are among the flowers longest favoured by man. The Ancient Greeks and Romans used the petals for perfume and even for carpeting. In the theory of signatures the thorn is said to resemble a dog's tooth, and, according to Pliny, a Roman soldier bitten by a mad dog applied the roots of a rose to the wound to cure it, hence the **Dog Rose** *(Rosa canina)* was credited with being a cure for hydrophobia. **Robin's Pincushion** is the gall or swelling often seen on the Dog Rose. It is caused by the Gall-wasp and is sometimes called a briar ball. Apothecaries used to powder them to make a drink to cure colic. The presence of the grub inside the gall was a bonus as it was dried, powdered and made into another drink which was used to 'drive forth the worms from the belly'.

 The white **Field Rose** *(R. arvensis)* has been a favourite for hundreds of years. It grows in woods and hedges, is very fragrant and is the rose Shakespeare referred to as the Musk Rose.

 The **Burnet Rose** *(R. pimpinellifolia)* is slightly fragrant and extremely spiny. It grows in dry open places, sometimes on sand dunes. It spreads quickly and is very difficult to eradicate from a garden, as we know. We have allowed it to stay but it is a constant struggle to keep it in the part of the garden allocated to it. **Sweet Briar** *(R. rubiginosa)* is sometimes called Eglantine. It grows in hedgerows and has scent glands on the back of the leaves so made a good strewing plant. **Downy Rose** *(R. tomentosa)* grows on hedges, generally in hilly districts. All the roses on these pages are native to Britain and are also generally found in Continental Europe except in the most northerly regions.

Field Rose

Burnet Rose

Downy Rose

Sweet Briar

Rosehips

Robin's Pincushion

161

Hawthorn

Wild Cherry

Sloes

Blackthorn

Our last representatives of the Rose family are these three trees. **Hawthorn** *(Crataegus monogyna)* is well known as a hedgerow tree in Britain and is found throughout Continental Europe. Because of its rapid growth as a hedging plant, it is also called Quickthorn. The subject of many legends and much folklore—many celebrations for the coming of summer are concerned with Hawthorn (hence yet another name, May Tree)—it is said to be the tree from which Christ's Crown of Thorns was made. Also according to legend, another member of the same genus, the Glastonbury Thorn, sprang from the staff of Joseph of Arimathea when he visited England after the Crucifixion. Until fertilization the scent of the Hawthorn is unpleasant—said to be like that of London during the plague—due to the presence of the chemical trimethylamine whose smell of putrefaction attracts midges and flies. After fertilization the scent changes to a very pleasant one.

Blackthorn *(Prunus spinosa)* grows on scrubland throughout Europe. It produces sloes as its fruit, from which is made that delicious liqueur sloe gin. Its very hard wood is used for tool handles, and the famous Irish shillelagh should be made of Blackthorn.

In the 16th century, branches of **Wild Cherry** *(P. avium)* were sold, complete with the fruit. It is little wonder, therefore, that the tree is not as common as it was. As long ago as the time of Dioscorides, cherry cough medicine was made from the gum which exudes from the wood. The tree grows in hedges throughout Europe.

The Pea and Flax families

The Pea family (Leguminosae) is a valuable one economically since it includes vegetables and clover forage crops for grassland as well as ornamental flowers for the garden. **Spotted Medick** *(Medicago arabica)* grows in southern Britain and Continental Europe on grass verges. It is sometimes found on sandy ground near the sea. The black spots which distinguish it from other medicks are said, like the marks on Persicaria, to come from Christ's blood falling upon them at the foot of the Cross. The pods, curled into a spiral and with spines, contain the seeds which have a built-in capability of several years' dormancy.

Another plant with unusual pods is the **Horseshoe Vetch** *(Hippocrepis comosa)* whose name is a literal translation from Greek, describing the pod as a series of horseshoes linked together. It is deep-rooted and grows on chalky grassland. Birdsfoot Trefoil *(Lotus corniculatus)*, illustrated on page 62, in Field Fare, has very straight narrow pods set at angles similar to those of the toes on a bird's foot. It is widespread in Europe.

Kidney Vetch *(Anthyllis vulneraria)* has yellow, orange, red, purple or white flowers, depending on its habitat. It grows at sea level, on cliffs and limestone mountains. As with so many flowers with a hairy calyx, it was used in the 16th century to dress wounds and to stop bleeding.

Sainfoin *(Onobrychis viciifolia)* is a British native legume and was widely cultivated as a forage crop. Its name is French, meaning 'wholesome or good hay', and it was coined into English in the 17th century.

Vetches are climbing or, often, scrambling plants with pinnate leaves, more-or-less long, flat pods and tendrils—sometimes branched—at the end of the leaves. It is the tendrils to look for when checking identification. The most commonly found is **Tufted Vetch** *(Vicia cracca)*. Pliny was not sure of its identity so he called it *cracca*, his standard term for plants of doubtful identity. Hairy Tare *(V. hirsuta)*, illustrated on page 40, in Wayside Weeds, has fewer and smaller flowers. It is the down on the pods which gives it its name.

Tufted Vetch

Sainfoin

Spotted Medick

Horseshoe Vetch

Kidney Vetch

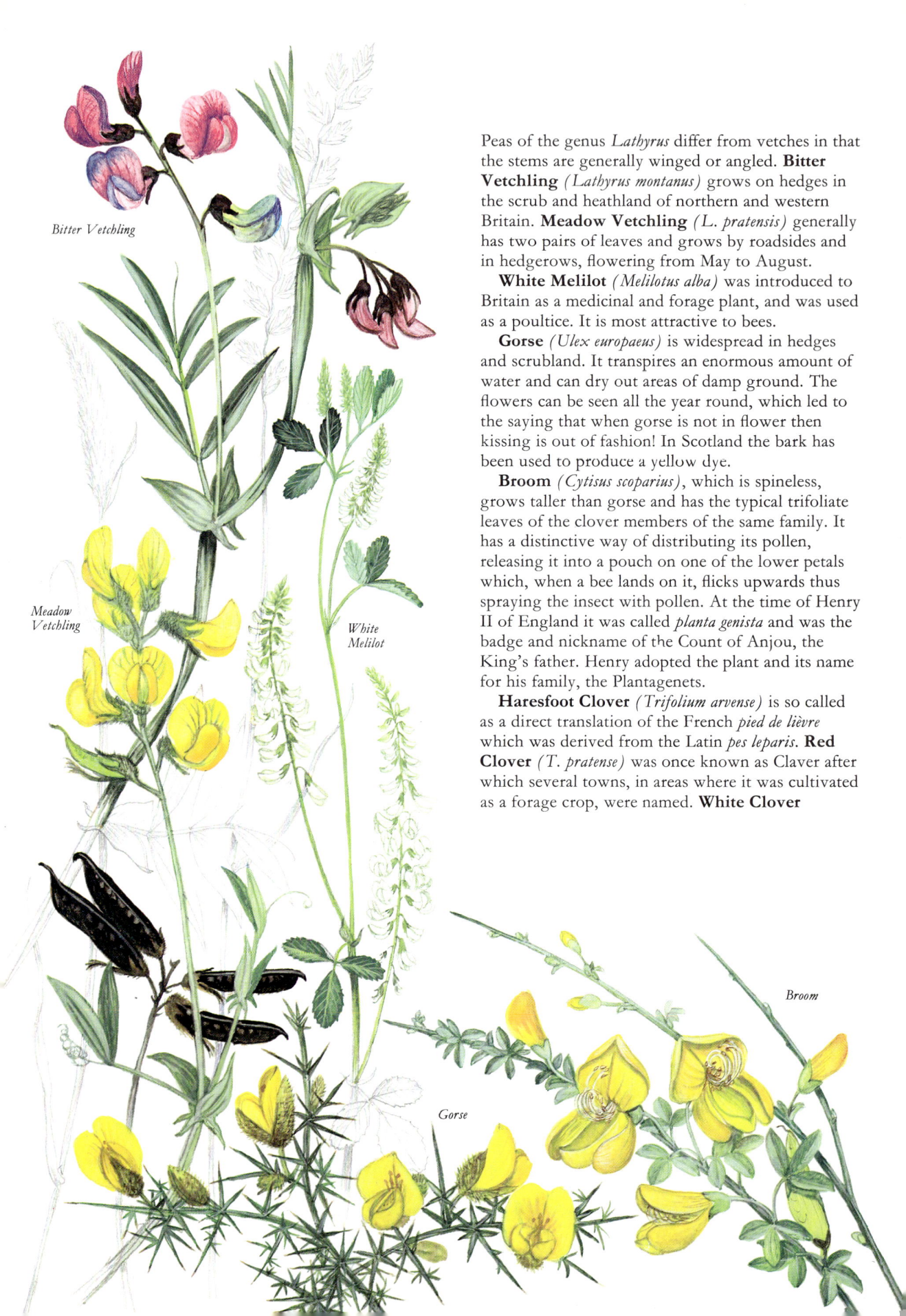

Peas of the genus *Lathyrus* differ from vetches in that the stems are generally winged or angled. **Bitter Vetchling** *(Lathyrus montanus)* grows on hedges in the scrub and heathland of northern and western Britain. **Meadow Vetchling** *(L. pratensis)* generally has two pairs of leaves and grows by roadsides and in hedgerows, flowering from May to August.

White Melilot *(Melilotus alba)* was introduced to Britain as a medicinal and forage plant, and was used as a poultice. It is most attractive to bees.

Gorse *(Ulex europaeus)* is widespread in hedges and scrubland. It transpires an enormous amount of water and can dry out areas of damp ground. The flowers can be seen all the year round, which led to the saying that when gorse is not in flower then kissing is out of fashion! In Scotland the bark has been used to produce a yellow dye.

Broom *(Cytisus scoparius)*, which is spineless, grows taller than gorse and has the typical trifoliate leaves of the clover members of the same family. It has a distinctive way of distributing its pollen, releasing it into a pouch on one of the lower petals which, when a bee lands on it, flicks upwards thus spraying the insect with pollen. At the time of Henry II of England it was called *planta genista* and was the badge and nickname of the Count of Anjou, the King's father. Henry adopted the plant and its name for his family, the Plantagenets.

Haresfoot Clover *(Trifolium arvense)* is so called as a direct translation of the French *pied de lièvre* which was derived from the Latin *pes leparis*. **Red Clover** *(T. pratense)* was once known as Claver after which several towns, in areas where it was cultivated as a forage crop, were named. **White Clover**

(T. repens), as its scientific name implies, is a creeping plant and liable to spread widely where it is not always wanted. Both Red and White Clover are attractive to bees, and as each flower is fertilized it turns brown and droops, as shown here on the White Clover. This is not the case with all clovers, however. Strawberry Clover *(T. fragiferum)*, for example, starts normally but the fruit swells when it is ripe, making it look like a pale strawberry. Occasionally a field can be seen full of a tall elongated clover flower. This is Crimson Clover *(T. incarnatum)*, an extremely heavy cropper and an excellent forage food.

Quite different is the simple flower of Flax. This is the plant from which linseed oil and linen fibre are produced. **Perennial Flax** *(Linum perenne)* grows in dry grassland. The much paler **Pale Flax** *(L. bienne)* has petals which drop very easily—at the slightest touch—and is often found with only one or two petals remaining. Both flower from May to August.

Perennial Flax

Pale Flax

Haresfoot Clover

Red Clover

White Clover

Dusky Cranesbill

Meadow Cranesbill

Bloody Cranesbill

166

The Geranium family
The Geranium family (Geraniaceae) is so called from the shape of the seed capsule, which resembles the beak of a crane—the word 'geranium' comes from the Greek for 'crane's bill', which, of course, is the name by which members of the family are known in Britain. It is a family which catapults its seeds, some plants being capable of throwing them up to twenty feet.

Many species were introduced to Britain from southern Europe, but **Meadow Cranesbill** *(Geranium pratense)* is probably native. Its range extends to Iceland and it is now spreading fast in North America. It grows in dry grassland on limey soil, flowers from June to September and dies down completely after seeding. It is a beautiful sight on some roadside verges and does well in the garden where it is easy to control and well worth growing. **Dusky Cranesbill** *(G. phaeum)* used to be considered a good wound herb, as were many plants of this family. It was probably a very early introduction and naturalized by the 16th century. It is often seen by the roadside in Central Europe. Both were grown by John Gerard, as was **Bloody Cranesbill** *(G. sanguineum)* which grows on sand dunes and limestone rocks and is often cultivated as a garden plant. The **Longstalked Cranesbill** *(G. columbinum)* has very long, thin flower stems and narrow, finely cut leaves.

More than a hundred other English names have been given to **Herb Robert** *(G. robertianum)* which grows in oak woods, hedges and verges. It has a strong foxy smell and the leaves turn red in winter. Named after Robert de Molesmes, an 11th-century healer and saint, it has a powerful astringent quality and was used to staunch wounds. It is a commoner weed than **Shining Cranesbill** *(G. lucidum)*, with its brilliant leaves and very small flowers, which grows on shady walls, banks and waste ground. One of the most delicately veined species is **Pencilled Cranesbill** *(G. versicolor)* which was introduced from Italy in the 17th century and is now naturalized in the hedges of Devon and Cornwall. Another species introduced from southern Europe, at the end of the 18th century, is **Hedgerow Cranesbill** *(G. pyrenaicum)*. A common roadside plant, it is also to be found in waste places, in company perhaps with **Dovesfoot Cranesbill** *(G. molle)*, a velvety plant and as such much used as a wound herb. It grows on arable land in corn-growing areas. **French Cranesbill** *(G. endressii)* escaped from gardens and is now naturalized in various parts of the country. **Cut-leaved Cranesbill** *(G. dissectum)* is another weed of arable land and dry grassland throughout Europe. It flowers from May to September.

1. Longstalked Cranesbill
2. Herb Robert
3. Shining Cranesbill
4. Pencilled Cranesbill
5. Hedgerow Cranesbill
6. Dovesfoot Cranesbill
7. French Cranesbill
8. Cut-leaved Cranesbill

The Spurge, Daphne and Buckthorn families

A treatise on the Spurge family (Euphorbiaceae), written by King Juba of Mauretania 2,000 years ago, detailed its great value as a medicine and purgative. He named it after his physician Euphorbius, and its English name comes from the Latin *purgare*, 'to purge'. In fact, its plants are such powerful purgatives that they are classified as poisonous. The milky latex which exudes from the stem and leaves of **Sun Spurge** *(Euphorbia helioscopia)* was used as a cure for warts—it has an alternative name of Wartweed—scurf, mange and other unpleasant things.
Caper Spurge *(E. lathyrus)* is particularly poisonous and is a weed of cultivation and wasteland but is rare in Britain. The seeds have been used as a substitute for capers, which they resemble— a very dangerous practice.

The Daphne family (Thymelaeaceae) is best known for its highly scented garden shrub Mezereon *(Daphne mezereum)*, a rare and also extremely poisonous plant of chalky woodland. **Spurge Laurel** *(D. laureola)* is as poisonous but not so scented. Both were once used as cures for cancer. It is native to Europe but does not grow in Scandinavia or northern Britain. Its insignificant flowers ripen into black poisonous berries.

Sea Buckthorn *(Hippophae rhamnoides)* is the only shrub of any size belonging to the sand-dunes habitat and is often planted to control and fix them. The male and female flowers appear in May and grow on different bushes. The bushes sucker freely and form into large thickets. The berries ripen in October; they are edible and rich in vitamin C but, as with all berries, best left to the birds.

Sun Spurge

Caper Spurge

Spurge Laurel flowers

berries

Sea Buckthorn

Female flower

Male flower

The Mallow family
The Mallow family (Malvaceae) is well known in gardens because of the tall Hollyhock *(Alcea rosea)*. Various forms of mallow have been bred; all are attractive and grow well. The Marsh Mallow *(Althaea officinalis)* is the genuine forerunner of the sugar and gelatine sweet of the same name. It was made from sections cut from the root of the plant, which were boiled to produce a sort of gluey toffee. Most members of the family produce this mucilage. Marsh Mallow is suffering, like many other wetland plants, from the effects of drainage schemes.

    Dwarf Mallow *(Malva neglecta)* has no herbal history. It flowers from June to September in wasteland where it is regarded as a weed.

    A much larger and very beautiful flower is **Musk Mallow** *(M. moschata)* which grows on road verges throughout Europe and in some grassland areas. The musk scent is not apparent until the plant is brought into a warm room.

    Also growing on roadsides in the south of Britain is **Common Mallow** *(M. sylvestris)*. Its edible seeds were what first attracted man to the plant, and then its soft tissues were found to make it a good poultice plant.

Musk Mallow

Common Mallow

Dwarf Mallow

St John's Wort family
St John's Wort (Guttiferae) is a family with much legend attached to it. Many magical attributes are also to its credit. Herbs of St John were said to protect animals, buildings, man and his family against demons and evil spirits, and on St John's Eve, 23rd June, they were passed through smoke to make them even more powerful.

Slender St John's Wort *(Hypericum pulchrum)* is found on heathland scrub, and it is one of the smallest of the family. The leaves have tiny translucent dots on them.

Perforate St John's Wort *(H. perforatum)*, sometimes called Common St John's Wort, is considerably larger. It acquired its name because the oil glands within the leaf extend almost from surface to surface, making the leaf appear to have holes in it. Because of the scent given off by the oil, it is sometimes also called Rosin Rose. The leaves are used to scent clothes-cupboards and books and are said to discourage moths.

Marsh St John's Wort *(H. elodes)* grows mainly near ponds and backwaters and in damp grassland but, in common with so many other plants found in wetlands, is endangered because of drainage schemes.

Tutsan *(H. androsaemum)*, looking rather like a small version of the famous Rose of Sharon *(H. calycinum)*, with red spots on the stems, flowers from June to August and produces beautiful berries. The English name comes from the French *tout sain*, 'all healthy'. This description reflects its previous herbal value. It grows rather in isolation and does not form large thickets or colonies, and can be found in shaded woods, mainly in western areas.

Slender St John's Wort

Perforate St John's Wort

Marsh St John's Wort

Tutsan flower

Tutsan berries

The Violet family

Violets and pansies are members of the same family (Violaceae), the main difference between the two being the shape of the leaves. Violet leaves are generally heart-shaped whereas pansy leaves are deeply toothed, narrow and tapering, or lanceolate. The very fragrant Sweet Violet *(Viola odorata)* grows in woods, on scrubland and in some hedgerows. **Field Pansy** *(V. arvensis)* is a weed on cultivated ground, flowering from April to November.

One of the most beautiful of all this family is **Wild Pansy** *(V. tricolor)* which we have seen in a great many habitats but usually on bare ground at all altitudes up to 4,000 feet. It is often known as Heartsease, which is its 16th-century name and the one used by Shakespeare. Another name he used was Love-in-Idleness which Parkinson thought 'a foolish name'. It grew widely in cornfields, according to farmers of the day, and is the flower from which the modern garden pansy was developed.

The most common violet found in Britain is the **Common Dog Violet** *(V. riviniana)*. Many flowers not considered to be the best, in the days when so many names were being coined, were often given the label of being good only for animals, and so it is with this one. Gerard named it thus because he knew and preferred the scented Sweet Violet and considered this one fit only for dogs. It hybridizes with other violets, making identification difficult.

There is no problem in identifying **Dwarf Pansy** *(V. kitaibeliana)*. It is rare and in Britain must be left to grow in its few homes without disturbance from anything but the Atlantic gales with which it copes so well.

Field Pansy

Wild Pansy

Common Dog Violet

Heath Dog Violet

Dwarf Pansy

Marsh Violet

Marsh Violet *(V. palustris)* grows in heath and moor bogs and flowers from April to July. Like other marshland plants, it faces problems because of drainage schemes. No such problems exist for the lovely pale-blue **Heath Dog Violet** *(V. canina)* which grows on dry heaths and coastal sand dunes. It has a close habit of growth and its seeds attract ants which collect and store them.

The Gourd family

The only member of the Gourd family (Cucurbitaceae) to be found wild in Britain is **White Bryony** *(Bryonia cretica)*. It grows in hedges from a large parsnip-type root which in days gone by was sometimes called Mandrake. It is in no way related to Black Bryony *(Tamus communis)* which is a member of the Yam family and illustrated on page 200. White Bryony climbs, by means of tendrils, in hedgerows and on scrubland. The name is derived from the old Greek word *bruo* meaning 'to burst forth', as the plant indeed does in the spring. The leaves are dull, as are the berries which are also extremely poisonous. The male and female flowers grow on separate plants. In this illustration the female flowers are shown above the male ones.

Cucumbers and marrows are also members of the Gourd family. Two other species are found wild in northern Europe—*Bryonia alba* is found in Germany, France and Scandinavia, while Prickly Cucumber *(Echinocystis lobata)* has been introduced to Germany from North America.

Female flowers

Male flowers

White Bryony

Rosebay Willowherb

The Willowherb family
We have mentioned **Rosebay Willowherb** *(Epilobium angustifolium)* many times before, in earlier chapters. Rarely found outside gardens until about 1860, it was originally grown by the Victorians as a decorative flower until it was realized what an invasive weed it is. The growth of travel by train and later by car has helped to spread it along railway embankments and roadsides, as its light feathery seeds, capable of considerable periods of dormancy, are wafted along by breezes.

Other members of this family also spread rapidly, for example, New Zealand Willowherb *(E. brunnescens)*, which is a low-growing plant, was first recorded in Britain near Edinburgh in 1904 and is now widespread in Ireland and northern

Alpine Willowherb

Rosebay seeds

and western Britain. The equally enthusiastic American Willowherb (*E. adenocaulon*) was first recorded in Leicester in 1891 and is now common on railway embankments and wasteland. Willowherbs hybridize freely but with no great success. The results are often sterile and stunted, frequently dying before they can flower.

Alpine Willowherb (*E. anagallidifolium*) grows on mossy cushions in mountain areas and flowers from June to August.

Contrasting completely in shape and colour is another member of the same family, the **Large-flowered Evening Primrose** (*Oenothera erythrosepala*) which was introduced from North America as a garden plant and which now grows by the roadside, on banks, in waste places and on dunes. In some areas it has colonized newly built road verges. The seeds can remain dormant for at least forty years. It is likely that new roadworks will bring them to the surface where they will germinate.

How **Enchanter's Nightshade** (*Circaea lutetiana*) became so called is rather a mystery. In folklore it has no connection with witches or enchanters, but its French name is *herbe à la magicienne*, and indeed the scientific name comes from that of the Greek enchantress Circe who turned the followers of Odysseus into pigs by giving them a drink made from this plant. A persistent and spreading weed, it is extremely difficult to eradicate. Having flowered and seeded, the main stem dies, whereupon underground roots form new plants. The seeds themselves are spread by means of barbs on the seed capsules, which become caught up in the fur of animals and the clothes of man.

Large-flowered Evening Primrose

Enchanter's Nightshade

The Carrot family

The Carrot family (Umbelliferae) has nearly 3,000 species throughout the world, most of them easily recognizable by their umbrella-type flower heads. Small, five-petalled flowers on stalks form either flat-topped or rounded umbels, the whole head being made up of many of these. Most of the family have white flowers, sometimes tinged with pink, but there are also several yellow species and other less typical plants. The leaves, which are generally pinnate, and the hard, dry seeds are a valuable guide to identification. Hedgerows and scrubland are their habitats.

Throughout history umbellifers have been useful plants. The seeds of some were burnt to freshen the atmosphere, and some are still used as spices and flavourings. The Wild Carrot *(Daucus carota)* is an ancestor of our modern carrot. The largest wild flower in Britain today is the Giant Hogweed *(Heracleum mantegazzianum)* which was introduced from southwest Asia and escaped to the wild. It can grow to a height of fifteen feet with an umbel eighteen inches across. Corn Parsley *(Petroselinum segetum)*, a member of the family, appears in our protected species.

The above examples demonstrate the great versatility of this family. Not all are good though, for Ground Elder *(Aegopodium podagraria)*, although edible, is one of the worst weeds of the garden and hardest to eradicate. Fool's Parsley *(Aethusa cynapium)* is poisonous and should be avoided. Both it and Hemlock *(Conium maculatum)* must be remembered when using any wild umbellifer for cooking.

Sanicle

Sea Holly

Marsh Pennywort

Three less typical umbellifers grow wild in Britain. **Sea Holly** (*Eryngium maritimum*) was common throughout Europe on sand dunes and shingle beaches, but over-picking and uprooting are eradicating it from beaches frequented by visitors. It is very attractive to bees and butterflies. It was once the source of considerable trade in the Colchester area where the candied roots were sold as an aphrodisiac and stimulant.

As unlike the rest of the family as Sea Holly is **Marsh Pennywort** (*Hydrocotyle vulgaris*). The only species in the family to have round leaves, it grows in damp grassland and shallow water throughout Europe. It was once thought to cause liver rot in sheep, but it is the liver fluke parasite in a water snail that is guilty, not the flower. **Sanicle** (*Sanicula europaea*) was once a herb of great medicinal value. Its name comes from the Latin *sano*, 'to heal', and was said 'to make whole and sound all inner hurts and outward wounds'. It is a small refined-looking plant which grows in and near deciduous woodlands throughout Europe.

The conventional umbellifer plant—if there is such a thing—is **Cow Parsley** (*Anthriscus sylvestris*) which lines so many roads, growing in hedges and on verges. The earliest flowering plant of the family, it is one of the most attractive with its delicate umbels of white flowers which have given it the more attractive common name of Queen Anne's Lace. It is closely related to Garden Chervil (*A. cerefolium*) which is a delicious wild herb.

Two of the yellow umbellifers are illustrated overleaf: **Wild Parsnip** (*Pastinaca sativa*), an ancestor of the domestic parsnip, is recognizable by its thick coarse growth and broad-toothed leaflets. Near the coasts of Britain, France and Germany grows one of the older vegetables, **Alexanders** (*Smyrnium olusatrum*), which was introduced to Britain from the Mediterranean in the 16th century as a pot herb and was soon established and naturalized. Concentrations of it can still be found on the sites of old monasteries and castles, confirming the locations of the kitchen gardens. It is most noticeable in autumn by the presence of the black spicy seeds. It was once called Parsley of Alexandria, hence its modern name. As noted in Field Fare, it may be used as celery.

Cow Parsley

Wild Parsnip

Alexanders seeds

Alexanders

The Wintergreen and Heath families

Common Wintergreen *(Pyrola minor)* is a member of a small family (Pyrolaceae) of only thirty species throughout the world. It has a history as a healing herb and grows in woods and marshes, on moors and mountains. It flowers from June to August in southern parts of Britain where it is locally common, but is much more widespread on the Continent. It is said that the name comes from the Greek *pyrus*, 'pear', after the similarity of the leaves.

Heathers belong to the Heath family, Ericaceae—the name is derived from the Greek word *ereikh*, 'heath', which sums up the habitat, for the plants grow on heathland, moorland and open woodland on acid soils. **Bell Heather** *(Erica cinerea)* grows on dry heath and acid moor, flowering from July to September. It is fairly widespread on the west coast of Britain, especially in Scotland, and it thrives in Continental Europe on the west and north coasts of France and Belgium. **Cross-leaved Heath** *(E. tetralix)* is so called because the narrow linear leaves are formed in a cross on the stem. In contrast to Bell Heather, it grows on wet moors and dune slacks primarily in the north and west areas of Britain and on the northern coastal belt of the Continent.

Heather *(Calluna vulgaris)*, sometimes called Ling, is a small shrub common throughout Europe, and has been useful economically ever since Neolithic times for beds, thatch, fuel, baskets, rope and brooms. An English alternative name was Broom, and the word *Calluna* is derived from the ancient Greek *kallona* meaning 'to cleanse'—presumably with a heather broom. Heather was also used to make an orange dye and even to flavour beer. It grows on heaths, moors and dunes, in open birch and pine woodland and on upper moors in Britain. It is regularly burnt to provide a good crop of new shoots for grouse to eat.

There are several other forms of heather and all grow in their own specialized areas. Cornish Heath *(Erica vagans)* grows only in western areas of France besides its special place in Cornwall, and Dorset Heath *(E. ciliaris)* is found in similar areas. Small shrubby plants which grow in association with heathers, for example, Bilberry, Cowberry and Cranberry, are looked at in earlier chapters. Larger shrubs which are also members of the Heath family and which have been bred for growing in gardens include rhododendrons and azaleas.

Common Wintergreen

Bell Heather

Cross-leaved Heath

Heather

The Primrose family
The Primrose family (Primulaceae) is altogether a beautiful one, best known for the species of the same name but including such delightful plants as Cyclamen, Scarlet Pimpernel and Alpine Snowbell.

Oxlip *(Primula elatior)* has been growing in Europe for many centuries but is rare in Britain, now found in only one place where it is locally common, the chalky boulder clay of East Anglia. It is often confused with the more common False Oxlip which is a hybrid of Primrose and Cowslip. It was noticed in the 16th century that the **Cowslip** *(P. veris)* grew particularly well in the close vicinity of cowpats, called then cow slips or flops, and so the name was coined.

The **Primrose** *(P. vulgaris)* has always been the acknowledged harbinger of spring. It has the most nostalgic scent of all the family and is something to look forward to during the dull winter months. It is not invariably pale yellow as there is a purple form which grows naturally in Wales and the north of England and a dusky pink we personally like to consider a wild Cornish form. There are many suggestions for the derivation of the name. One is that it comes from the Latin *prima rosa*, 'first rose'; another that the old French name *Primverole* was anglicized to Prymrose and then Primrose.

Oxlip

Primrose

Cowslip

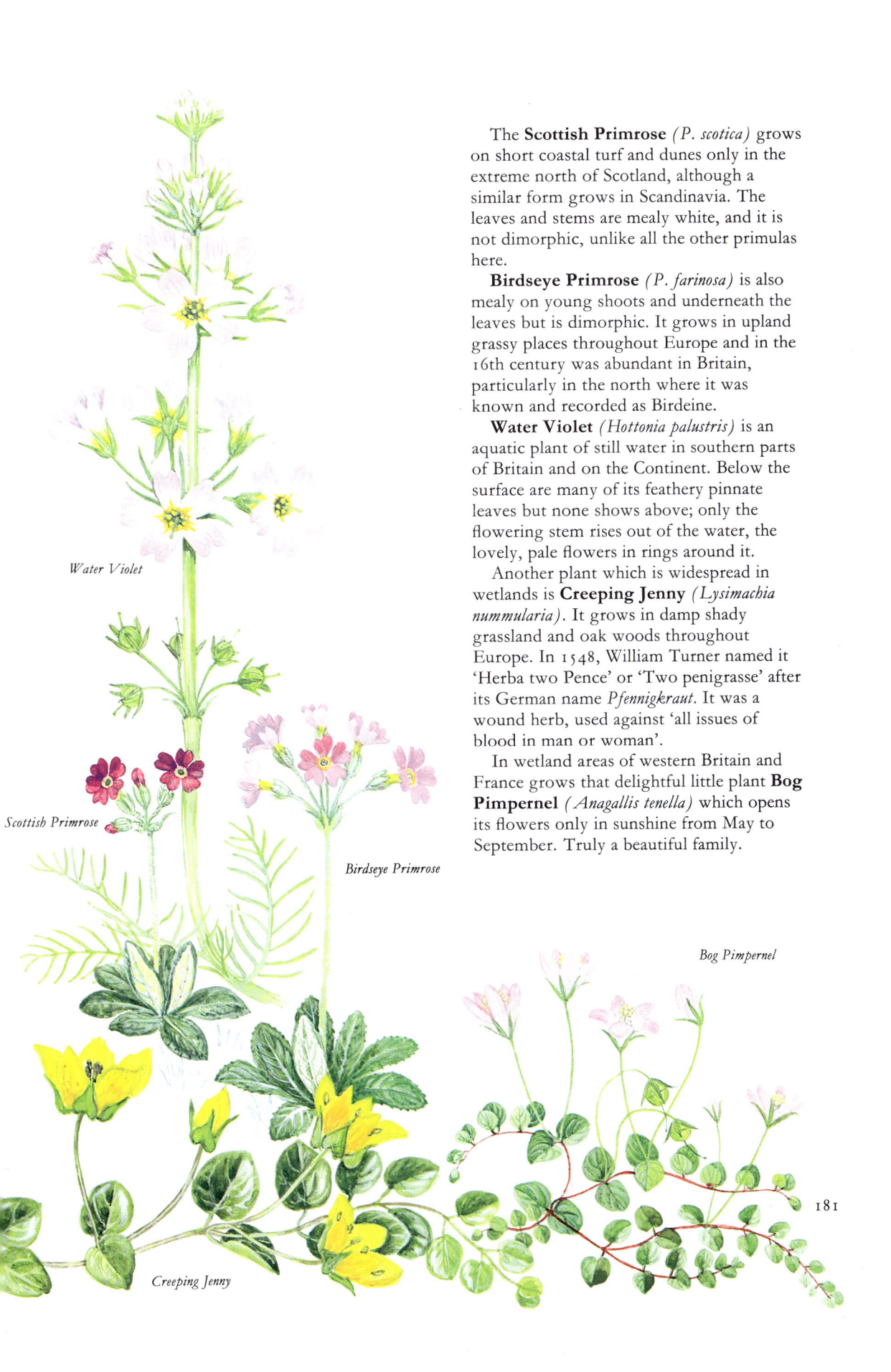

The **Scottish Primrose** (*P. scotica*) grows on short coastal turf and dunes only in the extreme north of Scotland, although a similar form grows in Scandinavia. The leaves and stems are mealy white, and it is not dimorphic, unlike all the other primulas here.

Birdseye Primrose (*P. farinosa*) is also mealy on young shoots and underneath the leaves but is dimorphic. It grows in upland grassy places throughout Europe and in the 16th century was abundant in Britain, particularly in the north where it was known and recorded as Birdeine.

Water Violet (*Hottonia palustris*) is an aquatic plant of still water in southern parts of Britain and on the Continent. Below the surface are many of its feathery pinnate leaves but none shows above; only the flowering stem rises out of the water, the lovely, pale flowers in rings around it.

Another plant which is widespread in wetlands is **Creeping Jenny** (*Lysimachia nummularia*). It grows in damp shady grassland and oak woods throughout Europe. In 1548, William Turner named it 'Herba two Pence' or 'Two penigrasse' after its German name *Pfennigkraut*. It was a wound herb, used against 'all issues of blood in man or woman'.

In wetland areas of western Britain and France grows that delightful little plant **Bog Pimpernel** (*Anagallis tenella*) which opens its flowers only in sunshine from May to September. Truly a beautiful family.

Water Violet

Scottish Primrose

Birdseye Primrose

Bog Pimpernel

Creeping Jenny

The Bogbean, Periwinkle and Gentian families

Bogbean *(Menyanthes trifoliata)* is a most attractive plant growing in shallow water or sphagnum-moss bog. It has thick fleshy roots with which it spreads over quite large areas. The shape of the leaf, which is divided into three leaflets, led to the name Bogbean since it is similar to the leaf of the broad bean and also accounts for the Latin *trifoliata*. It grew in Britain before the Ice Age and is also found in Iceland and into the Arctic.

A comparatively recent introduction into Britain is the periwinkle. It was first recorded in western parts of the country in the middle of the 16th century when it is said garlands made from it were worn by criminals on the way to the gallows. **Lesser Periwinkle** *(Vinca minor)* is not native but has naturalized from being a garden escape. We grow it as a ground-cover plant in a few places in our garden and it makes a very pleasant carpet through which other plants will grow.

There are few more beautiful sights than gentians growing high up in the mountains. Their blue at high altitudes seems more intense and clear. **Common Centaury** *(Centaurium erythraea)* is also a member of the Gentian family, its scented, clear pink flowers open only during the day. Until the 16th century or thereabouts, many medicines based on this family of plants were used as tonics and cleansers. The source of several of these medicines was the Great Yellow Gentian *(Gentiana lutea)*. **Field Gentian** *(Gentianella campestris)* flowers from June to October on fixed dunes in many parts of Britain and mainland Europe, but the **Marsh Gentian** *(Gentiana pneumonanthe)* is very local in a few wet heaths and bogs in Britain although it is quite common in other parts of Europe.

Marsh Gentian

Common Centaury

Field Gentian

Bogbean

Lesser Periwinkle

The Bindweed family
The familiar and, by gardeners, dreaded weed which winds and binds itself in and around other flowers and shrubs is well known. It is seen in hedgerows, on shingle or sandy beaches, in woodland and in arable land where it tangles itself and the sown crop into a solid mass. The member of the Bindweed family (Convolvulaceae) found on shingle beaches is the species **Sea Bindweed** *(Calystegia soldanella)* which also grows on sand dunes where its spreading roots help to bind and stabilize. The young shoots used to be gathered as a poor substitute for samphire. While in flower, from June to September, it will frequently be found with only its leaves because rabbits, which are particularly partial to the flowers, will not eat them.

The **Great Bindweed** *(C. sylvatical)*, illustrated overleaf, has large white flowers and inflated bracts. The beautiful flowers, which are sometimes pink or have pink stripes, are shown to best effect when the plant grows enthusiastically and anti-clockwise up the stay wire of a telephone pole. It has been shown that when growing with its usual vigour it will twine a full circle up such a wire in one and a half to two hours. It appears on waste ground and is most commonly found near human habitats. First recorded in 1548 by William Turner as a British wild flower, it was even then a pestilential garden weed.

Only one of the Bindweed family shown here is scented and that is **Field Bindweed** *(Convolvulus arvensis)*. It has alternative names which reflect countrymen's opinions of it: Withy Wind because it winds the withy, or willows, together, and Devil's Guts, coined from the German *Teufels Nohgern*. It spreads on bare arable ground and its capability is prodigious. In one season it has been known to cover thirty square yards.

Sea Bindweed

Great Bindweed

Field Bindweed

The Bedstraw family

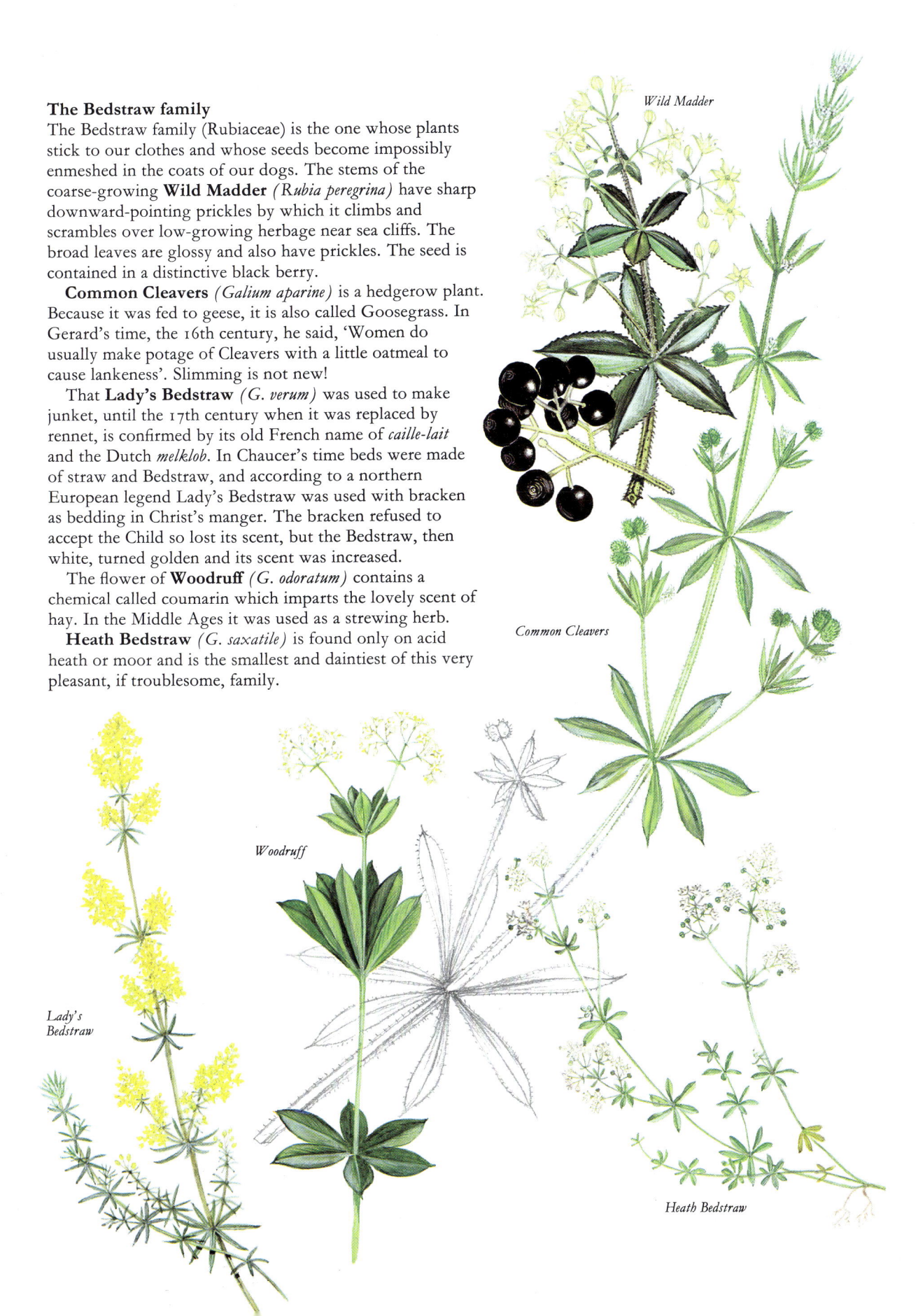

The Bedstraw family (Rubiaceae) is the one whose plants stick to our clothes and whose seeds become impossibly enmeshed in the coats of our dogs. The stems of the coarse-growing **Wild Madder** *(Rubia peregrina)* have sharp downward-pointing prickles by which it climbs and scrambles over low-growing herbage near sea cliffs. The broad leaves are glossy and also have prickles. The seed is contained in a distinctive black berry.

Common Cleavers *(Galium aparine)* is a hedgerow plant. Because it was fed to geese, it is also called Goosegrass. In Gerard's time, the 16th century, he said, 'Women do usually make potage of Cleavers with a little oatmeal to cause lankeness'. Slimming is not new!

That **Lady's Bedstraw** *(G. verum)* was used to make junket, until the 17th century when it was replaced by rennet, is confirmed by its old French name of *caille-lait* and the Dutch *melklob*. In Chaucer's time beds were made of straw and Bedstraw, and according to a northern European legend Lady's Bedstraw was used with bracken as bedding in Christ's manger. The bracken refused to accept the Child so lost its scent, but the Bedstraw, then white, turned golden and its scent was increased.

The flower of **Woodruff** *(G. odoratum)* contains a chemical called coumarin which imparts the lovely scent of hay. In the Middle Ages it was used as a strewing herb.

Heath Bedstraw *(G. saxatile)* is found only on acid heath or moor and is the smallest and daintiest of this very pleasant, if troublesome, family.

The Borage family

Nearly all the plants in the Borage family (Boraginaceae) are hairy on the leaves and stems and often produce pink flowers which turn to blue as they mature. There is no purer blue than **Borage** *(Borago officinalis)* itself. Native to the Mediterranean region, it was introduced to Britain very early as a pot herb with medicinal qualities. It was said to be a stimulant and 'to drive away melancholie' but its chief virtue is as a flavouring for drinks. It is not as common in the wild as it used to be as a garden escape, but is unmistakable when found, generally growing in dry bare places. A plant of it grown in a herb garden will provide many flowers full of nectar for bees which are very attracted to it.

Green Alkanet *(Pentaglottis sempervirens)* is a flower of the hedgerow which has naturalized in southwest Britain, having been introduced in the Middle Ages as a dye plant. Despite its English name, the root provides a brilliant red dye which substantiates the derivation of the name as being from the Spanish *alcanna* which in turn comes from the Arabic *al henna*, the henna plant. This is the source of the dye used by the women of Ancient Egypt as a cosmetic and used again today for tinting hair.

The most familiar flower of the family is the forgetmenot, three species of which are illustrated here. The name is said to come from a translation of the 16th-century German name *Vergissmeinnicht* which the French translated to *ne m'oubliez mye* and which Samuel Taylor Coleridge coined in a poem in 1802 as 'Forget-me-not'. As the flower unwinds it has a certain resemblance to a scorpion's tail, hence the alternative name of Scorpion Grass.

Early Forgetmenot *(Myosotis ramosissima)* is the smallest, and we have found it growing on the Isles of Scilly, with the minute viola, the Dwarf Pansy, both of them only one or two centimetres high and exposed to the full fury of the Atlantic gales. As a contrast, **Water Forgetmenot** *(M. scorpioides)* is one of the largest-flowering species and grows in wet places to a height of twelve inches. **Changing Forgetmenot** *(M. discolor)* differs from the rest of the genus by having yellow flowers which turn to blue from May to June, when the other species also will be flowering.

The Labiate family
The Labiate family (Labiatae) is one of the most important since it includes many species of herbs, such as mint, marjoram, sage, thyme and basil, to mention just the best known. Until the introduction of hops from Holland, **Ground Ivy** *(Glechoma hederacea)* was used as a flavouring for beer. It grows in woodland, on hedges and bare ground throughout Europe, flowering from March to June when the beauty of the labiate, or two-lipped, flowers can be appreciated.

Self-heal *(Prunella vulgaris)* is a flower of dry grassland and is more abundant on lime. It had a great reputation as a wound herb and cure for sore throats. Occasionally, but rarely, the flowers are pink or white.

The powder-blue flowers on a purplish spike belong to **Bugle** *(Ajuga reptans)* which is another wound herb from the Middle Ages. It appears in legends about thunder, lightning and fire; in Germany it is said that to bring it indoors when it flowers from April to June is to run the risk of fire consuming the house.

Wood Sage *(Teucrium scorodonia)* grows in woodland, heath and areas not on lime at heights up to 2,000 feet. It has little history as a culinary or medicinal herb, unlike other members of the family.

Wood Sage

Bugle

Self-heal

Ground Ivy

The flowers illustrated here show clearly the beauty of the Labiate family. Look into the individual flowers of any of these or the Large-flowered Hemp-nettle *(Galeopsis speciosa)*, illustrated on page 28 in Beginner's Botany, and you will see why we consider them to be just as lovely as some of the wild orchids which grow in Europe and why we are happy to have all the species described on this page growing together in our garden.

Several of the labiates are common in hedgerows where they are taken for granted. Those that are garden weeds are pulled up and cast on the compost heap without so much as a second look.

Hedge Woundwort *(Stachys sylvatica)* grows on hedges and is soon traced if it is in the garden because of the rather unpleasant smell which is given off when its square stem is crushed or broken. It blooms from June to October, when its flowers are best described as being beetroot in colour.

The **Common Hemp-nettle** *(Galeopsis tetrahit)*, which flowers from July to September, is paler and has swollen stems at the joint where the leaves and flower spikes branch out. Gerard called it Nettle Hemp in the late 16th century, but whether the fibre was ever used as a hemp we do not know.

Betony *(Betonica officialis)* was first recorded in the 14th century and flowers from June to October. According to the 17-century herbalist Nicholas Culpeper, it was an exceedingly valuable herb, curing a wide range of ailments from headache to the bites of mad dogs.

Marsh Woundwort *(Stachys palustris)* is very orchid-like, with creamy marks on its lips. It is only faintly aromatic and hybridizes with Hedge Woundwort to produce flowers which are often of the colour of Hedge but with the narrow leaves of Marsh Woundwort.

Common Hemp-nettle

Betony

Hedge Woundwort

Marsh Woundwort

Hybrid of Hedge and Marsh

Galeopsis bifida

A very similar plant to Common Hemp-nettle, but without an English name, is **Galeopsis bifida** but it differs in that the hairs are more evenly spread and the flower is smaller, with the lower lip narrower and notched.

Yellow Archangel *(Lamiastrum galeobdolon)* is strong-smelling, creeping and invasive, with long runners which root at every node. It grows in woods and flowers from May to June.

Henbit Dead-nettle *(Lamium amplexicaule)* is a weed of light arable land, flowering from March to October, which has rounded leaves usually unstalked and half-clasping the stem. The **Red Dead-nettle** *(L. purpureum)* is a widespread garden weed which grows on waste ground as well. It is short and flowers from March to October. It is aromatic like the **White Dead-nettle** *(L. album)* which is the taller of the two and flowers on into November.

Like the White Dead-nettle, **Bastard Balm** *(Melittis melissophyllum)* often grows by roads. It is locally common in Britain only in the southwest where it was first recorded, in Devon, in 1650. It was originally called Bug Balm because of its unpleasant smell, but it is a beautiful-looking flower, the magenta-purple patches varying greatly from plant to plant.

Yellow Archangel

White Dead-nettle

Henbit Dead-nettle

Red Dead-nettle

Bastard Balm

The Nightshade family
The Nightshade family (Solanaceae) includes the most important vegetables used by man—potato, tomato, pepper, aubergine—as well as some of the most poisonous plants, including Henbane and tobacco. The two species shown here are poisonous.

Bittersweet *(Solanum dulcamara)* can be found climbing or scrambling in hedgerows, on waste ground and on shingle beaches. It is extremely poisonous and a very ancient charm. German farmers would put garlands of the plant around the necks of their cattle to ward off witches and disease. It seems that these attributes had been handed down through the centuries because it has been found threaded on strings of date-palm leaf in Ancient Egyptian tombs—even in Tutankhamen's third coffin. In Germany it was also used by doctors against rheumatism and as a purgative, and in England Culpeper recommended it for dizziness.

The even more poisonous **Deadly Nightshade** *(Atropa bella-donna)* grows in scrub on limey soil and in woodland. Henry Lyte called it a 'naughtie and deadly plant', and Gerard suggested that 'being a plant so furious and deadly' it should be banished from the garden. In the 19th century it was realized that it contained a valuable ophthalmic drug, atropine, for dilating the pupils of the eyes. This property had already been discovered by the ladies of Venice in the Middle Ages, for they used it cosmetically to make their eyes appear larger and thus enhance their beauty—to make them *bella donnas*, hence the scientific name.

Bittersweet

Deadly Nightshade

The Figwort family
Digitalin, the drug used in the treatment of heart disease, comes from the Foxglove *(Digitalis purpurea)*, one of the members of the Figwort family (Scrophulariaceae).

The flowers of **Common Toadflax** *(Linaria vulgaris)* are similar to those of the antirrhinum, also a member of the family. It is most invasive and was a serious weed in flax fields when that was a major European crop. **Ivy-leaved Toadflax** *(Cymbalaria muralis)* introduced from southern Europe about 1617 as a garden plant, by the end of the 19th century was flourishing throughout the Thames basin and now flowers from April to November on walls throughout Europe.

Speedwells, well known and often grouped as birdseyes, form a genus of many species. **Germander Speedwell** *(Veronica chamaedrys)* flowers from April to June when its pronounced white 'eye' can be seen. The most recent of the genus to be recorded here, **Common Field Speedwell** *(V. persica)*, comes from western Asia and was first found in Berkshire in 1825. By the end of the century it had spread throughout Britain as a weed of cultivation. **Brooklime** *(V. beccabunga)*, whose name comes from the old English 'brok' (brook) and 'lemok' (plant), grows well in Scandinavia where it was called *bekkrbung*, 'brook-bung', as it was said to block up streams. Linnaeus presumably Latinized it to *beccabunga*.

Lousewort *(Pedicularis sylvatica)*, semi-parasitic on grass and sedge, flowers from April to July. It was once thought to infest cattle with lice, but in fact it contains a powerful natural insecticide.

Common Toadflax

Germander Speedwell

Common Field Speedwell

Brooklime

Ivy-leaved Toadflax

Lousewort

The Honeysuckle family

The Honeysuckle family (Caprifoliaceae) is best known for the sweetly scented climber which bears the family name, and the fruitful Elder.

The **Wayfaring Tree** *(Viburnum lantana)* grows to a height of twelve feet, and was so named by Gerard who had seen it growing by the roads as he travelled the country. The leaves are oval and the flowers, which are scented, open from April to June. The berries turn from red to black as they ripen.

The berries of the **Guelder Rose** *(V. opulus)*, on the other hand, remain a shiny brilliant red. The plant grows to the same height as the Wayfaring Tree and the flowers are also white, but considerably larger, and open from pink buds. It was introduced from the Guelders province of Holland in the 16th century.

A total contrast is the delightful little **Twinflower** *(Linnaea borealis)*, a low-growing mat-forming, fragrant undershrub. It has aptly been called the 'gem of the Scottish pine wood'. It is common in the great coniferous forests of Scandinavia but is not found in more southerly areas of Europe. It was the favourite flower of Linnaeus, after whom it was named.

The Teasel and Bellflower families

It was the Romans who first used the Teasel family (Dipsacaceae) as industrial tools for raising the nap on woollen cloth. The common **Teasel** *(Dipsacus fullonum)* has straight ends to the spines on the head, but the best for its industrial purpose and still in use, is Fuller's Teasel, a subspecies.

Like the Teasel, found in damp, grassy places, is **Devilsbit Scabious** *(Succisa pratensis)*. Culpeper reported it to be excellent for curing the plague, fever and freckles, among other things. It was said to annoy the Devil who took revenge by biting off the end of the taproot which is not as pointed as usual.

The **Field Scabious** *(Knautia arvensis)* flowers from June to October in dry, cornfield areas. It, too, had good qualities and was used to relieve sores, snake bites and other nasty complaints. The seeds are often spread by ants.

Sheepsbit Scabious *(Jasione montana)* superficially resembles the other scabious-named plants but is one of the Bellflower family (Campanulaceae). It grows in dry, grassy areas at altitudes up to 3,000 feet.

The bellflowers are beautiful, variable flowers. The **Harebell** *(Campanula rotundifolia)*, on page 143, is a weed difficult to eradicate from the garden. It grows on dry, chalky grassland as does the **Clustered Bellflower** *(C. glomerata)*, overleaf, whose alternative name is Dane's Blood because it was said to grow in areas attacked by Vikings. It is cultivated in gardens. The **Spreading Bellflower** *(C. patula)* can be found in woods and grassy places throughout Europe but is rare in Britain. **Nettle-leaved Bellflower** *(C. trachelium)* is in flower in midsummer like all the bellflowers and lasts well into September. It is a tall perennial, in contrast to the delightful little **Ivy-leaved Bellflower** *(Wahlenbergia hederacea)* which is found in damp woods and moors in most parts of Europe. **Heath Lobelia** *(Lobelia urens)* is very rare in Britain, protected in a nature reserve in Cornwall.

Teasel

Devilsbit Scabious

Field Scabious

Sheepsbit Scabious

Nettle-leaved Bellflower

Heath Lobelia

Spreading Bellflower

Clustered Bellflower

Ivy-leaved Bellflower

The Daisy family

The largest botanical family, covering the world with a fantastic array of flowers, is the Daisy family (Compositae). The **Daisy** (*Bellis perennis*) was known in Anglo-Saxon times as Day's Eye since it opens with the dawn and closes at dusk. Linnaeus named it *Bellis perennis*, 'beautiful perennial'.

Many of the family have good medicinal records and none better than **Feverfew** (*Tanacetum parthenium*). In the 16th century it was found to be slightly analgesic and became the 'aspirin' of the day. It is a highly aromatic, short to medium perennial, growing on walls and in waste places and flowering from June to September.

Yarrow (*Achillea millefolium*) grows in grassland and has flowers, either white or pink, from June to November. Achilles found it cured his soldiers' wounds with its application, hence its generic name.

Sneezewort (*A. ptarmica*) grows in damp grassland on acid soil and flowers from July to September. It was used to combat toothache and, due to its ability to cause sneezing, as a snuff.

Scentless Mayweed (*Tripleurospermum inodorum*) is one of a group of plants which are all aromatic and growing on waste places but unlike them is not aromatic.

Common Fleabane

Winter Heliotrope

The strong vanilla scent of **Winter Heliotrope** *(Petasites fragrans)* belies the damage done by the plant with its invasive and smothering habits. It flowers only seldom in some places but produces prodigious quantities of leaves, like its equally persistent cousin Coltsfoot *(Tussilago farfara)*. It was first found on Mont Pilor in France in 1806 and introduced to Britain as a winter flower. It became a favourite Victorian pot plant and was soon found to grow satisfactorily in the open. It has proved to be another Victorian garden disaster for as well as being invasive, it is virtually impossible to eradicate. It is a true winter flower, in bloom from November to March, and a delight to find growing on wasteland or in hedges—well away from the garden.

Common Fleabane *(Pulicaria dysenterica)* grows in damp grassland, flowering from June to September. In the 16th century Turner wrote that, by burning, it had been used as an insecticide against fleas and midges since Roman times. There are many natural insecticides which are members of the Daisy family, secreting a type of the chemical thiophene.

At first glance it is easy to forget that the thistle belongs to the Daisy family but remembering the general definition of a composite flower, with heads made up of a central disc of hundreds of tiny flowers, but without strap-shaped ray-flowers, they are clearly so. One of the few scented species **Musk Thistle** *(Carduus nutans)* has a pleasant almond-like perfume. Its flowers nod on spineless top stalks above very spiny leaves. It is also known as Nodding Thistle. We have seen them in plenty on the roadside growing up to four feet tall. It is a very handsome weed and is also found on bare places and grassland where it flowers from June to September, the same period as the **Spear Thistle** *(Cirsium vulgare)*. This dreadful weed of agriculture was described as one of the worst by William Pitt in 1809, and is listed as such to this day. The seeds are most attractive to goldfinches and flocks of the birds may be seen attending to them in the autumn. An equally noxious weed of agriculture is the Creeping Thistle *(C. arvense)* which has a honey scent when it flowers, from June to September.

The **Prickly Sow-thistle** *(Sonchus asper)* looks more like a tall, prickly dandelion than a thistle. Plants of the Sow-thistle group are so called because they were once fed to pregnant sows to increase their milk. The leaves are soft and the prickles do not pierce any but the most delicate skin. It grows on bare ground and waste places and is another weed of cultivation.

Spear Thistle

Musk Thistle

Prickly Sow-thistle

197

Leafy Hawkweed

Chicory

Goatsbeard

198

Because of its habit of closing its flowers at about noon, **Goatsbeard** *(Tragopogon pratensis)* has earned another name, Jack-go-to-bed-at-noon. It was known to Dioscorides as *Barba hirci* which John Turner translated as Goatsbeard. Before the beautiful, completely spherical seed head develops, the pappus (the ring of feathery hairs surrounding the seed, enabling it to be carried on the wind) forms a beard. Joseph, husband of the Virgin Mary, is usually depicted with a beard, giving the flower another name—now rarely used—of Joseph's Flower. In the Middle Ages the taproot was eaten as a carrot.

One of the few clear blue flowers of this predominantly yellow family is **Chicory** *(Cichorium intybus)* which also has the distinction of being one of the few of the group which do not exude a milky juice. It flowers from June to September in waste places and is a delightful plant to see in the countryside. Its roots, roasted, are blended with coffee to impart a bitter flavour, and it has been used medicinally since the Middle Ages. It is the endive of the kitchen garden and its new young shoots are blanched and eaten as a vegetable. It is a natural litmus paper: Curtis wrote in his *Flora Londinensis* that boys delighted in picking the flowers and holding them over ants' nests which they then disturbed with sticks. The ants would spray up their defensive formic acid thereby turning the flowers pink.

An enormous section of the Daisy family covers the dandelion-like flowers of the hawkbits, hawkweeds and hawksbeards, and the Dandelion itself. **Leafy Hawkweed** *(Hieracium umbellatum)* flowers from May to September and grows on acid grassland and heaths. There is nothing hawkish about this plant or any other member of this group, and it has been suggested that the name comes from the Greek word *hierex* meaning 'hawk', since legend has it that birds of prey would use the juice of the plant to sharpen their sight.

The Lily family

Unless the leaves are crushed, the familiar onion scent is not always much in evidence with plants of the onion genus, part of the Lily family (Liliaceae). Chives (*Allium schoenoprasum*) is a member of the family, well known to gardeners.

Three-cornered Leek (*A. triquetrum*) was not recorded in Britain until late in the 18th century when it was found in west Cornwall and the Isles of Scilly. It was introduced from the Mediterranean and is such a pest to horticulture in some areas that growers can be fined for having it on their land. Woods and banks are its habitats where it flowers sometimes with **Ramsons** (*A. ursinum*) from April to June. On the Continent, particularly in the north and east, the name was *rams* which implies the same derivation as the Old English name of 'hramsan'. Gerard said the leaves made a good sauce to eat with fish but it was fit only for those with a strong constitution and for 'labouring men'. Two types of roots are produced: fibrous ones in the autumn absorbing nutrients and moisture; and in the spring fleshy taproots grow deep and eventually contract, thereby pulling the bulb farther into the ground. This ability to adjust its depth is shared by several bulbous plants, which is sometimes a help to those who may plant bulbs too shallow in their garden.

The **Sand Leek** (*A. scorodoprasum*) grows on sandy hedge banks and cultivated places throughout Europe. The long-stalked umbel also contains bulbils and may be seen from June to August when the flowers are blooming.

Crow Garlic (*A. vineale*) sometimes does not flower and then the bulbils take over the loosely formed umbel completely. It has been a noxious weed on the farm since Roman times and this has earned it its derogatory Crow epithet. It reproduces in five ways—from spring-sown seeds, aerial bulbils, underground bulbs growing in the axils, or 'armholes', of the leaves, offsets from the main bulb and from the main bulb itself.

A similar plant, with pink-purple flowers, **Keeled Garlic** (*A. carinatum*) was introduced into Britain in the 16th century.

In addition to having these troublesome pests, the Lily family has some of the most beautiful flowers there are, their names as lovely as the flowers.

Sand Leek

Keeled Garlic

Crow Garlic

Ramsons

Three-cornered Leek

Berries in August

Male flowers

Female flowers

Berries in January

Black Bryony

The Yam family

The Yam family (Dioscoreaceae), which produces the staple diet of many regions in Asia, Africa and South America, is represented in Europe by one inedible species **Black Bryony** *(Tamus communis)*, first recorded in Britain by Gerard. It is an unusual plant because although it is a monocotyledon, it has net-veined leaves instead of parallel veins. The poisonous root, which is large and tuberous, is black, which accounts for the plant's name. The stems twine in a clockwise direction (with the sun), climbing without tendrils. The leaves are very variable in shape and the flowers are open from May to August, with male and female flowers on separate plants. The flowers are followed by green, poisonous berries which turn red as they ripen. It climbs in woods, scrub and hedges, and throughout the winter dead leaves and red berries may still be seen clinging to the brown, flattened stems.

The Iris, Daffodil and Lily families

The unfortunately named **Stinking Iris** *(Iris foetidissima)*, which grows in woodland, scrub and on sea cliffs in Britain and France, and the Yellow Iris *(I. pseudacorus)* are the two most common members of the Iris family (Iridaceae) growing wild in Britain. The Stinking Iris is so called because the leaves, when crushed, give off a sweet sickly smell which some think is like meat and accounts for an alternative name of the Roast Beef Plant. William Turner called it Spurgewort after its purgative powers. The berries in their open capsules last a long time.

'There hath beene great confusion among many of our moderne Writers of plants, in not distinguishing the manifold varieties of Daffodils', so wrote Parkinson in his *Paradisus* in 1629. He followed this statement with forty pages of classification which includes the **Wild Daffodil** *(Narcissus pseudonarcissus)*. Destruction of its habitat and removal to gardens has reduced this lovely spring flower to its modern comparative scarcity. With the exception of the very rare Tenby Daffodil *(N. obvallaris)* it is the only native wild daffodil in Britain. The other species are often garden escapes or naturalized and hybridized forms of plants originally introduced from southern Europe. The Snowdrop *(Galanthus nivalis)* and the Spring and Summer Snowflakes *(Leucojum vernum* and *L. aestivum)* are also members of the Daffodil family (Amaryllidaceae).

A beautiful plant of the Lily family is the **Lily of the Valley** *(Convallaria majalis)*. It has an unforgettable perfume and grows in fairly dry woodland in soil rich in humus. The bell-like flowers always nod to one side of the main flower stalk. Legend has it that they represent the tears of the Virgin Mary shed at the foot of the Cross.

The flowers of **Meadow Saffron** *(Colchicum autumnale)* appear in woods and damp grassy places in August and September before the leaves which grow in spring. The apparent stems of the flower are actually part of the flower itself, and are weak, resulting in a rather floppy habit of growth. They are often grown in gardens and are variously known as Naked Ladies, Naked Boys or Naked Nanny. Dioscorides said it was sufficiently poisonous to kill a man in one day. Apothecaries and herbalists proceeded with due caution and found it relieved gout. Beneficial under proper control, it is still listed as a palliative in the British Pharmacopoeia.

Stinking Iris and berries

Wild Daffodil

Meadow Saffron and bud

Lily of the Valley

INTRODUCTION TO ORCHIDS

If there are any other flowers growing on this earth more certain to attract attention, more complicated in their construction, more fascinating, variable, vulnerable and altogether more captivating than orchids, then we have yet to find them. Their very name conjures up thoughts of wealth and luxury to many people, but we are not dealing with the exotic beauties of the rain forests or the cool sculptured perfections from the hot house, but the more simple wild orchids of Britain and Europe which are small and insignificant in comparison, and yet have such a strong appeal for us that annual orchid forays have become an essential part of our lives.

There are fifty species of orchid in this country and no other family can produce so many widely different and captivating flowers, each one an individual with its own peculiarities, smell, design, colour, shape, habit of growth and its own particular appeal. No flower family in Britain is more hunted and collected than the orchid; no other family has so many members on the list of protected species and so many more which may one day have to join them if they are to survive; and yet it is a family which also includes several species which are relatively common over a wide area of Britain and Europe, or in small localized communities.

The life story of the orchid is closely linked with that of a soil fungus called Mycorrhiza, meaning literally 'fungus root'. Mycorrhizal fungi obtain their nutrients parasitically from rotting and decaying vegetable matter in the soil, which we call humus. Part of the fungus lives outside the orchid, obtaining life-sustaining nutrients from the humus, which it passes on to the other part which penetrates deep into the roots and underground stems of the orchid

1 Lesser Butterfly Orchid
2 Greater Butterfly Orchid
3, 4, 5, 6 Lady Orchid showing variations of lip
7 Burnt Orchid
8 Heath Spotted Orchid
9 Coral-root Orchid
10 Birdsnest Orchid
11 Southern Marsh Orchid
12, 13, 14 Lizard Orchid
15, 16, 17 Fragrant Orchid
18 Fly Orchid
19 Common Twayblade
20 Lesser Twayblade
21 Bee Orchid
22 Narrow-lipped Helleborine
23 Broad-leaved Helleborine
24 Violet Helleborine

plant. The orchid has actually learnt to turn this parasitic situation to its own advantage, by digesting some of the advancing fungus and so acquiring an additional, valuable supply of second-hand food. The seed of the wild orchid is so fine and dust-like that it cannot store within itself any reserves of food, and so it too relies on this fungus to provide the nourishment for the tiny and slow-growing seedling, from the critical moment of germination until it has green leaves of its own to supply the food, which may not be for months, or even years in the case of some orchids. Many orchid seeds cannot even germinate, let alone grow, without the bolstering-up effect of the fungus.

The seedling starts life as a minute projection or bud, followed by the roots and then, after several months or years have passed, aerial stems and the first leaves are produced, but no flowers at this stage. The time between germination and flowering may be many years. Because of this, an orchid needs all the extra help the fungus can give it.

Most orchids die down after flowering, although some, like Autumn Lady's Tresses, develop their leaves during the autumn, and these remain all winter until the flower stem rises in the following year. The food required to nourish some orchid plants is stored in underground tubers, as in the case of the Marsh and Lizard Orchids. These have one tuber to produce food for leaves and flowers, and any nutrients over and above their requirements are stored in a second tuber which is produced later in the year to take over the role of the first one when it has exhausted its supply. Other orchids have an extensive network of underground stems and roots growing either horizontally or vertically, and in these they store their food. They include Lady's Slipper, the twayblades, Creeping Lady's Tresses and the helleborines. Another group, which includes the Bee, Fragrant and Early Purple Orchids, builds up a store of food during development but this becomes so depleted by the time the first flowers have been produced that some of the plants die of malnutrition. These species, called monocarpic, rely on the production of vast amounts of seed after one glorious flowering to carry on their race.

Root systems

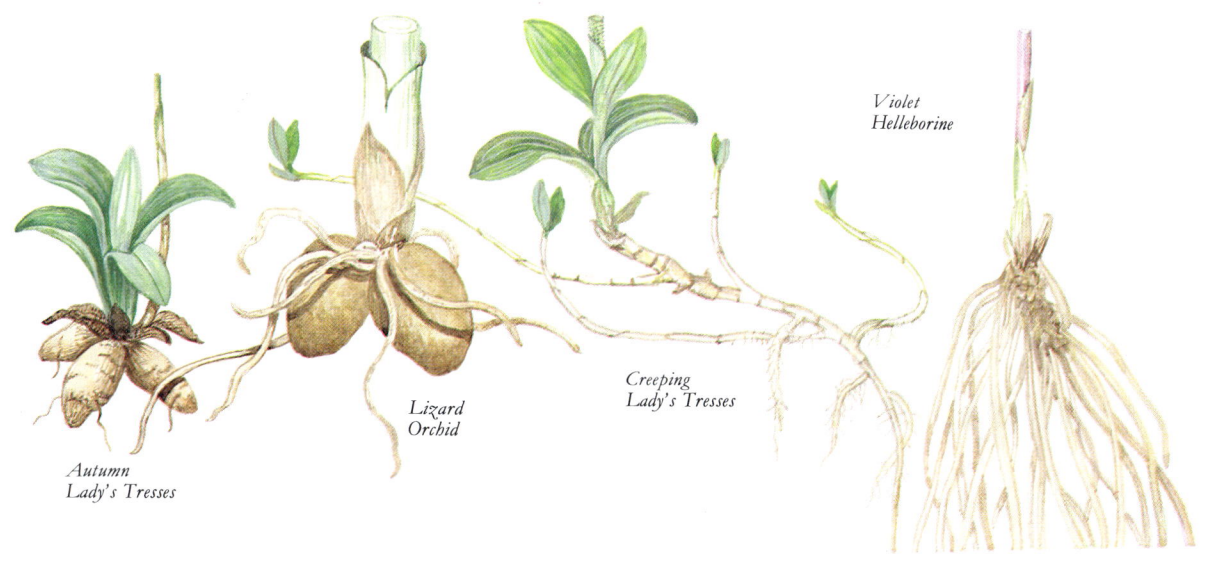

Violet Helleborine

Creeping Lady's Tresses

Lizard Orchid

Autumn Lady's Tresses

Some orchids are more heavily dependent than others on the fungus. If the woodland canopy above the Red Helleborine, for example, becomes too dense over the years, it has not enough light from which to manufacture chlorophyll and has to rely more and more on the fungus in order to survive, let alone to flower. Roots continue to grow but no stems appear, and this underground existence may continue for many years, some say for as long as twenty, until the felling of trees allows sufficient light to fall again upon the woodland floor, when the flowers will reappear as if by magic. Other orchids become self-supporting after they have passed the juvenile stage, notably the Common Twayblade and the Lady's Slipper.

At the opposite end of the scale there are three orchids in Britain which are dependent upon the fungus for the whole of their lives. These are called saprophytic orchids; all are leafless and so cannot manufacture food for themselves, a case of parasites living off parasites. They grow in deep, dense woodlands, in a soil very rich in humus from which the invader draws the food that feeds both itself and the host plant. This food is stored in the roots of the orchid and in the nodules which develop upon them until there is sufficient to produce a flower stem, although this may not occur every year. The three orchids are the Birdsnest—which is fairly regular in its flowering habits—the Common Coral-root, and the tiny, aptly named Ghost Orchid, of great rarity, with its pale almost transparent stem, its strange and not very beautiful flowers. The Ghost may bloom one year and then not be seen for a further ten or even twenty years.

Identification of orchids can be a problem because of their habit of hybridizing—particularly among the genus *Dactylorhiza*, the marsh and spotted orchids—and also because of many variations in colour and markings. A few orchids occasionally produce complete or partial albinos, mainly among the red, purple and pink-flowered species. Leaves can vary in the number of spots present but as a rule not in the actual shape, and some species can even produce plants with plain leaves.

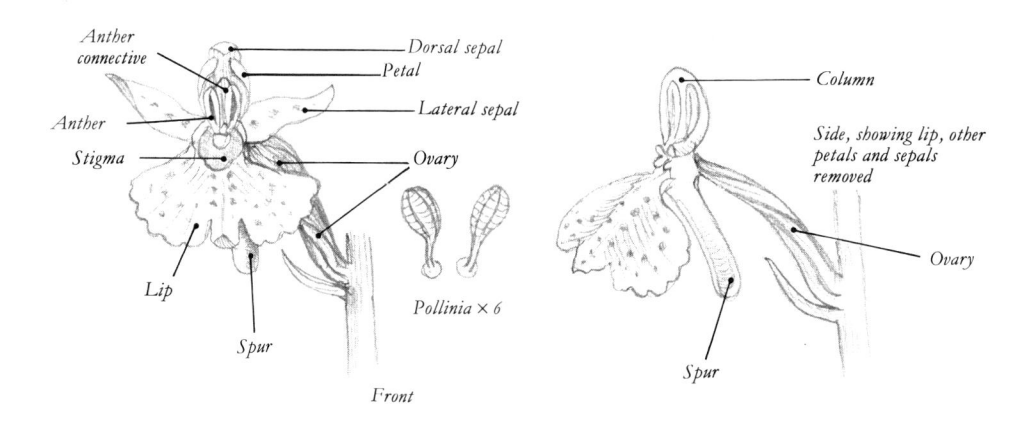

Orchid flowers are intricate pieces of engineering, with the male and female organs joined together in a single column—one of the general characteristics of this family. The pollen produced by the orchids is as fine as dust, but instead of being in separate grains and blowing about in the wind it is fused into small groups called pollinia. Each mass—the size of a pin's head—contains thousands, even millions, of sticky pollen grains. The flowers are pollinated by many different species of insects, from tiny and not very intelligent, creeping ones, which visit the least complicated flowers, to the large butterflies and moths whose long proboscises are tailor-made to fit into the nectar-bearing spurs of some orchids. Finally, at the top end of the intelligence scale there are the highly developed bees which pollinate the most complicated and intricately designed flowers in the most efficient way possible. The pollination mechanism of the Common Twayblade serves as a good example. It has a nectar-producing groove down the centre of its small yellow-green lip, which provides delectable food for a variety of small, short-tongued insects, and it is one of those rare types of plants which is visited by ichneumon wasps. These visitors suck their way up the lip until they reach the point where it turns sharply downwards under the column. Here, a small beak-like projection, called the rostellum, is situated in such a position that the insect cannot fail to touch it, however lightly and briefly, and this triggers off an explosion which forces a drop of very sticky liquid from the tip of the rostellum on to the head of the insect, thus enabling the pollen, which is situated conveniently nearby, to become firmly attached to the insect on impact. The glue hardens in a matter of seconds, and the insect, being so startled by the whole procedure, usually flies away to a different plant, either to be bombarded yet again with more pollen or to cross-pollinate any mature and receptive flower whose sticky stigma is so positioned as to accept readily the clumps of pollen which are transferred to it from the insect's head. It needs only one pollinium or, at the most, two, placed on a receptive stigma to pollinate the vast numbers of ovules awaiting fertilization within a single ovary. It is astonishing that the entire world is not covered with orchids for each stem supports several flowers, from one or two in Spider Orchids to Lizard Orchids with up to seventy.

Orchids work hard to survive—some harder than others. A Common Twayblade produces a mere 500 seeds per capsule, but it can have as many as a hundred flowers on its stem. A Bee Orchid can average a staggering 10,000 and a really large capsule can produce 25,000 but there may not be more than six flowers on one stem. Tropical orchids outdo our European ones in a really spectacular way, for according to some experts the *Cymbidium* orchids may have as many as $1\frac{3}{4}$ million seeds in each capsule, and the Swan Orchid of America probably holds the record with 4 million in a capsule measuring six inches long and two inches in diameter. Self-pollination can take place in some orchids—it is common among the helleborines and also among the various *Ophrys*—but only as a last resort. For instance, as the flowers of the Bee Orchid mature, the pollen stalk shrivels and causes the pollen-bearing part to become dislodged from its bag, or container, and to bend over the stigma, after which any small breeze will cause the grains to touch and stick to the stigma.

When the seeds of orchids are ripe, the capsule containing them splits lengthways into six divisions, or valves, which are still attached at each end of the capsule. Any breeze or movement of the stem causes the seeds to be shaken out between the slits, and currents of warm air bear them to a great height and disperse them far and wide in the upper atmosphere from where they gently float down to land, we hope, on good earth.

The orchid which probably gives most pleasure when seen for the first time is the **Bee Orchid** *(Ophrys apifera)*. More common and widespread than the other members of its genus, the *Ophrys*, it is however elusive, sometimes flowering in large numbers in one particular area before disappearing for a few years or even forever. It is found mainly on chalk or limestone and sometimes on dunes and in woods. A rosette of leaves forms in the autumn and lasts throughout the winter. The flower stem, appearing in the spring, reaches heights from six inches to well over a foot, with as few as two flowers or as many as six and sometimes seven. They bloom from late May to June with their strangely beautiful, delicate-pink sepals and the velvet 'bee' body much in evidence. Many variations occur in the colour of the sepals and the marking on the lip. The flowers are said to be pollinated by bees which have also been observed trying to mate with the flower bee, but this we have not seen and we have heard doubts cast upon the role of the bee as the pollinator. It is far more commonly self-pollinated.

The **Wasp Orchid** *(O. apifera* var. *trollii)* is regarded as a subspecies of the Bee. It can be recognized by the pointed, dagger-shaped lip, the tip of which does not curl back as in the Bee Orchid. The colour of the lip is a mixture of hazy, mottled browns and green with a less noticeably velvety texture.

The **Late Spider Orchid** *(O. fuciflora)* is like the Bee in colour but the lip is larger, more spread out and curves slightly forward at the tip. It is frequently found in central and southern Europe and in very small colonies in the southeast tip of England where it grows only on chalkland with a short-cropped turf. Undergrazing has caused a marked decline in its numbers, making it exceedingly local and rare. It blooms from late May through June, growing from four to twelve inches tall. The two to six, beautiful flowers on the stem are so large that they make the little plant look top-heavy.

The **Early Spider Orchid** *(O. sphegodes)* is more easily overlooked, for it is sombre green and brown in colour and only three to nine inches tall as a rule, with two or three flowers on a stem, although up to six or seven have been found. The individual flowers, which appear in late April, are longlasting but do not always open at the same time. Its distribution is much the same as that of the Late Spider, although it was once probably widespread over several counties and can still be found in Dorset, Sussex and Kent. It grows well in coastal areas.

A favourite of ours is the **Fly Orchid** *(O. insectifera)* which is also easily overlooked. Its narrow, delicate, flowering stem is hung with small, brown 'flies' and grows from six to twenty-four inches tall. It is more widely distributed than the spiders although it is local and never common in Britain. It may be found near woodland edges, often in shade and always on chalk or limestone.

The **Frog Orchid** *(Coeloglossum viride)* is another inconspicuous plant. It is not really frog-like except in its colouring which varies from green to brownish, often tinged with red. Sometimes the whole plant, which is only a few inches tall, is suffused with this reddish colour. Widely distributed through central Europe and in Britain, although it grows in quite large numbers in a few small areas, it is not common. It is in flower from June to August and is pollinated by small insects including beetles.

White-sepalled form of the Bee Orchid

Fly Orchid

Wasp Orchid

Early Spider Orchid

Late Spider Orchid

Frog Orchid

Bee Orchid

The **Man Orchid** *(Aceras anthropophorum)* is one of those fascinating orchids with many florets—up to ninety have been recorded—which can be found in southern Britain. The shape of the floret gives it its name since the hood is said to resemble the head and the lip the body of a person, with its four projections as the arms and legs. It grows on chalk soils in eastern England, but curiously enough it is not so confined in Continental Europe where it will grow on soil which is not particularly chalky. It flowers in May and June, dying down soon after in the open grassland and scrub in which it flourishes. The chemical coumarin is contained in its leaves which give off the pleasant scent of new-mown hay.

The distribution of the **Lizard Orchid** *(Himantoglossum hircinum)* is similar to that of the Man Orchid but it has had a varied history in Britain. The number of florets depends on the height and vigour of the plant—as many as seventy have been found but this is rare. In Britain the plant may be as small as twelve inches but on the Continent it grows to three feet. During the first thirty years of this century, the winter climate in Britain warmed very slightly with more rain coming before a less frosty spring. In the same period the Lizard Orchid extended its range considerably to the north and west, and it is reasonable to suggest that the two are linked since the improved weather pattern matches that in which the orchid grows in profusion in other countries. It is confined to calcareous soils and over limestone rocks, and we have found well-grown specimens in some of the sand dunes on the west coast of France. On one occasion we picked up a large plant which had just been cut down by a hay machine and took it to our caravan where we left it. On returning later that hot sunny day we were made aware of the reason for the species name of *hircinum,* a 'goat'. The smell of billy goat was with us for several days.

Some orchids produce a pair of large leaves before the flower stalk appears to grow up through them. The **Common Twayblade** *(Listera ovata)* has these two large ovate leaves (hence the species name) which make identification simple. Many flowers of this orchid are sterile, especially if they grow in more shady areas of woodland, requiring the plant as it matures to develop a lateral root system from which buds and later stems can grow. The flowers appear from May to July in the varying habitats which this species will tolerate. The Lesser Twayblade *(L. cordata)*, whose 'face' appears on page 202, is only a third of the size of the Common species and its flowers, which appear from June to August, have a reddish tinge to them. It grows on slightly acid soils, in open meadow and wet boggy places, often hidden by heather and bracken.

The **Greater Butterfly Orchid** *(Platanthera chlorantha)* also flowers from June to August. This is a beautiful plant—tall, white and fragrant with the scent of vanilla. It has a pair of leaves at the base which, being shiny and elliptical, cannot be mistaken for those of other orchids. It grows on moors and marshy ground alongside its relative the Lesser Butterfly Orchid *(P. bifolia)*. Although a stunted Greater may be smaller than a vigorous Lesser, they can still be told apart. The pollen masses in the Greater are divergent whilst in the Lesser they are parallel. This identification clue can be clearly seen on page 202. Gerard first recorded it 'growing on a heath between London and Henden, at a place called Hampstead'.

Man Orchid

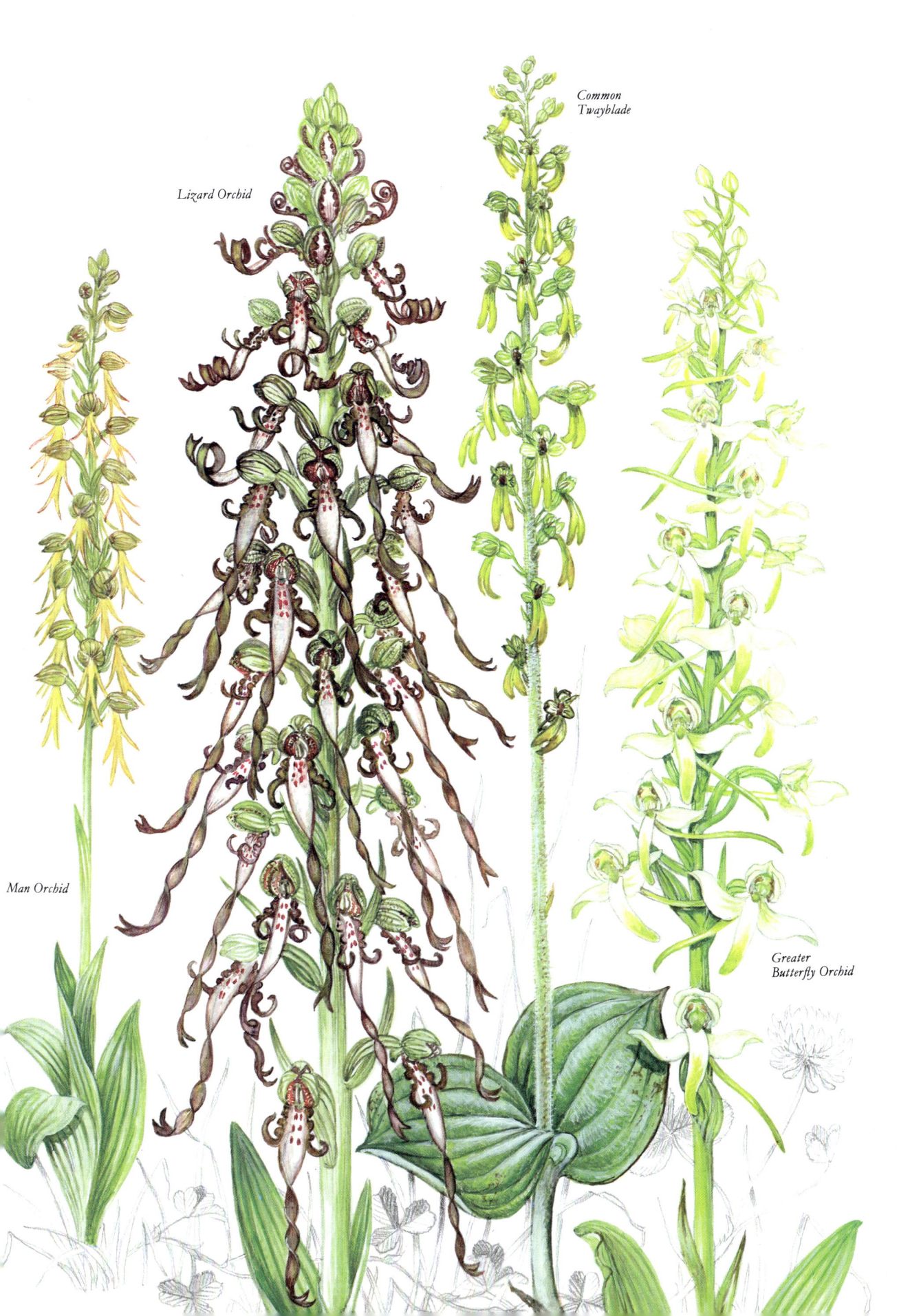

Lizard Orchid

Common Twayblade

Greater Butterfly Orchid

Lady Orchid

One of the largest of our orchids is the **Lady Orchid** *(Orchis purpurea)*. It is often a robust plant, reaching a height of three feet, with large leaves and a massive spike of flowers which can itself be up to five inches long. The individual large florets are most attractive, with dark chocolate-maroon hoods and purple-spotted lips which can vary in shape. It grows in woods on chalky soil and is widespread though local in southeast Britain. It is less common than it was because of overpicking and the destruction of its habitats. In late May we like to visit these flowers in a small wood in France where they are allowed to grow to their full majestic height, unmolested and unpicked. They are a magnificent sight.

The **Burnt Orchid** *(Orchis ustulata)* is often described as the Lady Orchid in miniature. There is a similarity in the colours of the flowers, but the hood of this species is redder on the fully opened flowers and a distinctive black-maroon when in bud, this latter feature giving it its common name of Burnt Orchid and its even more descriptive one of Burnt-tip. It grows on chalk and limestone and can reach a height of eight inches in a well-grown specimen but sometimes may not exceed two inches. The sweetly scented flowers appear from mid-May onwards, if you can find them, for their colonies are decreasing and although they may appear in large numbers on a few sites they cannot be relied upon to repeat the performance every year. They require short-cropped, well-drained soil, so the undergrazing of grass by sheep and rabbits has contributed to their decline as much as the ploughing-up of old pastures.

Of the two spotted orchids, the Heath *(Dactylorhiza maculata)*, is usually found on acid or neutral soil and grows equally well in bogs or on dry moorland. The **Common Spotted Orchid** *(D. fuchsii)*, on the other hand, grows on chalky soil in marshes, light woodlands, downs and roadside verges, and is widespread throughout Britain, being fairly common in some areas. It is said to grow as tall as thirty inches, but the plant in

Burnt Orchid

our garden, which annually produces more and more flowers, does not exceed fifteen. The lowest leaf is always the smallest and most rounded, the leaves above being progressively narrower and more sharply pointed. They are usually heavily blotched and spotted although plants with plain leaves can be found.

Among our favourite orchids the **Fragrant Orchid** *(Gymnadenia conopsea)* ranks high for it is extremely dainty. The flowers are delightful, long-spurred and scented, and the plant grows to about eighteen inches tall with leaves hooded at the tip and fanning out from the lower part of the flowering stem. Once, and once only, the Short-spurred Fragrant Orchid *(G. odoratissima)* flowered in Britain, in 1922. It has never appeared again, but we live in hope that one day some Continental seed may drift down to start a new colony. It has smaller flowers, shorter spurs and narrower leaves.

An orchid rarely overlooked is the bright pink **Pyramid Orchid** *(Anacamptis pyramidalis)* which grows on chalk downland and in limestone areas, often in quite large numbers. The flower is usually distinctly pyramidal to start with, but the shape spreads out as the top flowers open. The height varies from six to eighteen inches. It may be found from June to August; the colour varies from a soft pale pink to a brilliant pure cerise.

One of the best-known orchids is the widespread and often abundant **Early Purple Orchid** *(Orchis mascula)* which flowers early in the year. It is as much at home on sea cliffs, in woodlands and on downland as in hedgerows. It can be found throughout Britain and is widespread in many other parts of the world. It has collected many local names including Long Purples in Shakespeare's time and Kettle Cases in the Isle of Wight. The upcurved spur is very characteristic and the plant is easily recognized by its usually well-spotted leaves and, in April, its magenta-purple flowers.

Fragrant Orchid

Common Spotted Orchid

Pyramid Orchid

Early Purple Orchid

White Helleborine

Autumn Lady's Tresses

Creeping Lady's Tresses

The helleborines are a slightly different group within the Orchid family and are divided into two genera—*Cephalanthera* and *Epipactis*. The former has larger and more colourful flowers, particularly the Red Helleborine *(Cephalanthera rubra)*, a beautiful and graceful plant, very rare in Britain (see Protected Flowers, page 123).

The **White Helleborine** *(C. damasonium)* is the most typical beech-wood orchid and is widespread in south and east Britain, being abundant on chalky soils. It has a considerable root stock producing a mass of underground growth which can cope with dry conditions. It has greyish leaves when mature, but sometimes with a reddish tinge at first. It can carry up to sixteen flowers on each spike, but more usually half that number, and grows from six to fifteen inches tall. The flowers, which rarely fully open, are white and sometimes creamy with orange or yellow ridges of the lip, and appear in May and June.

The lady's tresses were so named by William Turner because the characteristic spiralling reminded him of the way ladies wore their hair.

The fragrant **Autumn Lady's Tresses** *(Spiranthes spiralis)* is widespread in southern Britain. A rosette of leaves grows in early autumn and overwinters, to wither and die before the flower spike blooms in August and September; sometimes the leaves of the following year's rosette grow beside the flowering stem. It is heavily dependent on fungal activity, for the buds on the spreading roots to form new colonies. The flower spike usually grows to six inches but can reach twelve, with about fifteen flowers. Summer Lady's Tresses *(S. aestivalis)* is now extinct in Britain. First recorded in 1840 in southern England where it was fairly abundant, by 1914 it had a precarious hold in the Channel Islands and was recorded in 1926 when the last colony of four plants was dug up complete with its roots. Irish Lady's Tresses *(S. romanzoffiana)* grows almost entirely in Ireland, but there are a few places in the southern Outer Hebrides where it flourishes. It has a much denser flower spike with three rows of spiralling flowers.

Creeping Lady's Tresses *(Goodyera repens)* has slender creeping roots from which the stem arises. It has attractively veined leaves and a sweetly scented flower spike, three to four inches tall, whose spiral is not so well formed. Native to Scandinavia and eastern Europe, in Britain, with one exception, it grows only in Scottish pine forests. The exception is a pair of sites in a pine plantation in East Anglia where it probably arrived on the roots of transplanted trees.

The **Marsh Helleborine** *(Epipactis palustris)* is not typical of its genus. It has larger flowers of a better colour with a yellow patch at the back of the lip instead of ridges. It has a creeping habit of growth. The stem is usually twelve to eighteen inches tall with about ten florets, but larger plants have been recorded. It is widespread in Europe and in Britain away from shady places. It is pollinated by bees when it flowers from June to September.

The **Dark Red Helleborine** *(E. atrorubens)* grows on limestone rock and scree, sometimes appearing to come straight out of the rock. Its short thick roots give rise to a large amount of thin ones which spread through crevices in search of nutrition. In Britain there is usually one stem per plant but on the Continent up to six may grow, with up to twenty slightly vanilla-scented florets. It is shorter than the Broadleaved Helleborine *(E. helleborine)* for which it is occasionally mistaken, but when in flower, in June and July, the broad red sepals should clear any doubt. The attractive Violet Helleborine *(E. purpurata)* grows in woods, often beech, in clumps of purple-tinted stems around which the flowers loosely spiral. The flowers are pale green and white inside, with a mottled violet cup. It can be found mainly in southern Britain, France and Germany.

Dark Red Helleborine

Marsh Helleborine

GLOSSARY

Achene	Small, dry indehiscent single-seeded fruit.
Alien	A plant which has obviously been introduced by man but maintains itself.
Annual	A plant which completes its life cycle within one year.
Anther	The terminal part of the stamen, containing the male pollen.
Axil	The upper angle formed by the joining of stem and leaf or leaf stalk.
Berry	A fleshy indehiscent fruit with two or more seeds, e.g. Hawthorn, Elderberry.
Biennial	A plant which takes two years to complete its life cycle, usually growing in the first year and flowering in the second, e.g. Scottish Primula, Wild Pansy.
Blade	The flat part of the leaf (also lamina).
Bract	Small leaf-like structures just below the flower.
Bulb	An underground storage organ, of fleshy scales, enclosing next year's bud.
Bulbils	Small bulbs which grow in axils, e.g. Drooping Saxifrage, or among florets, e.g. Crow Garlic.
Calyx	The collective term for the sepals which enclose the flower bud.
Capsule	A dry dehiscent fruit, composed of more than one carpel.
Carpel	The female reproductive organ of flowering plants, comprising ovary, style and stigma.
Chlorophyll	The green colouring matter manufactured in leaves.
Cleistogamy	Self-pollination of an unopened flower, e.g. Violet family.
Column	The fused style and stigma, e.g. Orchids.
Coniferous	Those trees and shrubs bearing cones and evergreen leaves.
Corolla	The collective name for the petals of a flower.
Cotyledon	A leaf or pair of leaves present within a seed.
Deciduous	Those trees and shrubs which shed their leaves every autumn.
Dehiscence	The spontaneous splitting open of ripe seed containers to release seeds.
Dicotyledons	Plants of one of the two groups to which flowering plants belong, with two seed leaves and usually broad, net-veined and stalked mature leaves.
Dioecious	Having the male and female organs in separate flowers on separate plants.
Disc-florets	Small fertile flowers packed into the disc-shaped centre of composite flowers.
Drupe	A fleshy fruit with the seed encased in a hard cover, e.g. plum.
Endemic	A plant which is native only in one country or region.
Filament	The stalk to which is attached the male anther.
Floret	Each individual flower within a compound head of flowers.
Flower	The complete reproductive organs of a plant.
Fruit	A general term to describe the ripe ovary of a plant, i.e. the seeds and the structures which enclose them.
Hermaphrodite	A flower which has both functional stamens and ovary.
Hybrid	A plant resulting from the fertilization of one species by another.
Inflorescence	The part of a plant that consists of the flower-bearing stalks, such as a panicle, spike or umbel, etc.
Lamina	The flat part of a leaf (also blade).
Leaf	The blade-like structure of a plant, generally green, primarily concerned in food production for the plant by photosynthesis.
Midrib	The central and main vein of a leaf.
Monocarpic	Those plants which die after the first fruits are produced.

Monocotyledons	Plants of the second of the two groups to which plants belong, with one seed leaf and mature leaves usually narrow, unstalked and nearly always parallel-veined.
Monoecious	Having the male and female organs in separate flowers on the same plant.
Mycorrhiza	The symbiotic association of a fungus and the roots of certain plants, e.g. orchids.
Native	A plant which has not been introduced by man.
Nectar	The sugary substance secreted by many flowers to attract insects. The basic material of honey.
Node	The point on a stem from which leaves grow.
Ovary	The hollow region at the base of a carpel containing one or more ovules.
Ovule	The structure in the ovary containing the egg, which develops into the seed after fertilization.
Panicle	A branched compound raceme of flowers.
Pappus	A ring of fine feathery hairs surrounding the fruit in composite plants.
Pedicel	The stalk bearing a single flower of an inflorescence.
Peduncle	The stalk bearing an inflorescence or solitary flower.
Perennial	A plant which lives for more than two years and usually flowers every year.
Perianth	The floral envelope round a flower, consisting of the calyx and corolla.
Petal	The usually colourful and conspicuous separate parts which make up the corolla.
Petiole	The stalk of a leaf.
Photosynthesis	The process by which green plants make sugar from carbon dioxide and water using light energy absorbed by chlorophyll.
Pistil	The female reproductive organ.
Pod	The long cylindrical fruit of a plant, e.g. the Pea family.
Pollen	The microspores produced by the anthers of a flowering plant.
Pollinium	A fused mass of pollen grains.
Pome	A fruit where the seeds are contained in a tough but not stony covering, the whole encased in a large fleshy receptacle, e.g. apple.
Raceme	An unbranched inflorescence, with a main stem with single flowers arranged alternately or spirally on pedicels of about the same length.
Radical	Those leaves which arise from the base only of a plant.
Ray florets	The flowers which surround the disc florets and which usually have a long strap-shaped petal, e.g. Corn Marigold.
Rhizome	A horizontal underground stem which lives on from one year to the next and produces roots and stems, e.g. Yellow Iris.
Rosette	The radiating circular cluster of basal leaves.
Runners	Horizontal above-ground stems (also stolons) which often produce roots.
Saprophyte	A plant which obtains nutriment from decaying vegetation.
Sepal	An individual segment of the calyx.
Sessile	Lacking a stalk, e.g. leaves without petioles.
Spathe	A bract that encloses an inflorescence.
Stamen	The male organ of a flower, consisting of a filament (stalk) bearing an anther.
Stigma	The tip of the style which receives the pollen.
Stolon	Horizontal above-ground stem (also runner).
Style	The column connecting the ovary and the stigma.
Taproot	A large single vertical root which bears smaller lateral roots.
Umbel	A type of inflorescence which is flat topped or umbrella-shaped.

BIBLIOGRAPHY

Allan, M. *The Gardener's Book of Weeds* Macdonald and Jane's, London 1978
Blamey, M., Fitter, A. and Fitter, R. *The Wild Flowers of Britain and Northern Europe* Collins, London 1974
Blamey, M. and Grey-Wilson, C. *The Alpine Flowers of Britain and Europe* Collins, London 1979
Blunt, W. *The Art of Botanical Illustration* Collins New Naturalist Series, London 1950
Clapham, A. R. etc. *Flora of the British Isles* Cambridge University Press, Cambridge 1962
Coats, A. M. *Flowers and Their Histories* A & C Black, London 1968
Craig, S. Ross- *Drawings of British Plants* 9 vols, Bell, London 1974
Culpeper, Nicholas *Complete Herbal* Foulsham, Slough 1952
Danesch, O. and E. *Orchideen Europas – Südeuropa* Hallwag, Berne
Danesch, O. and E. *Orchideen Europas – Mitteleuropa* Hallwag, Berne
Duddington, C. L. *Beginner's Guide to Botany* Pelham Books, London 1970
Ellis, E. A. *Jarrolds Nature Series* Jarrold, Norwich 1971–76
Ettlinger, D. M. T. *British and Irish Orchids* Macmillan, London 1976
Fitter, A. *Atlas of the Wild Flowers of Britain and Northern Europe* Collins, London 1978
Genders, R. *Scented Wild Flowers of Britain* Collins, London 1971
Gilmour, J. S. L. and Walters, M. *Wild Flowers* Collins New Naturalist Series, London 1973; Fontana, London 1972
Greenoak, F. *Wild Flowers* Macdonald Guidelines, London 1977
Grigson, G. *A Dictionary of English Plant Names* Allen Lane, London 1974
Grigson, G. *The Englishman's Flora* Hart-Davis, London 1975; Paladin, London 1975
Hepburn, I. *Flowers of the Coast* Collins New Naturalist Series, London 1952
Heywood, V. H. *Flowering Plants of the World* Oxford University Press, Oxford 1978
Huxley, A. J. *Plant and Planet* Allen Lane, London 1974
Hyde, M. *Hedgerow Plants: The History, Identification, Usage and Folklore of Wayside Flowers, Grasses and Trees* Shire, Princes Risborough 1976
Lousley, J. E. *Wild Flowers of Chalk and Limestone* Collins New Naturalist Series, London 1969
Mabey, R. *Street Flowers* Kestrel Books, London 1976
Mabey, R. *Roadside Wild Life Book* Sphere, London 1978
Mabey, R. *Food for Free: A Guide to the Edible Wild Plants of Britain* Collins, London 1972; Fontana, London 1975
Mabey, R. *Plants with a Purpose* Collins, London 1977; Fontana, London 1979
Prime, C. T. *Plant Life* Collins, London 1977
Parkinson, John *A Garden of Pleasant Flowers* London 1629
Proctor, M. and Yeo, P. *The Pollination of Flowers* Collins New Naturalist Series, London 1972
Salisbury, Sir Edward *Weeds and Aliens* Collins New Naturalist Series, London 1961
Summerhayes, V. S. *The Wild Orchids of Britain* Collins New Naturalist Series, London 1968
Turrill, W. B. *British Plant Life* Collins New Naturalist Series, London 1948
Tutin, T. G. etc. (Ed.) *Flora Europaea* Cambridge University Press, Cambridge 1964–76
Walters, M. and Raven, J. *Mountain Flowers* Collins New Naturalist Series, London 1956

INDEX

*Figures in italics
denote illustrations*
Aceras anthropophorum. See
  Man Orchid
Achillea millefolium. See
  Yarrow
  ptarmica. See Sneezewort
Aconitum napellus. See
  Monkshood
  vulparia. See Wolfsbane
Acorn, *65*, 65, *66*, *70*, 71
Actaea spicata. See Baneberry
Adonis annua, *101*.See also
  Pheasant's-eye
Aegopodium podagraria. See
  Ground Elder
Aethusa cynapium. See Fool's
  Parsley
Agrimonia eupatoria. See
  Agrimony
Agrimony, *158*, 158
Ajuga reptans. See Bugle
Alcea rosea. See Hollyhock
Alder, 71, 78, 131
  catkins, *70*, 71
Alder Buckthorn, 52
Alexanders, 55, 129, 177, *178*
Allium carinatum. See Keeled
  Garlic
  schoenoprasum. See Chives
  scorodoprasum. See Sand Leek
  triquetrum. See Three-
    cornered Leek
  ursinum. See Ramsons
  vineale. See Crow Garlic
Alpine Bistort, 140
Alpine Cinquefoil, 140
Alpine Clematis, *85*, 85
*Alpine Flowers of Britain and
  Europe*, 86, 108, 143
Alpine garden, 76, 77, 78
Alpine Gentian, 117, *119*, 120
Alpine Lady's Mantle, *25*, 77,
  140, 140
Alpine Snowbell, *85*, 87
Alpine Sow-thistle, 117, 121,
  122
Alpine Willowherb, *174*, 175
Alpine Woodsia, 117
Althaea officinalis. See Marsh
  Mallow
American Willowherb, 174
Amphibious Bistort, 131
Anacamptis pyramidalis. See
  Pyramid Orchid
Anagallis arvensis. See Scarlet
  Pimpernel
  tenella. See Bog Pimpernel
Anemone apennina. See Blue
  Anemone
  hepatica. See Hepatica
  nemorosa. See Wood
    Anemone
Angelica, 56
Angleshades caterpillar, 43

Annual Seablite, 130
Annual Wall Rocket, 133,
  157, 157
Anthriscus cerefolium. See
  Garden Chervil
  sylvestris. See Cow Parsley
Anthyllis vulneraria. See
  Kidney Vetch
Apple, 66
Aquilegia vulgaris. See
  Columbine
Arrowhead, 27, 80, 130, *131*
Ash, 78, 137
Atropa bella-donna. See Deadly
  Nightshade
Autumn Crocus, 73
Autumn Lady's Tresses, 132,
  203, 203, *212*, 212
Autumn Squill, 129

Baneberry, 52
Barren Strawberry, 46, 137,
  159, 159
Basil, 84
Bastard Balm, 28, 73, *189*,
  189
Bauer, Ferdinand, 17
  Francis, 17
Beaked Hawksbeard, *47*, 47
Bearded Bellflower, *86*, 87
Bedstraws, 63, 94, 128, 133,
  139, *185*, 185
Bee Orchid, 30, 41, *132*, 202,
  203, 205, 206, *207*
Beech, 66, 78, 94, *95*, 96, 135,
  137
Bell Heather, 138, *179*, 179
Bellflowers, *41*, 84, 86, 87,
  132, 137, 193, *194*
Bellis perennis. See Daisy
Bents Grass, 94
Beta vulgaris, 54
Betonica officinalis. See Betony
Betony, *188*, 188
Betula pendula. See Silver
  Birch
Bilberry, *57*, 57, *70*, 71, 137,
  139
Bindweeds, 28, 40, 45, *46*, *98*,
  106, *126*, 126, 127, *183*, 183,
  184
Birch, 138
  Silver, *65*, 66, 74, 79, 94
Birds. See individual entries
Birdseye Primrose, 28, 77,
  181, 181
Birdsfoot Trefoil, 62, 128,
  129, 133, 163
Birdsnest Orchid, 137, *202*,
  204
Biting Stonecrop, 127, 128,
  157, 157
Bitter Vetchling, *164*, 164
Bittercresses, *37*, 134, *157*,
  157

Bittersweet, 46, *52*, 52, 127,
  190, 190
Black Bryony, *52*, 52, 173,
  200, 200
Black Currant, *57*, 58
Black Mustard, *40*, 40, 95
Black Nightshade, 52
Blackberry, 35, *37*, *57*, 57, 64,
  96
Blackbird, 66
Blackthorn, 58, *162*, 162
Bladder Campion, *147*, 147
Bladderworts, *48*, 49
Blood-drop Emlets, 81
Bloody Cranesbill, 137, *166*,
  167
Blue Anemone, *85*, 85
Blue Woodruff, *39*, 39
Bluebell, 68, 78, 94, 96, 129,
  137
Bog Asphodel, 33, *138*, 139
Bog Myrtle, 68, 139
Bog Orchid, *138*, 139
Bog Pimpernel, 139, *181*, 181
Bog Pondweed, 139
Bog Rosemary, *138*, 139
Bogbean, 80, *182*, 182
Borages, 73, *83*, 83, *186*, 186
Borago officinalis. See Borage
Botanical Magazine, 14, 17
Botanists, 13, 14
Bracken, *70*, 71, 139
Bramble, 62, 135
Brandy Bottle. See Yellow
  Water-lily
Brassica oleracea. See Wild
  Cabbage
Bridewort. See Meadowsweet
Brimstone Butterfly, 61
British Pharmacopoeia, 201
Broad-leaved Dock, 45
Broad-leaved Helleborine,
  202, 213
Brooklime, 130, *191*, 191
Broom, *164*, 164
Broomrape, *49*, 51, 77
Bryonia alba, 173
  cretica. See White Bryony
Bryony, 94
Buckshorn Plantain, *126*, 126
Buckthorns, 52, 60, 168, *169*
Buddleia, 62
Bug Balm. See Bastard Balm
Bugle, *187*, 187
Bulbous Buttercup, *151*, 151
Bullace, *53*, 58
Bullfinch, 66
Burdock, 64, 66, 134
Burnet Rose, 96, 128, 160,
  161
Burnt Orchid, 28, *132*, 202,
  210, 210
Burnt-tip Orchid. See Burnt
  Orchid
Burr, 36

Butcher's Broom, 26, *27*
Butterbur, 130
Buttercups, 19, 22, 27, 28, 36,
  37, *46*, 52, 74, 89, 94, *132*,
  132, 149–53
Butterflies. See individual
  entries
Butterfly Orchids, 30, 41, 77,
  111, 132, *202*, 208, *209*
Butterworts, 28, *48*, 48, 139
Buttonhole Flower. See
  Spring Beauty

Cabbages, 53, 118, 128, *156*,
  156, *157*
Cakile maritima. See Sea
  Rocket
Calluna vulgaris. See Heather
Caltha palustris. See Marsh
  Marigold
Calystegia soldanella. See Sea
  Bindweed
  sylvatica. See Great
    Bindweed
Camomile, 77, 84
Campanula barbata. See
  Bearded Bellflower
  cochlearifolia, *86*, 87
  glomerata. See Clustered
    Bellflower
  patula. See Spreading
    Bellflower
  rotundifolia. See Harebell
  trachelium. See Nettle-leaved
    Bellflower
Campions, 62, 94, *95*, 126,
  128, 140, *146*, 146, *147*,
  147
Canadian Fleabane, *47*, 47
Cannabis sativa, 145
Caper Spurge, *168*, 168
Cardamine amara. See Large
  Bittercress
  hirsuta. See Hairy Bittercress
  pratensis. See Cuckoo Flower
Carduus nutans. See Musk
  Thistle
Carline Thistle, 77, 96
Carrot family, 28, 176–78
Caterpillars. See individual
  entries
Celandine, 46, 78
  Lesser, 136, 137, *151*, 151
Centaurium erythraea. See
  Common Centaury
Cephalanthera damasonium. See
  White Helleborine
  rubra. See Red Helleborine
Cerastium fontanum. See
  Common Mouse-ear
Changing Forgetmenot, *186*,
  186
Charlock, 40, *40*, 45, *65*, 66
Cheddar Pink, 117, *122*, 122,
  148

Cherries, 35, 37, 58, 65, 66, 162
Chickweeds, 19, 30, 40, 45, 52, 55, *146*, 146
Chickweed Wintergreen, 138
Chicory, *198*, 198
Children and Flowers, 88–90
Chiltern Gentian, 133
Chinery, Michael, 43
Chives, *83*, 83, 84, 199
Cicerbita alpina. See Alpine Sow-thistle
Cichorium intybus. See Chicory
Cicuta virosa. See Cowbane
Cinnebar caterpillar, 42, 45, *64*, 64
moth, *64*
Cinquefoils, 40, *40*, 131, 140, *158*, 158, *159*, 159
Circaea lutetiana. See Enchanter's Nightshade
Cirsium arvense. See Creeping Thistle
vulgare. See Spear Thistle
Clematis, 28, *85*, 85, 94, 95. See also Traveller's Joy
Clematis alpina. See Alpine Clematis
vitalba. See Traveller's Joy
Cloudberry, *57*, 57
Clouded Yellow caterpillar, 61
Clove-scented Broomrape, *49*
Clove Scented Pink, 56, 67, *148*, 148
Clovers, *25*, 61, 74, 128, 132, 164, *165*
Clusius, 13
Clustered Bellflower, 193, *194*
Cochlearia officinalis. See Common Scurvy-grass
Cocksfoot Grass, 94
Codex Vindobonensis, 15
Coeloglossum viride. See Frog Orchid
Colchicum autumnale. See Meadow Saffron
Colour sense, 99–101
Coltsfoot, *38*, 46, 134, 196
Columbine, 52, *152*, 153
Comma butterfly, 44, 61
Common Blue butterfly, 61, *62*
Common Butterwort, 28, *48*, 48, 139
Common Centaury, *127*, 128, *182*, 182
Common Chickweed, 30, 45, 55, *146*, 146
Common Cleavers, 36, *37*, 185, *185*
Common Comfrey, *53*, 55, 131
Common Cow-wheat, 139
Common Dog Violet, 128, 137, *172*, 172
Common Duckweed, 134

Common Field Speedwell, 46, *47*, 47, *191*, 191
Common Fleabane, *196*, 196
Common Fumitory, *154*, 155
Common Hemp-nettle, *188*, 188
Common Mallow, *170*, 170
Common Meadow-rue, 130
Common Mouse-ear, *146*, 146
Common Poppy, *100*, *154*, 155
Common Rock-rose, 133
Common St John's Wort, 133, *171*, 171
Common Scurvy-grass, 128, *156*, 156
Common Spotted Orchid, 15, *28*, 210, *211*
Common Storksbill, *127*, 127, 128, 129
Common Toadflax, *191*, 191
Common Twayblade, *202*, 205, 208, *209*
Common Water Crowfoot, 130, 131, *150*, 150
Common Wintergreen, 138, *179*, 179
Conium maculatum. See Hemlock
Conservation, 113–117
Convallaria majalis. See Lily of the Valley
Convolvulus arvensis. See Field Bindweed
Convolvulus Hawkmoth, 63
Coral-root Orchid, 138, *202*, 204
Corn Cockle, *39*, 39, 47, 118
Corn Marigold, *39*, 39
Corn Mint, 67
Corn Parsley, 118, 176
Cornfield Weeds, 39
Cornflower, *39*, 39, *41*, 41, 47
Cornish Heath, 179
Cotton-grass, 139
Couch Grass, 94
Cow Parsley, 30, 56, 94, *177*, 177
Cowbane, 52
Cowberry, *57*, 57, 139
Cowslip, 14, *28*, 38, 73, 133, *180*, 180
Crab Apple, 36, *37*, *53*, 58
Cranberry, *57*, 57, *138*, 138, 139
Cranesbills, 73, 75, *107*, 137, *166*, *167*, 167
Crataegus monogyna. See Hawthorn
Creeping Bellflower, *41*
Creeping Buttercup, *151*, 151
Creeping Cinquefoil, 40, *40*, *159*, 159
Creeping Jenny, 135, *181*, 181
Creeping Lady's Tresses, 138, *203*, 203, *212*, 213
Creeping Thistle, *42*, 44, 45, 128, 197

Creeping Willow, 128
Crimson Clover, 165
Crocus, 65, 75, 79
Cross-leaved Heath, 138, *179*, 179
Crow Garlic, *199*, 199
Crowberry, *65*
Cruydeboek, 13
Cuckoo Flower (Lady's Smock), 60, 61, 73, 74, 131, *157*, 157
Culpeper, Nicholas, 43, 188, 190, 193
Curled Dock, *42*, 42, 43, 45, 127, 134
Curtis, William, 14, 198
Cut leaved Cranesbill, *167*, 167
Cyclamen, *25*, *28*, *72*, 72, 78, 79
Cymbalaria muralis. See Ivy-leaved Toadflax
Cypripedium calceolus. See Lady's Slipper Orchid
Cytisus scoparius. See Broom

Dactylorhiza fuchsii. See Common Spotted Orchid
maculata. See Heath Spotted Orchid
Daffodils, 65, 74, *75*, 75, 78, *201*, 201
Daisies, 19, 30, 36, *38*, *46*, 62, 74, 94, 97, *102*, *132*, 132, *195*, 195–198
Daisy, *38*, 97, *195*, 195
Dame's Violet, 73
Dandelion, 12, 45, *46*, 52, 54, 64, 128, *132*, 132, *133*, 134
Dane's Blood. See Clustered Bellflower
Daphne family, 52, 73, 168
Daphne laureola. See Spurge Laurel
mezereum, 73. See also Mezereon
Dark Mullein, 133, 135
Dark Red Helleborine, *213*, 213
Darnel Rye-grass, 52
Darwin, Charles, 23, 32, 34
Datura stramonium. See Thorn-apple
Daucus carota. See Wild Carrot
Deadly Nightshade, 51, *52*, *190*, 190
Dead-nettles, *189*, 189
De Materia Medica, 11, 15
Deptford Pink, *148*, 148
Devil's Guts. See Field Bindweed
Devilsbit Scabious, *193*, 193
Dianthus armeria. See Deptford Pink
caryophyllus. See Clove Scented Pink
deltoides. See Maiden Pink

gratianopolitanus. See Cheddar Pink
plumarius. See Wild Pink
Diapensia, 117, *119*, 121
Diapensia lapponica. See Diapensia
Digitalis purpurea. See Foxglove
Dill, 84
Dioscorides, 11, 12, 15, 158, 159, 162, 198, 201
Diplotaxis muralis. See Annual Wall Rocket
Dipper, 82
Dipsacus fullonum. See Teasel
Docks, 40, *42*, 42, 45, 64, 127, 130, 134, 145
Dodder, *49*, 51
Dodonaeus, 13
Dog Rose, 57, 96, *160*, 160
Dog's Mercury, 34, 52, 69, *136*, 136, 137
Dog's Tooth Violet, *85*, 87
Dog violets, 128, 137, *172*, 172
Dogwood, 96
Dormouse, *65*, 65, 66
Dorset Heath, 179
Dovesfoot Cranesbill, *167*, 167
Downy Rose, 57, 160, *161*
Dragonflies, 82
Drying flowers, 94–7
Drooping Saxifrage, 117, *119*
Dropwort, 133
Duckweed, 134
Dune Helleborine, 128
Dürer, Albrecht, 16
Durmast Oak, *136*, 137
Dusky Cranesbill, 75, *166*, 167
Dutch Elm disease, 115
Dwarf Gorse, 138
Dwarf Mallow, *170*, 170
Dwarf Pansy, 103, 128, *172*, 172, 186
Dyes, 70, 71, 186

Early Dog Violet, 137
Early Forgetmenot, *127*, 127, 128, *186*, 186
Early Gentian, 133
Early Marsh Orchid, 131
Early Purple Orchid, *75*, 75, 132, 203, *211*, 211
Early Spider Orchid, 206, *207*
Eglantine. See Sweet Briar
Ehret, Georg, 16, 17
Elder, 58
-berry, *57*, 58, 96
Elephant Hawkmoth, *46*, 46, 61, 62, 147, 174
Emperor Moth caterpillar, *60*, 62
Enchanter's Nightshade, 36, *175*, 175
Endangered Species, 117, 118–124, *119*

218

English Stonecrop, 25, 129, *157*, 157
Epilobium adenocaulon. See American Willowherb
anagallidifolium. See Alpine Willowherb
angustifolium. See Rosebay Willowherb
brunnescens. See New Zealand Willowherb
Epipactis atrorubens. See Dark Red Helleborine
helleborine. See Broad-leaved Helleborine
palustris. See Marsh Helleborine
purpurata. See Violet Helleborine
Epipogium aphyllum. See Ghost Orchid
Eranthis hyemalis. See Winter Aconite
Erica ciliaris. See Dorset Heath
cinerea. See Bell Heather
tetralix. See Cross-leaved Heath
vagans. See Cornish Heath
Ermine caterpillar, 43
Eryngium maritimum. See Sea Holly
Erythronium dens-canis. See Dog's Tooth Violet
Estuaries, 129
Eucalyptus, 97
Euonymus europaeus. See Spindle-tree
Euphorbia helioscopia. See Sun Spurge
lathyrus. See Caper Spurge
European Favourites, 85, 86
European Weeds, 41
Extinct Species, 115
Eyebright, 49, 50, 128

Fairy Moss, 81
Fairy's Thimble. See *Campanula cochlearifolia*
False Oxlip, 180
Fat Hen, 38, 40, *53*, 54, 134
Fen Violet, 131
Fenlands, 130, 131
Fennel, 56, *83*, 84, 129
Fennel Pondweed, 131
Fertilization, 34, 69
Feverfew, 19, 46, *195*, 195
Field Bindweed, 28, 40, 45, *46*, 98, 183, *184*
Field Cow-wheat, *39*, 39, 49, 50, 118
Fieldfare, 66
Field Forgetmenot, *40*, 40
Field Gentian, *182*, 182
Field Maple, 96
Field Pansy, *172*, 172
Field Pennycress, 22, *37*, 38
Field Rose, *57*, 160, *161*
Field Scabious, *193*, 193

Figworts, 95, 191
Filing system, 109
Filipendula ulmaria. See Meadowsweet
Fine-leaved Water Dropwort, 52
Fitch, Walter, 17
Five Hundred Points of Husbandry, 42
Flanders Poppy. See Common Poppy
Flaxes, 75, 135, *165*, 165
Fleabanes, 47, 47, *196*, 196
Flora Londinensis, 14, 198
Flower Arranging, 90
Flowering Rush, 64, *79*, 80, 130
Flowers, 28–34. See also individual entries
Fly Orchid, *202*, 206, *207*
Foam Poppy. See Sea Campion
Food Chain, 113
Food plants, 53–66
Fool's Parsley, *51*, 51–52, 56, 176
Forests, 115
Forgetmenots, 36, 40, *40*, 62, 66, 81, 97, *127*, 127, 128, 130, *131*, 137, *186*, 186
Foxglove, *28*, 46, 52, 78, 94, *136*, 137, 191
Fragaria vesca. See Wild Strawberry
Fragrant Evening Primrose, 118
Fragrant Orchid, 69, *202*, 203, *211*, 211
Frangula alnus. See Alder Buckthorn
French Cranesbill, *167*, 167
Fritillaria meleagris. See Fritillary
Fritillary, 52, 96
Fritillary butterfly, 61
Frog Orchid, 206, *207*
Frogbit, 131
Fruits, 35, 36, *37*, *57*, 58
Fuchs, Leonard, 15
Fumaria officinalis. See Common Fumitory
Fumitory family, *154*, 155

Galanthus nivalis. See Snowdrop
Galeopsis bifida, *188*, 189
Galeopsis speciosa. See Large-flowered Hemp-nettle
tetrahit. See Common Hemp-nettle
Galinsoga ciliata. See Shaggy Soldier
parviflora. See Gallant Soldier
Galium aparine. See Common Cleavers
odoratum. See Woodruff
saxatile. See Heath Bedstraw

verum. See Lady's Bedstraw
Gallant Soldier, *47*, 47
Garden Chervil, 177
Garden Tiger caterpillar, 64
Garden Weeds, 46
Garlic Mustard, 54
Garlics, *199*, 199
Gatekeeper butterfly, 64
Gentians, 28, *85*, 86, 97, 117, 118, *119*, 120, 133, *182*, 182
Gentiana acaulis. See Trumpet Gentian
lutea. See Great Yellow Gentian
nivalis. See Alpine Gentian
pneumonanthe. See Marsh Gentian
verna. See Spring Gentian
Gentianella campestris. See Field Gentian
Geranium family, 36, 167
Geranium columbinum. See Longstalked Cranesbill
dissectum. See Cut-leaved Cranesbill
endressii. See French Cranesbill
lucidum. See Shining Cranesbill
molle. See Dovesfoot Cranesbill
phaeum. See Dusky Cranesbill
pratense. See Meadow Cranesbill
pyrenaicum. See Hedgerow Cranesbill
robertianum. See Herb Robert
sanguineum. See Bloody Cranesbill
versicolor. See Pencilled Cranesbill
Gerard, John, 13, 148, 153, 157, 158, 167, 172, 185, 188, 192, 199, 200
Germander Speedwell, 28, *191*, 191
Geum rivale. See Water Avens
urbanum. See Herb Bennet
Ghost Orchid, 117, *123*, 123, 204
Giant Hogweed, 176
Gipsywort, 130
Gladiolus illyricus. See Wild Gladiolus
Glasswort, *53*, *130*, 130
Glaucium flavum. See Yellow Horned-poppy
Glechoma hederacea. See Ground Ivy
Globe Flower, 80, *150*, 150
Goatsbeard, *198*, 198
Golden Samphire, 128, *129*
Golden-rod, 134, 137
Goldfinch, *65*, 66
Good King Henry, 40, *53*, 55
Goodyera repens. See Creeping Lady's Tresses

Gooseberry, 35, *37*, *57*, 58
Goosefoots, 69, 145
Goosegrass. See Common Cleavers
Gordon, Seton, 121
Gorse, 26, 51, 68, 129, 138, 139, *164*, 164
Gourd family, 173
Grasses, 94, *95*, 127
Grass of Parnassus, 28, *131*, 131
Grassland, 132, 133
Grass snake, 82
Great Bindweed, *106*, 183, *184*
Great Tit, 88
Great Willowherb, *62*
Great Yellow Gentian, 182
Greater Butterfly Orchid, 77, *111*, *202*, 208, *209*
Greater Knapweed, 133
Greater Meadow-rue, *28*
Greater Stitchwort, *146*, 146
Green Alkanet, *186*, 186
Green Helleborine, 52, 78, 97, 136, *149*, 149
Green Sandpiper, 82
Greenfinch, 66
Green-winged Orchid, 132
Grew, Nehemiah, 23
Grey Wagtail, 82
Ground Elder, 45, 176
Ground Ivy, 137, *187*, 187
Groundsel, 38, 40, 45, *46*, 134
Guelder Rose, *65*, 66, *192*, 192
Gymnadenia conopsea. See Fragrant Orchid
odoratissima. See Short-spurred Fragrant Orchid

Habitats, 125–140
Hairy Bittercress, *37*, *157*, 157
Hairy St John's Wort, 137
Hairy Tare, *40*, 40, 163
Hairy Violet, 133
Halimione portulacoides. See Sea Purslane
Harebell, 133, *138*, 139, *143*, 193
Haresfoot Clover, 164, *165*
Harestail Grass, 94, *95*
Hawkweeds, 46, 128, *198*, 198
Hawthorn, 18, 58, *65*, 66, 67, 69, 78, *162*, 162
Hazel, *33*, 33, 34, 65, 78, 88, 94, 107
nuts, *57*, 53, 59, *65*, 65, 66
Heartsease. See Wild Pansy
Heaths, 117, *119*, 120, 138, *179*, 179
Heath Bedstraw, 128, 133, 139, *185*, 185
Heath Dog Violet, *172*, 173
Heath Lobelia, 97, 193, *194*
Heath Milkwort, 128, 138
Heath Spotted Orchid, 34, 77, 139, *202*, 210

219

Heather, *49*, 51, *60*, 71, 137, 138, 139, *179*
Heathland, 138
Hedera helix. See Ivy
Hedge Mustard, 134, *156*, 156
Hedge Parsley, 64
Hedge Woundwort, *188*, 188
Hedgerows, 135
Hedgerow Cranesbill, *167*, 167
Hellebores, 52, 69, 78, 97, 136, *149*, 149
Helleborines, 41, *111*, 117, *123*, 123, 128, 131, 137, *202*, *203*, 203, 204, *212*, 212, *213*, 213
Helleborus foetidus. See Stinking Hellebore
viridus. See Green Hellebore
Hemlock, *51*, 52, 56, 69, 176
Hemp family, 145
Hemp Agrimony, 62
Hemp-nettles, *28*, *188*, 188
Henbane, 12, *51*, 52, 69
Henbit Dead-nettle, *189*, 189
Hepatica, *85*, 86
Hepatica nobilis. See Hepatica
triloba. See Hepatica
Heracleum mantegazzianum. See Giant Hogweed
Herb Bennet, 137, *158*, 158
Herb Paris, *136*, 137
Herb Robert, *46*, 135, *167*, 167
Herbals, 13, 16
Herbs and Spices, 56, 83
Hieracium umbellatum. See Leafy Hawkweed
Himalayan Balsam, *47*, 47, 130
Himantoglossum hircinum. See Lizard Orchid
Hippocrepis comosa. See Horseshoe Vetch
Hippophae rhamnoides. See Sea Buckthorn
Historia Naturalis, 11
Hogweeds, 28, 176
Holly, 26, *27*, 64, *65*, 66
Holly Blue butterfly, 64
Hollyhock, 170
Honeysuckles, 62, *63*, 68, 78, 135, 192
Hop, 94, 132, *144*, 145
Hornbeam, 97
Horse Hoeing Husbandry, 42
Horseradish, 54, 134
Horseshoe Vetch, *163*, 163
Hottentot Fig, *25*
Hottonia palustris. See Water Violet
Humming-bird Hawkmoth, 63
Humulus lupulus. See Hop
Huxley, Anthony, 33
Hydrocotyle vulgaris. See Marsh Pennywort
Hyoscyamus niger. See Henbane

Hypericum androsaemum. See Tutsan
elodes. See Marsh St John's Wort
perforatum. See Perforate St John's Wort
pulchrum. See Slender St John's Wort

Iceplant, 62–63
Illustrators, 15–17
Intermediate Wintergreen, 138
Irises, *79*, 79, 80, 81, 95, 128, 131, *201*, 201
Iris foetidissima. See Stinking Iris
kaempferi, 81
laevigata, 81
pseudacorus. See Yellow Iris
Irish Lady's Tresses, 212
Isle of Man Cabbage, 118
Ivy, 52, 64, *65*, 66, 94, *136*, 137
Ivy-leaved Bellflower, *193*, *194*
Ivy-leaved Speedwell, *40*, 40
Ivy-leaved Toadflax, *28*, *133*, 134, *191*, 191

Jack-by-the-hedge, 60, *62*. See also Garlic Mustard
Jack-go-to-bed-at-noon. See Goatsbeard
Jasione montana. See Sheepsbit Scabious
Johnson, Thomas, 158

Keeled Garlic, *199*, 199
Kidney Vetch, *45*, 129, *163*, 163
Killarney Fern, 117
Kingcup. See Marsh Marigold
Kingfisher, 82
Knapweeds, 62, 95, 133
Knautia arvensis. See Field Scabious
Knotgrass, 40, 126, *144*, 145

Labiate family, 187–189
Laburnum, 52
Lady Orchid, *28*, *202*, 210
Lady's Bedstraw, 63, 94, 128, *185*, 185
Lady's Mantle, *25*, 94
Lady's Slipper Orchid, 20, 117, 118, *123*, 123, 203, 204
Lady's Smock, *60*, 61, 132, 157. See also Cuckoo Flower
Lady's Tresses, 132, 138, *203*, 203, *212*, 212, 213
Lamiastrum galeobdolon. See Yellow Archangel
Lamium album. See White Dead-nettle
amplexicaule. See Henbit Dead-nettle

purpureum. See Red Dead-nettle
Larch, 74, 78
Large Bittercress, *157*, 157
Large Blue butterfly, *114*, 114
Large-flowered Butterwort, *28*, 48
Large-flowered Evening Primrose, *175*, 175
Large-flowered Hemp-nettle, *28*, 188
Large Quaking-grass, 94, *95*
Late Spider Orchid, 206, *207*
Lathyrus montanus. See Bitter Vetchling
pratensis. See Meadow Vetchling
Lavender, 62
Leafy Hawkweed, *198*, 198
Least Lettuce, 118
Leaves, *25*, 25, *26*, 26, *27*, 27
Lemon Balm, 83
Lesser Butterfly Orchid, *202*, 208
Lesser Celandine, 136, 137, *151*, 151
Lesser Periwinkle, *182*, 182
Lesser Spearwort, *150*, 150
Lesser Twayblade, *202*, 208
Leucojum aestivum. See Summer Snowflake
vernum. See Spring Snowflake
Lichens, 71, *113*
Ligustrum vulgare. See Wild Privet
Lilium martagon. See Martagon Lily
pyrenaicum. See Yellow Turk's-cap
Lilies, 65, *85*, 87, 117, *119*, 121, 199, 201
Lily of the Valley, 52, 68, 72, 78, 137, *201*, 201
Lime, 61
Lime Hawkmoth, 62, *63*
Linaria vulgaris. See Common Toadflax
Ling. See Heather
Linnaea borealis. See Twinflower
Linnaean system, 14–15
Linnaeus, 14, 23, 191, 192, 195
Linum bienne. See Pale Flax
perenne. See Perennial Flax
Listera cordata. See Lesser Twayblade
ovata. See Common Twayblade
Little Mouse-ear, 127
Lizard Orchid, 41, *202*, *203*, 203, 205, 208, *209*
Lloydia serotina. See Snowdon Lily
L'Obel, Matthias de, 155
Lobelias, 87, 97, 193, *194*
Lobelia urens. See Heath Lobelia

Lolium temulentum. See Darnel Rye-grass
Long-headed Poppy, *154*, 155
Longstalked Cranesbill, *107*, *167*, 167
Lords and Ladies, *32*, 32, *52*, 52, 135
Lotus corniculatus. See Birdsfoot Trefoil
Lousewort, *191*, 191
Love in a Mist, 73, 96, 97
Lungwort, *25*
Lychnis floscuculi. See Ragged Robin
Lysimachia nummularia. See Creeping Jenny
Lyte, Henry, 13, 190

Mabey, Richard, 43, 89, 90
Madagascan Orchid, 32
Maiden Pink, *28*, 28, *148*, 148
Mallows, 64, 128, *170*, 170
Malva moschata. See Musk Mallow
neglecta. See Dwarf Mallow
sylvestris. See Common Mallow
Man Orchid, 208, *209*
Mandrake. See White Bryony
Maple, 36, 97
Marigolds, *39*, 39, 83
Marjoram, 56, 68, *83*, 83
Marram Grass, 127
Marsh Cinquefoil, 131, *158*, 158
Marsh Felwort, 132
Marsh Gentian, *28*, *182*, 182
Marsh Helleborine, 131, *213*
Marsh Mallow, 170
Marsh Marigold, 27, 72, 79, 80, 132, *150*, 150
Marsh Orchids, 131, *202*, 203
Marsh Pea, 131
Marsh Pennywort, *25*, *176*, 177
Marsh St John's Wort, *171*, 171
Marsh Samphire, 55
Marsh Violet, *28*, *131*, *172*, 173
Marsh Woundwort, 130, *188*, 188
Martagon Lily, 65, *85*, 87
May Tree. See Hawthorn
Mayweeds, *40*, 40, *47*, 47, 126, 128, *195*, 195
Meadow Buttercup, *132*, 132, *151*, 151
Meadow Clary, *28*, *41*, 41, 132
Meadow Cranesbill, 75, *166*, 167
Meadow garden, 74, 75
Meadow Grass, 94
Meadow-rues, *28*, 130
Meadow Saffron, 52, *201*, 201
Meadow Vetchling, *164*, 164
Meadowsweet, 56, 75, 80, 132, *158*, 158

220

Meadwort. *See* Meadowsweet
Meconopsis cambrica. See Welsh Poppy
Medicago arabica. See Spotted Medick
Medicinal properties of Plants, 11, 12, 14, 44, 67, 150, 155, 158, 159, 160, 162, 167, 182, 188, 193, 195, 198, 201
Melilotus alba. See White Melilot
Melittis melissophyllum. See Bastard Balm
Menyanthes trifoliata. See Bogbean
Mercurialis perennis. See Dog's Mercury
Merian, Maria, 16
Mezereon, *52*, 52, 66, 73, 117, *122*, 122, 137, 168
Mice, 65, 75, 80
Michaelmas Daisy, 62
Military Orchid, 28, 41, 117, *124*, 124
Milk Parsley, 131
Milkworts, 128, 138
Mints, 56, 67, 77, *79*, 81, 83, 130
Minuartia stricta. See Teesdale Sandwort
Mistletoe, *50*, 50, *65*
Monkey Flower, 47, *47*, 81, 130
Monkey Orchid, 117, *124*, 124
Monkshood, 31, *51*, 51, 52, 73, *152*, 153
Montia perfoliata. See Spring Beauty
sibirica. See Pink Purslane
Moondaisy. *See* Ox-eye Daisy
Moorhen, 82
Moorland, 139
Moschatel, *136*, 137
Moss Campion, 140
Moths. *See* individual entries
Mountain Ash, 96
Mountain Avens, 77, *140*, 140
Mountain Everlasting, 84
Mountain Heath, 117, *119*, 120
Mountain Pansy, 140
Mountains, 140
Mouse-ears, 128, 129, *146*, 146
Mouse-ear Hawkweed, 128
Mouse-eared Chickweed. *See* Common Mouse-ear
Mud banks, 130
Mugwort, 134
Muller, Fritz, 23
Musk Mallow, *170*, 170
Musk Rose. *See* Field Rose
Musk Thistle, *197*, 197
Mustards, 40, *40*, 45, 54, 94, *133*, *156*, 156
Myosotis discolor. See Changing Forgetmenot

ramosissima. See Early Forgetmenot
scorpioides. See Water Forgetmenot

Naked Boys, Ladies or Nanny. *See* Meadow Saffron
Narcissus obvallaris. See Tenby Daffodil
pseudonarcissus. See Wild Daffodil
Narrow-lipped Helleborine, 202
Navelwort. *See* Wall Pennywort
Nectar, 31
Nettles, 22, *25*, 27, 42, 44, 46, 52, 55, 61, 64, 71, 145
Nettle-leaved Bellflower, 137, 193, *194*
New Zealand Willowherb, 174
Nightshades, 51, *52*, 52, 190
Enchanter's, 36, *175*, 175
Nipplewort, 94
Nodding Thistle. *See* Musk Thistle
Nottingham Catchfly, *146*, 146
Nuphar lutea. See Yellow Water-lily
Nuts, 59
Nymphaea alba. See White Water-lily

Oak, 71, 78, 131, 132, 136
Oblong Woodsia, 117
Oblong-leaved Sundew, *25*
Oenanthe aquatica. See Fine-leaved Water Dropwort
crocata. See Hemlock Water Dropwort
Oenothera erythrosepala. See Large-flowered Evening Primrose
Old Lady caterpillar, 43
Old Man's Beard. *See* Traveller's Joy
Onobrychis viciifolia. See Sainfoin
Ophrys apifera. See Bee Orchid
apifera var *trollii. See* Wasp Orchid
fuciflora. See Late Spider Orchid
insectifera. See Fly Orchid
sphegodes. See Early Spider Orchid
Orache, 126
Orange-tip butterfly, 61, *62*
Orchids, 19, *28*, 28, 30, 32, 34, 41, 69, *72*, 74, 77, 111, 117, 118, *123*, 123, *124*, 124, 131, *132*, 132, 137, *138*, 139, 202–213
Orchis mascula. See Early Purple Orchid
militaris. See Military Orchid

purpurea. See Lady Orchid
simia. See Monkey Orchid
ustulata. See Burnt Orchid
Oxalis, 19
Ox-eye Daisy, 19, 30, *46*, 74, 94, *102*, *132*, 132
Oxford Ragwort, 47, *47*, 134
Oxlips, *136*, *180*, 180
Oyster Plant, 126

Painted Lady butterfly, 44, 61, *62*, 64
Pale Butterwort, *48*, 48
Pale Flax, 75, *165*, 165
Pansies, *28*, 74, 84, 103, 128, 140, *172*, 172, 186
Papaver argemone. See Prickly Poppy
dubium. See Long-headed Poppy
hybridum. See Rough Poppy
rhoeas, 100. See also Common Poppy
Paradisus, 13, 201
Parasites, 50
Parietaria judaica. See Pellitory of the Wall
Parkinson, John, 13, 14, 150, 201
Parmelia omphalodes, 71
Parsleys, 30, *51*, 51–2, 56, 64, 118, 131, 176, *177*, 177
Pasque Flower, 28, *152*, 153
Pastinaca sativa. See Wild Parsnip
Patio garden, 83, 84
Peas, 127, 131, 163–5
Peacock butterfly, 44, 61, *60*, 64
Pedicularis sylvatica. See Lousewort
Pedunculate Oak, 136
Pellitory of the Wall, *144*, 145
Pemptades, 13
Pencilled Cranesbill, *167*, 167
Pennycresses, 22, *37*, 38
Pennyroyal, 67
Pentaglottis sempervirens. See Green Alkanet
Pepper Saxifrage, 135
Perennial Flax, *165*, 165
Perforate St John's Wort, 28, *171*, 171
Perfumes, 67–69
Periwinkles, 73, *182*, 182
Persicaria, 40, *144*, 145
Petasites fragrans. See Winter Heliotrope
Petroselinum segetum. See Corn Parsley
Pheasant, 66
Pheasant's-eye, *39*, 39, *101*, 101
Photographing flowers, 110–112
Phyllodoce caerulea. See Mountain Heath
Pimpernels, 40, *40*, *101*, 101, 139, *181*, 181

Pine, 66, 137
Pineapple Mayweed, 47, *47*
Pink Purslane, *47*, 47, *145*, 145
Pinks, *28*, 28, 56, 62, 67, 117, *122*, 122, *148*, 148
Plantains, *126*, 126, *133*, 134
Plant and Planet, 33
Plants with a Purpose, 89, 90, 179
Plantanthera bifolia. See Lesser Butterfly Orchid
chlorantha. See Greater Butterfly Orchid
Pliny, 11, 12, 67, 158, 160, 163
Plume Moth larvae, 62
Poisonous Plants, 12, *51*, 51–52, *65*, 69, 137, *149*, 149, *152*, 153, *168*, 168, *173*, 173, 176, *190*, 190, *201*, 201
Pollen, 31–34
Pollination, 22, 23, 29–32, 33, 204, 205
Polygonum aviculare. See Knotgrass
hydropiper. See Water-pepper
persicaria. See Persicaria
Pondweeds, 131, 139
Poplar, 61
Poplar Hawkmoth caterpillar, *60*, 61
Poppy family, 155
Poppies, 36, *37*, *41*, 41, 45, 96, 99, *100*, 103, 127, 132, *154*, *155*, 155
Potentilla erecta. See Tormentil
palustris. See Marsh Cinquefoil
reptans. See Creeping Cinquefoil
sterilis. See Barren Strawberry
Potpourri, 68
Pressing flowers, 109, 110
Prickly Cucumber, 173
Prickly Poppy, *154*, 155
Prickly Saltwort, 126
Prickly Sow-thistle, *197*, 197
Primroses, *28*, *31*, 31, 61, 68, 73, 77, *78*, 78, 88, 94, *102*, 135, 136, *180*, 180, *181*, 181
Evening, 118, *175*, 175
Primula elatior. See Oxlip
farinosa. See Birdseye Primrose
scotica. See Scottish Primrose
veris. See Cowslip
vulgaris. See Primrose
Privet Hawkmoth caterpillar, *60*, 62
Protected Plants, 117
Prunella vulgaris. See Self-heal
Prunus avium. See Wild Cherry
spinosa. See Blackthorn
Pulicaria dysenterica. See Common Fleabane
Pulsatilla vulgaris. See Pasque Flower

Purging Flax, 135
Purple Loosestrife, *31*, 31, 81, 130
Purple Saxifrage, 140
Purslanes, 47, 47, *145*, 145
 Sea, 129, *145*, 145
Pussmoth caterpillar, *60*, 61
Pussy Willow, 94, 96
Pyramid Orchid, 41, 69, 132, *211*, 211
Pyrola minor. *See* Common Wintergreen

Quaking-grasses, 94, *95*
Queen Anne's Lace. *See* Cow Parsley
Quickthorn. *See* Hawthorn

Ragged Robin, *28*, 28, 62, *107*, 132, *147*, 147
Ragworts, *42*, 45, *47*, 47, *64*, 64, *107*, 134
Ramonda, 86
Ramonda myconi. *See* Ramonda
Rampions, 87, 118
Ramsons, 137, *199*, 199
Ranunculus acris. *See* Meadow Buttercup
 aquatilis. *See* Common Water Crowfoot
 bulbosus. *See* Bulbous Buttercup
 ficaria. *See* Lesser Celandine
 flammula. *See* Lesser Spearwort
 repens. *See* Creeping Buttercup
Raspberry, 35, *57*, 57
Ray, John, 14, 23
Recording flowers, 107–109
Red Admiral butterfly, 44, 61, *64*, 66
Red Campion, *46*, 62, 94, *95*, *147*, 147
Red Clover, 132, 164, *165*
Red Currant, *57*, 58
Red Dead-nettle, *189*, 189
Red Helleborine, 41, *111*, 117, *123*, 123, 204, 212
Red Hemp-nettle, *28*
Redouté, Pierre-Joseph, 17
Redpoll, 66
Redshank. *See* Persicaria
Red-veined Dandelion, 128
Redwing, 66
Rest-harrow, *127*, 128
Rhamnus catharticus. *See* Buckthorn
Ribwort Plantain, *133*
Ringlet butterfly, 62, 64
Rivers and Fenlands, 130, 131
Roast Beef Plant. *See* Stinking Iris
Robin's Pincushion, 161, *161*
Rock Samphire, 128, *129*
Rock Sea-lavender, 128
Rock Sea Spurrey, *129*, 129
Roots, 24, 53

Rosa arvensis. *See* Field Rose
 canina. *See* Dog Rose
 pimpinellifolia. *See* Burnet Rose
 rubiginosa. *See* Sweet Briar
 tomentosa. *See* Downy Rose
Roses, 27, 57, 68, 96, 128, 158–62, *160 161*
 Guelder, *65*, 66, *192*, 192
Rosebay Willowherb, 19, 45, 46, *95*, *111*, 112, *133*, 134, *174*, 174
Rosehips, *37*, *57*, 57, *65*, 66, *161*
Rosemary, 68, 84
Rosin Rose. *See* Perforate St John's Wort
Rough Poppy, *134*, *135*
Round-headed Rampion, 118
Round-leaved Common Sundew, *25*
Round-leaved Wintergreen, 128
Rowan, *35*, 58, *65*, 66
Royal Botanic Gardens, Kew, 17, 110
Rubia peregrina. *See* Wild Madder
Rugosa Rose, 96
Rumex acetosa. *See* Sorrel
 crispus. *See* Curled Dock
 scutatus, 55
Rye Grass, 94

Sages, 62, 84, 137, *187*, 187
Sagittaria sagittifolia. *See* Arrowhead
Sainfoin, *163*, 163
St John's Worts, *28*, 36, 130, 133, 137, *171*, 171
Salads and Vegetables, 54, 55
Sallow, 61
Salt marshes, 130
Sand dunes, 127, 128
Sand Leek, *199*, 199
Sandworts, 22, 117, *119*, 119, 126
Sandy and Shingle beaches, 126, 127
Sanicle, 137, *176*, 177
Sanicula europaea. *See* Sanicle
Saponaria officinalis. *See* Soapwort
Saxifraga, cespitosa. *See* Tufted Saxifrage
 cernua. *See* Drooping Saxifrage
Saxifrages, 117, *119*, 119, 120, 140
 Pepper, 135
Scabiouses, 127, 128, 132, *193*, 193
 Sheepsbit, *193*, 193
Scarlet Pimpernel, *101*, 101
Scented plants, 67–69
Scentless Mayweed, *40*, *195*, 195
Scorpion Grass. *See* Forgetmenot

Scots Lovage, 128
Scottish Primrose, *181*, 181
Sea Aster, *130*, 130
Sea-beet, *53*, 54, 128
Sea Bindweed, *126*, 126, 127, *183*, 183
Sea Buckthorn, 168, *169*
Sea Campion, 126, 128, *146*, 146
Sea cliffs, 128, 129
Sea Holly, 73, 127, *176*, 177
Sea Kale, *53*, 55, 126
Sea-lavenders, 94, 128, *130*, 130
Sea Mayweed, 126, 128
Sea Pea, 127
Sea Plantain, 126
Sea Purslane, 129, *145*, 145
Sea Radish, 126, 128
Sea Rocket, 126, *156*, 156
Sea Sandwort, 126
Sea Spurge, *126*, 126
Sea Wormwood, 127, 128
Sedum acre. *See* Biting Stonecrop
 anglicum. *See* English Stonecrop
 spectabile. *See* Iceplant
Seeds, 36
Self-heal, *187*, 187
Shaggy Soldier, 47
Sheep's Sorrel, 128, 139
Sheepsbit Scabious, *127*, 128, *193*, 193
Shepherd's Purse, *37*, 38, *40*, 40, 45, 134
Shining Cranesbill, *167*, 167
Short-spurred Fragrant Orchid, 211
Signatures of flowers, 12, 160
Silene alba. *See* White Campion
 dioica. *See* Red Campion
 maritima. *See* Sea Campion
 nutans. *See* Nottingham Catchfly
 vulgaris. *See* Bladder Campion
Silver Birch, *65*, 66, 74, 79, 94
Silver Y moth, 63
Silverweed, *40*, 40, 128
Sisymbrium officinale. *See* Hedge Mustard
Sketching flowers, 102–105
Slender St John's Wort, *171*, 171
Sloes, *57*, 58, *162*, 162
Small Copper butterfly, *42*, 43, *60*, 61
Small-flowered Catchfly, *28*, 28, *39*, 39
Small Scabious, 133
Small Tortoiseshell butterfly, 44, 61, 63, *64*
Smyrnium olusatrum. *See* Alexanders
Snakeshead Fritillary, *72*, 75, 118

Sneezewort, *195*, 195
Snipe, 83
Snowdon Lily, 117, *119*, 121
Snowdrop, 18, *72*, 72, 78, 88, 201
Soapwort, *147*, 147
Solanum dulcamara. *See* Bittersweet
 nigrum. *See* Black Nightshade
Soldanella alpina. *See* Alpine Snowbell
Solomon's Seal, 78
Sonchus asper. *See* Prickly Sow-thistle
Sorrels, 43, 44, 52, 55, 61, 94, 128, 132, 138
 Wood-, 30, *78*, 78, 85
Southern Marsh Orchid, 202, 203
Sow-thistles, 40, 117, *122*, 122, *197*, 197
Spear Thistle, *25*, *42*, 44, 45, 128, *197*, 197
Speedwells, *40*, 40, 46, 47, 74, 117, *122*, 122, *191*, 191
Sphagnum Moss, 139
Spices and Herbs, 56
Spider Orchids, 41, 205, 206, 207
Spiked Rampion, 118
Spiked Speedwell, 117, *122*
Spiked Water Milfoil, 131
Spindle-tree, *52*, 52
 berries, 96, *101*, 101
Spiny leaves, 27
Spiranthes aestivalis. *See* Summer Lady's Tresses
 romanzoffiana. *See* Irish Lady's Tresses
 spiralis. *See* Autumn Lady's Tresses
Spotted Medick, *163*, 163
Spotted Orchids, 15, *28*, 34, 77, 139, 202, 210, 211
Spreading Bellflower, 193, *194*
Spring Beauty, *145*, 145
Spring Gentian, 77, 117, 118, *119*, 120
Spring Snowflake, *72*, 75, 201
Spring Squill, *129*, 129
Spry, Constance, 92
Spurges, 52, *126*, 126, 136, *168*, 168
Spurge Laurel, *52*, 52, 137, *168*, 168
Spurgewort. *See* Stinking Iris
Squills, *129*, 129
Stachys palustris. *See* Marsh Woundwort
 sylvatica. *See* Hedge Woundwort
Starry Saxifrage, *140*, 140
Stellaria holostea. *See* Greater Stitchwort
 media. *See* Common Chickweed
Stems, 24, 24, 55

Stinging Nettle, *25*, 27, 44, *46*, 55, 71
Stinking Goosefoot, 69
Stinking Hellebore, 52, 69, 78, 136, *149*, 149
Stinking Iris, 95, *201*, 201
Stinking Mayweed, *40*
Stitchworts, *25*, 94, 135, *146*, 146
Stonecrops, *25*, 127, 128, 129, *157*, 157
Strangler Vetch. See Hairy Tare.
Strawberries, 36, *37*, 46, *57*, 57, 137, *159*, 159
Strawberry Clover, 165
Succisa pratensis. See Devilsbit Scabious
Summer Lady's Tresses, 212
Summer Snowflake, *72*, 75, 201
Sundews, *25*, *48*, 49, 61, 139
Sun Spurge, *168*, 168
Superstitions and legends, 11, 18, 149, 158, 162, 171, 187, 201
Swallowtail butterfly, 131
Sweet Briar, 57, 160, *161*
Sweet Chestnut, 59, 96
Sweet Cicely, 56
Sweet Flag, 67
Sweet Gale. See Bog Myrtle
Sweet Rocket, 62
Sweet Violet, 172
Sweet Woodruff, 137
Sycamore, 36

Tamus communis. See Black Bryony
Tanacetum parthenium. See Feverfew
Tansy, *83*, 84, 94
Taxus baccata. See Yew
Teasels, 46, 66, 96, *193*, 193
Teesdale Sandwort, 117, *119*, 119
Tenby Daffodil, 201
Teucrium scorodonia. See Wood Sage
Thickening Grass. See Butterwort
Thistles, *27*, 27, *37*, *40*, *42*, 44, 45, *46*, *65*, 66, 77, 96, 128, *197*, 197
Thorn hedge, 135
Thorn-apple, *51*, 52
Thorow-wax, *39*, 39
Three-cornered Leek, *199*
Thrift, 82, 84, 128, *129*, 130
Thrush, 66
Thyme Broomrape, *49*, 77
Tigermoth caterpillar, 43
Timothy Grass, 94
Toadflaxes, 12, 28, *133*, 134, *191*, 191
Toothwort, 51

Tormentil, 128, 133, 139, *159*
Tortoiseshell caterpillar, *42*
Town Clock. See Moschatel
Town and Wasteland, 133, 134
Tragopogon pratensis. See Goatsbeard
Trappers, 48–9
Traveller's Joy, 95, *152*, 153
Tree Mallow, 128
Trefoils, 61, *62*, 128, 129, 132, 163
Trichomanes speciosum. See Killarney Fern
Trifolium arvense. See Haresfoot Clover
fragiferum. See Strawberry Clover
incarnatum. See Crimson Clover
pratense. See Red Clover
repens. See White Clover
Tripleurospermum inodorum. See Scentless Mayweed
Trollius europaeus. See Globe Flower
Trumpet Gentian, *85*, 86
Tufted Saxifrage, 117, *119*, 120
Tufted Vetch, 107, *163*, 163
Tull, Jethro, 42
Turner, John, 198
Turner, William, 14, 145, 181, 183, 201, 212
Turpin, Pierre Jean, 17
Tusser, Thomas, 42
Tussilago farfara. See Coltsfoot
Tutsan, *171*, 171
Twayblades, 139, *202*, 203, 204, 205, 208, 209
Twinflower, *192*, 192

Ulex europaeus. See Gorse
Umbilicus rupestris. See Wall Pennywort
Useless. See Persicaria

Valerian, *62*, 63
Veronica beccabunga. See Brooklime
chamaedrys. See Germander Speedwell
persica. See Common Field Speedwell
spicata. See Spiked Speedwell
Vetches, 45, 61, 74, 107, 129, 135, *163*, 163
Vetchlings, 135, *164*, 164
Viburnum lantana. See Wayfaring Tree
opulus. See Guelder Rose
Vicia cracca. See Tufted Vetch
hirsuta. See Hairy Tare
Vinca minor. See Lesser Periwinkle

Viola, 30
Viola arvensis. See Field Pansy
canina. See Heath Dog Violet
kitaibeliana. See Dwarf Pansy
odorata. See Sweet Violet
palustris. See Marsh Violet
riviniana. See Common Dog Violet
tricolor. See Wild Pansy
Violets, 17, *25*, *28*, *46*, 46, *53*, 56, 61, 68, 78, *85*, 87, 128, *131*, 131, 132, 135, 137, *172*, 172
Dame's, 73
Water, 80, *131*, 131, 181, 181
Violet Helleborine, *202*, *203*, 213
Viper's Bugloss, 41, *62*, 64

Wahlenbergia hederacea. See Ivy-leaved Bellflower
Wall Brown butterfly, 64
Wall Pennywort, *157*, 157
Wallpepper. See Biting Stonecrop
Walnut, 59
Wartweed. See Sun Spurge
Wasp Orchid, *206*, *207*
Water Avens, 137, *158*, 158
Watercress, 54, 134
Water Dock, 130
Water Dropworts, 52
Water Forgetmenot, 130, *131*, *186*, 186
Water garden, 79–82
Water-lilies, 22, 81, *131*, *149*
Water Mint, *79*, 81, 130
Water-pepper, *144*, 145
Water-plantain, 80
Water Violet, 80, *131*, 131, *181*, 181
Wayfaring Tree, 58, *192*, 192
Weeds, 38–47
Weld, *70*, 71
Welsh Poppy, 96, *154*, 155
White Bee Orchid, *207*
White Bryony, *52*, 52, *107*, *173*, 173
White Campion, *147*, 147
White Clover, 128, 132, 164, 165
White Dead-nettle, *189*, 189
White Helleborine, *212*, 212
White Melilot, *164*, 164
White Water-lily, 79, *149*, 149
Whitlow-grass, 133
Wild Cabbage, *53*, 128, *156*, 156
Wild Carrot, 28, 176
Wild Cherry, 58, *162*, 162
Wild Daffodil, 65, *72*, 74, 75, 78, *201*, 201
Wild Flowers of Britain and Northern Europe, 108, 121, 143
Wild Gladiolus, 117, *122*, 122

Wild Iris, 80
Wild Larkspur, *39*, 39, 47
Wild Madder, *185*, 185
Wild Pansy, *28*, 74, 84, *172*, 172
Wild Parsnip, 28, 54, 177, *178*
Wild Pink, *148*, 148
Wild Plum, *53*
Wild Privet, *52*, 52, *62*, 96
Wild Radish, *40*, 40, 45, 94
Wild Spinach, 54
Wild Strawberry, 137, *159*
Wild Thyme, 56, 77, *83*, 83, 84, *114*, 114, 128
Willowherbs, 19, 45, *46*, 46, 61, *62*, 95, *111*, 112, *133*, 134, 137, *174*, 174, 175
Winter Aconite, 79, 136, *149*, 149
Wintergreens, 128, 138, 139, *179*, 179
Winter Heliotrope, 46, 68, *196*, 196
Winter Savory, 83
Withy Wind. See Field Bindweed
Woad, *70*, 70
Wolfsbane, 153
Wood Anemone, 36, 78, *85*, 136, *152*, 153
Woodcock, 83
Woodland, 135–137
Woodland garden, 78, 79
Woodland St John's Wort, 137
Wood Millet, 94
Wood Pigeon, 66
Woodruffs, *39*, 39, 68, *185*, 185
Wood Sage, *62*, 137, *187*, 187
Woodsia alpina. See Alpine Woodsia
ilvensis. See Oblong Woodsia
Wood-sorrel, 30, *78*, 78, 85
Wood Spurge, 136
Woolly Bear caterpillar, 64

Yam family, 200
Yarrow, 134, *195*, 195
Yellow Archangel, 78, *189*
Yellow Birdsnest, 128, *136*
Yellow Horned-poppy, 103, 127, *155*, 155
Yellow Iris, *79*, 79, 81, 128, 132, 201
Yellow Rattle, *49*, 50, 132
Yellow Rocket, 134
Yellow Saxifrage, *140*, 140
Yellow Turk's-cap, 87
Yellow Underwing caterpillar, 43
Yellow Vetchling, 135
Yellow Water-lily, *149*, 149
Yellow-wort, 133
Yew, 51, 52, *65*

223

FULL CIRCLE

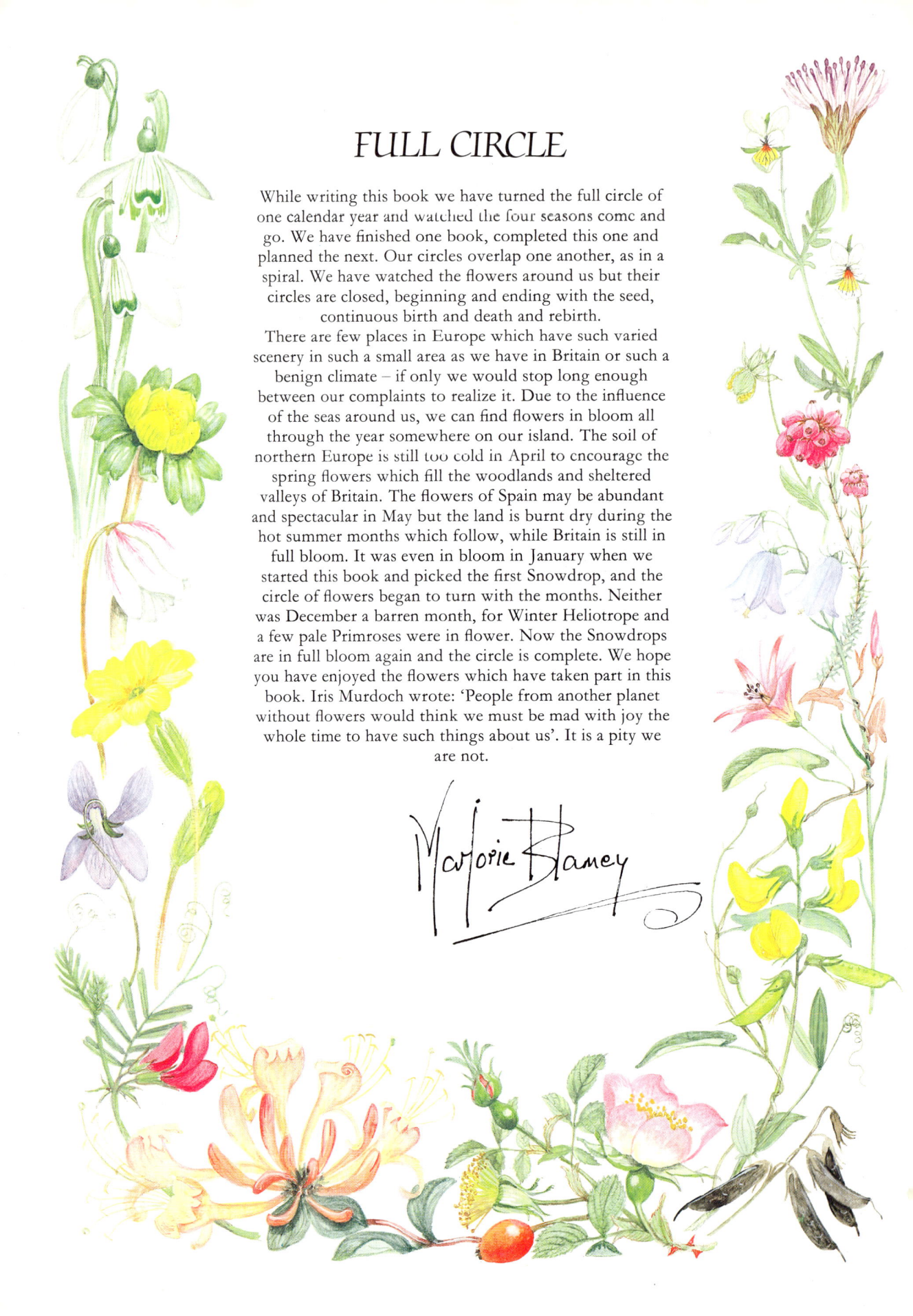

While writing this book we have turned the full circle of one calendar year and watched the four seasons come and go. We have finished one book, completed this one and planned the next. Our circles overlap one another, as in a spiral. We have watched the flowers around us but their circles are closed, beginning and ending with the seed, continuous birth and death and rebirth.

There are few places in Europe which have such varied scenery in such a small area as we have in Britain or such a benign climate – if only we would stop long enough between our complaints to realize it. Due to the influence of the seas around us, we can find flowers in bloom all through the year somewhere on our island. The soil of northern Europe is still too cold in April to encourage the spring flowers which fill the woodlands and sheltered valleys of Britain. The flowers of Spain may be abundant and spectacular in May but the land is burnt dry during the hot summer months which follow, while Britain is still in full bloom. It was even in bloom in January when we started this book and picked the first Snowdrop, and the circle of flowers began to turn with the months. Neither was December a barren month, for Winter Heliotrope and a few pale Primroses were in flower. Now the Snowdrops are in full bloom again and the circle is complete. We hope you have enjoyed the flowers which have taken part in this book. Iris Murdoch wrote: 'People from another planet without flowers would think we must be mad with joy the whole time to have such things about us'. It is a pity we are not.

Marjorie Blamey